Consumption and Public Life

Series Editors
Frank Trentmann
Birkbeck, University of London
London, UK

Richard Wilk
Indiana University
Bloomington, IN, USA

The series will be a channel and focus for some of the most interesting recent work on consumption, establishing innovative approaches and a new research agenda. New approaches and public debates around consumption in modern societies will be pursued within media, politics, ethics, sociology, economics, management and cultural studies.

More information about this series at
http://www.palgrave.com/gp/series/14914

Dale Southerton

Time, Consumption and the Coordination of Everyday Life

palgrave
macmillan

Dale Southerton
University of Bristol
Bristol, UK

Consumption and Public Life
ISBN 978-0-230-57251-5   ISBN 978-1-349-60117-2   (eBook)
https://doi.org/10.1057/978-1-349-60117-2

This Palgrave Macmillan imprint is published by the registered company Springer Nature Limited.
The registered company address is: The Campus, 4 Crinan Street, London, N1 9XW, United Kingdom

In loving memory of George Grant for whom time was short but who always danced like there's nobody watching.

Acknowledgements

For a book focused on time published 10 years after its original deadline, there are many possible puns: not least that it is about time the book was published! In the terms of my own analysis, this book has had a long *duration*, its content has been *synchronized* with many parallel projects and activities, the *tempo* of my writing has been a mix of bursts of activity and many more times staring at a screen. Sequences of many kind have been a challenge, from the sequential ordering of the content of this book (which theory belongs best to what chapter) through to whether to begin the working day by clearing emails to focus on book writing or push them to the end of the day (I never did find the most effective sequence). The greatest challenge was *coordinating* the *periodicities* of book writing with all the other *social practices* of which my day-to-day life consists: whether reserving particular days of the week for book writing or the constant delaying 'until the summer' in the hope that my academic responsibilities would wane enough for me to devote concentrated periods to the book. Of course, the summer is also the time for holidays and an opportunity to spend it with my family, and so 10 years late feels somewhat acceptable!

One consequence of the temporalities of the writing process is that I have a huge number of people to thank—too many to properly recognize in these acknowledgements. The initial ideas for this book took shape through many conversations with colleagues at the ESRC Centre for

Research on Innovation and Competition and the European Sociological Association's Consumption Research Network. Notable amongst the many colleagues that shared ideas were Judy Wajcman, Mark Harvey, Jukka Gronow and Bente Halkier. I have also benefitted enormously from many colleagues who helped me to find time and develop good practices to perform the empirical work that underpins this book: Brian Heaphy, Wendy Bottero, Colette Fagan, Fiona Devine, Carol Smart, Chris Orme and Alistair Ulph. I must thank all members of the Sustainable Consumption Institute and Economic and Social Research Council (ESRC) Sustainable Practices Research Group who have challenged, added and inspired further thinking on time, consumption and practices. The influence of these colleagues will be noticeable from the corpus of material reported in the pages that follow, but a thank you for the many conversations relevant to this work is especially warranted for Frank Trentmann, Ted Schatzki, Dan Welch, Luke Yates, Nicola Spurling and Stanley Blue. Throughout this project, and especially towards the end when the book was taking shape, there have been many additional colleagues who have offered insights into new literatures, empirical studies and theories. This includes my colleagues at Consumption Research Norway (SIFO), especially Arne Dulsrud. Lotte Holm, with whom I shared an office during the final months of writing this book, offered huge inspiration in bringing together ideas on temporal rhythms, practices and consumption. Our meandering conversations are a sharp reminder of the real pleasures of academic practice. I must also thank the excellent team at Palgrave, Phillipa Grande in the early days and Poppy Hull in recent years, all of whom have shown amazing patience and made the process of 'getting the book done' a pleasant experience.

The statement that 'this book would never have happened if it wasn't for' is often written in acknowledgements. In this case there are several people for whom this is undoubtedly the case. Alan Warde and Elizabeth Shove have offered inspiration, support and advice—telling me what I needed, as opposed to what I wanted, to hear. I will forever be grateful to Andrew McMeekin for his immeasurable support in listening, challenging and talking through many ideas only some of which can be found in the pages of this book. I want to especially thank Mark Tomlinson and Josephine Mylan, co-authors of studies that form an important part of the empirical evidence that underpins this book and whose intellectual contributions cannot be understated. I owe a hefty debt of gratitude to David Evans and Jennifer Whillans, both of whom have collaborated on multiple research activities and whose approach to writing has informed my own. Together with Alan Warde they both read and offered invaluable comments on a draft typescript of the book that significantly sharpened the articulation and clarified the flow of its argumentation.

There are many friends and family members outside of academia who have shown interest and shared experiences from their own lives relevant to my thinking. It is however my partner Kerry for whom the final thank you must be reserved. Not just for the incredible patience and tolerance while I worked late or remained absorbed in 'the book', for the constant support and encouragement or for her capacity to help me put work into perspective during my 'gloomier' moments. Kerry's contribution to discussing and working through ideas, sharing her perspectives and experiences and in challenging my interpretations of everyday life have been crucial to the development of my writing at all stages.

Contents

1

Introducing Time, Temporality and Societal Change

1.1 Introduction

Lewis Carroll's white rabbit from *Alice in Wonderland*—the white rabbit who frantically dashes around holding a clock claiming '*I'm late, I'm late, for a very important date*'—conjures the image of being a slave to time, of time being something against which actions in daily life are measured and judged. The 'white rabbit' has come to symbolically represent dominant interpretations of time in contemporary societies because it captures the common perception that the pace of daily life is accelerating and that there is an increasing shortage of time. Time famine, the time squeeze, the harried leisure class and the search for quality time are popular topics of public discussion and of more and less popular social science books (e.g. Colville 2016; Demos 1995; Gleick 1999; Hewitt 1993; Linder 1970; Schor 1992; Schulte 2015). The time squeeze has become a contemporary malady for which a range of prescriptions have been spawned which promise to help alleviate its effects. Examples include time management books, websites and consultants; gadgets of various descriptions including labour-saving technologies, traffic warning devices that allow you to find a quicker route to your destination and the replacement of

© The Author(s) 2020   1
D. Southerton, *Time, Consumption and the Coordination of Everyday Life*,
Consumption and Public Life, https://doi.org/10.1057/978-1-349-60117-2_1

'snail mail' by email; a range of services have emerged that offer convenience, whether that relates to the delivery of groceries or assistance with the selection of gifts for one's partner or children. In response, various social movements and ethical concerns have emerged that espouse the slowing down of daily life (e.g. the Slow Food Movement), mindfulness and the 'downshifting' of lifestyles, while governments and firms seek to offer their employees flexible working arrangements in order to facilitate work-life balance policies.

The reasons for concern are multiple and profound. The time squeeze is held either directly or indirectly responsible for a wide range of contemporary social problems. Families are torn asunder because couples do not have the time available to spend with one another, while parents struggle to spend meaningful time with their children. Busy lifestyles are forever being cited as a principal reason for the breakdown of intimate relationships, and it is commonly implied that children watch too much television and spend too much time playing computer games simply because their parents are too busy with work and domestic commitments to do other, presumably more virtuous, cultural activities with them. Communities also suffer. Finding time to spend with friends, for idle chat with neighbours, is often assumed to be connected in some way or other with people having a 'lack of time'. There are simply too many competing demands on our time such that we prioritize consuming and working, rationing our time accordingly, and wider community relationships suffer most. People live in communities where they know a few of their neighbours in any form other than to say a passing 'hello'. Unsurprisingly, given the aforementioned set of associations between a time squeeze and the decline of family and community relationships, senses of well-being are undermined. The popular discourse of contemporary life as being 'stressful' is well established and often, at least indirectly, correlated with the rise of mental illness (Rosa 2017). Even leisure, that segment of social life associated with rest, recuperation and pleasure, is often described as being 'less leisurely' as people rush to fit it into their hectic lives (Roberts 1976).

Broader still, the time squeeze has profound implications for the organization of societies. Social capital, which refers to degrees of trust in others and the strength of social networks, are eroded as people lack time to participate in community activities and civil society, leading scholars such as Robert Putnam (2000) to complain that '*Bowling Alone*' leads to the fragmentation of public life and political disinterestedness. Indeed, in 2006 the Power Inquiry into British Democracy drew a direct correlation between the presumed decline of time spent eating together and political apathy because people do not have the time to discuss and debate key political issues. Crudely speaking, the time squeeze further exacerbates a contemporary process of individualization whereby individuals become increasingly self-aware and compelled to make choices in contexts of weakening social rules or norms to guide or constrain their actions (Beck and Beck-Gernsheim 2001). The perceived need to manage one's time reinforces processes of individualization and exacerbates senses of personal responsibility to manage that time effectively, intensifying our awareness and focus on time as a resource (or commodity) to be used purposefully. Concerns around climate change and environmental sustainability represent a further case where the perceived lack of time is held to be a barrier to pro-environmental lifestyle choices (Southerton 2013). People constantly report being concerned about the environment but also report feeling helpless in their response because they do not have the time to adopt a more sustainable lifestyle—to substitute slower transportation methods for car driving or carefully sourcing local products from markets as opposed to the one-stop trip to supermarkets.

The popular image presented in these contemporary maladies of time is a social world so tightly calibrated and filled with so many activities and commitments that critical features of social, cultural and political life have been squeezed out. Those activities have not disappeared, people still eat together, parents do spend time with their children and people still engage in community events. But, according to popular commentary, they do so more seldomly than in the past and such engagement is performed within contexts of rush and haste.

There are many competing diagnoses of the time squeeze predicament, most of which assume there to be some substantive basis for these concerns. Many try to explain why, despite it being possible for most people to have more free time and a more relaxed pace of life, people perversely opt to remain harried. Critical to such accounts is the rising significance of consumer culture, with people becoming locked-in to 'work-spend' cycles as they seek to earn the money required to fund the ever-rising expectations of a consumer lifestyle. The claim that people are working more is a vexed issue and, as will be argued, limits our understandings of socio-temporal change. The puzzle is, however, deepened by much time diary evidence. For example, Robinson and Godbey (1997) show that, paradoxically, Americans felt more rushed in 1985 than in 1965 despite having substantially more free time. Gershuny's (2000) cross-cultural analysis replicates this finding—most people spend less time in paid work than did the workers of 50 years ago.

Other accounts focus on economic restructuring and changing domestic divisions of labour. As more women enter paid employment, they find themselves juggling the roles, responsibilities and associated activities of an employee, mother, homemaker and partner. Working mothers especially experience a dual burden of juggling work and domestic life. A strong argument is presented regarding the rationalization of everyday life, with more domestic and social tasks becoming subject to the time-disciplining effects of technologies, such as washing machines and email. Accounts of the 'acceleration of everything' (Gleick 1999) attempt to demonstrate that the pace of change creates a condition in which social, economic and cultural life is experienced as one of perpetual and ever-faster change. And, finally, there are accounts which attempt to correct against a largely negative view of time scarcity. Being busy, harried and rushed can lead to senses of achievement and offer a form of social status (Gershuny 2005). A busy lifestyle demonstrates a 'full and valued life' to the self and to others.

These broad theoretical accounts of profound societal changes employ 'clock time' as the conceptual basis for their analyses. The precise measurement of the passage of time in seconds, minutes, hours, days, weeks, months and years is a dominant feature of modern life. Societies are calibrated around clock time: trains arrive and disembark at given times; meetings are scheduled for a particular time of a particular day and, often, are allocated a particular duration; family life is organized around the specific timings of the school day, the work day, childcare and mealtimes; the organization of any workplace is dependent on people, goods and services arriving and leaving at designated times. Not only is clock time inescapable in modern life, our social and economic systems would, quite literally, grind to a halt without it.

This book takes the time squeeze as its substantive starting point. It distinguishes between time scarcity and time pressure to explore the extent to which contemporary everyday lives are experiences of time being squeezed. It has three principal aims. First, it provides a systematic review of social scientific theories that seek to explain the changing significance of time in social life. Second, it presents empirical studies that examine socio-temporal experiences of everyday life. The term temporal is nebulous in that it refers to perceptions of social phenomena related to or of time, and thus opens up empirical analysis to consider a wide range of interconnected dimensions through which daily activities can be analysed. Principal dimensions considered in the analysis of this book are timing, tempo, periodicity, sequence, synchronization (of activities), coordination (of participants) and durations. Finally, this book aims to advance theoretical understandings of the socio-temporal organization of daily lives through the application of social practice theories. In doing so, it will be argued that the patterns of consumption embedded in contemporary arrangements and performances of social practices should be conceptualized as formations of socio-temporal rhythms. The implications of such an approach move social theory beyond the dominance of clock time and towards explanations focused on the coordination and synchronization of social practices.

1.2   Thinking Time

Daily life has not always been so regimented by objective (e.g. clock) measures of time. Historical archives that document the canonization process (the inquiry through which a deceased person was judged whether or not they should be made a saint) provide a rich source of data on 'time reckoning' in medieval times. In 1287, the Welshman William Cragh was hung outside the walls of Swansea, only to be revived by the Bishop of Hereford, Thomas de Cantilupe. In 1307, the now dead Bishop was to be considered for canonization, on account of his miracle revival of William Cragh. What is interesting about the archives is not whether this was actually a miracle, but the evidence provided by nine witnesses that Cragh was indeed dead before being revived by the good Bishop. When asked for how long he hung on the gallows, the witnesses gave answers such as 'for the space of time that a man would have gone a quarter mile at an ordinary pace'. The witnesses also found it difficult to pinpoint when the 'miracle' happened with some claiming it was 15 years earlier, while others suggested 16 or 18 years previously (Bartlett 2004).

The example of the canonization enquiry for the Bishop of Hereford is instructive for two reasons. First, and especially when juxtaposed with the representation of time evoked by Lewis Carroll's white rabbit, it vividly highlights the extent to which our everyday understandings and perceptions of time has come to be dominated by the clock. Secondly, and more importantly for present purposes, is that the example highlights there are other ways in which time in everyday social lives can be understood. In the testimonies of witnesses of William Cragh's hanging, time was presented based on subjective interpretations of shared social practices that acted as a reference point for indicating temporal features of daily lives. In these examples the practices mentioned were typical, shared, everyday experiences such as walking. As will be argued in the latter chapters of this book, examining the relationship between time and society through the theoretical lens of shared social practices offers instructive insights into the organization and experiences of contemporary daily life.

Given that a central focus of this book is temporality (i.e. perceptions of social phenomena related to or of time), it is useful to briefly consider five different ways in which the temporal has been understood and conceptualized: (1) understanding change and measuring motion, (2) contrasting past and future dimensions of time, (3) intercultural comparison, (4) progression through 'life times' and (5) socio-temporal rhythms. While each approach connects the temporal to ways of analysing forms of societal organization and change, it is the analysis of socio-temporal rhythms that forms the core consideration of this book.

Philosophical theories of time can be traced back to the sixth century BC and with the concerns of Greek philosophers with understanding the relationship between persistence and change, permanence and ephemerality, mortality and immortality. Plato (c.429–347 BC) distinguished between the realms of 'form' and 'ideas'. On the one hand the form of a tree, for example, changes with the seasons—growing and dying—but the idea of the tree is 'timeless': '*[t]he idea endures, while its particular expression is perishable*' (quoted in Adam 2004: 27). The tree that lives and dies, and which is therefore temporal (changes through time), can only be known through reference to the timeless idea of a tree; '*time does not exist in its own right but is an integral part of the universe*' (ibid.: 27). The work of Aristotle (384–322 BC) was, by contrast, concerned with the relationship between time and motion and how we might measure change. Time is known through the difference between 'before and after', and without change we cannot recognize time, while without time we cannot identify change (Adam 2004).

That time does not exist in its own right but can only be understood in relation to form and ideas was critical to Newton's scientific concern with the measurement of motion. Newton was not concerned with time per se, but rather with the application of time as a unit for measuring motion. For Newton, time is a quantity, measurable in length and expressible in number. An absolute and mathematical concept of time allows for the precise measurement of rates of change because it is a form of time that is independent from the transformations that it reveals. Motions may be accelerated or delayed, but this has no effect on the passage of absolute time. The Newtonian concept of time has been critical in the development of Western understandings of time as an objective unit of measurement. Understandably, given Newton's concerns, this concept fails to consider subjective experiences of time. Hegel makes the point that physics cannot reveal the 'meanings' of time. Rather, he argues, that things are finite and therefore temporal. Time is not abstract to things but part of things (Adam 2004). Like Plato's tree, things grow, wither and die; their meanings and cultural significance change over time, and they cannot, therefore, be understood as anything other than being constituted 'in and of time'. One important implication of Hegel's work is that to understand time it is necessary to understand the social relations between things and people: to explore how time is socially constructed.

A second approach to understanding time can be described as the contrast between past and future. Bergmann (1992), for example, characterizes societies in terms of successive forms of societal organization such as traditional and modern or agrarian and industrial, to which could be added modern and late modern or industrial and post-industrial (see van Tienoven [2019] for an overview). Such categorizations refer to change over time and imply social forms with different temporal orientations. These orientations are sometimes applied to societies but can also be applied to particular social groups within a society, hence terms like progress, advanced, developed, entrepreneurial or even revolutionary being applied to generically describe societies or groups that are future-oriented, and terms such as conservative, orthodox, conventional and traditional to describe those with a past or present orientation (Bergmann 1992). In this approach, temporality is employed to capture and characterize successive (and broad) forms of societal change (from agrarian to industrial modes of socio-economic organization) and to characterize differences between socio-cultural groups.

Contrasting past and future temporalities present societal change as a form of linear succession and continuum, which has come to dominate the conceptualizations of the future that underpin policy, innovations and government or business strategy. This is expressed in Luhmann's (1976: 139) argument that future time horizons are inseparable from the present: 'the future cannot begin but travels together with the present'. Predictions of the future (such as climate change or market demand) are almost always extrapolated from 'present' trends, while images of the future captured in films and literature are often based on the imagined maturation of specific aspects of present society (e.g. genetic engineering or robotic technologies) and present a future where the main focus is a critique of the present. Planning strategies, particularly with regard to technologies, focus on 'future presents' (Luhmann 1976) where the future is often represented as 'technological advanced' versions of present forms of social life and the future is understood as the present located in a future temporal context. As contemporary debates about climate change demonstrate, the present threatens the future while the representation of how societies can respond to those threats is always rooted in our conceptualizations of the past and the present (Bergmann 1992). One implication of this line of reasoning is that while the present is indeterminate of the future (Schatzki 2010), imaginations or anticipations of the future act on the present because they shape our understandings and decisions about actions in the present.

Intercultural comparisons represent a third approach in which the temporal perspectives of different cultural groups are identified as a basis of fundamental societal difference. Evans-Pritchard's (1969) influential anthropological study of the Nuer, for example, showed how their understandings of time were represented through the changing seasons. Bourdieu's (1979) account of the Kabyle in Algeria revealed hostility to any notion of 'clock time', which was referred to as the *'devil's mill'*. Reverence for the timings of nature dominated the way that the Kabyle organized time; *'submission to nature is inseparable from submission to the passage of time scanned in the rhythms of nature'* (ibid.: 57). Hence, the Kabyle's philosophy was that a rainstorm, sunset, a harvest or a child's rate of growth cannot be controlled, rushed or slowed down, they had no notion of designated times for meeting or set times for eating and any sense of haste was regarded as *'a lack of decorum combined with a diabolical ambition'* (ibid.: 57). Time diary studies represent another approach to comparing different cultures based on the organization and experience of time. For example, Warde et al. (2007) use time diary data to show how the temporal organization of food consumption in different societies is representative of cultural variations in the social structure and stratification of the practice of eating. The temporalities of eating are symbolic of social status in France and the UK, but not in Norway, the Netherlands or the USA. Such differences may partly be explained by Gershuny's (2000) analysis of time use in 20 Organisation for Economic Co-operation and Development (OECD) countries, which suggests that cultural variations in the use of time relate to differences in socio-political regimes (e.g. based on mixes of liberal market economics and socio-democratic welfare systems).

'Lifetimes" capture a fourth set of approaches often applied to the analysis of time and includes considerations of the body, generation and life-course. The significance of 'lifetimes" cannot be described in any more profound sense than Heidegger's (1927) observation that human existence finds its meaning in its temporal character: that being human is made visible through the progressive movement towards death. Barbara Adam (1989, 1990) also highlights how biological and social times are inseparable. For instance, the ageing body is often at odds with the contemporary (cultural) celebration of youthful bodies. While our bodies reveal the 'biological times' of ageing, numerous technologies enable us to attempt to overcome that process; and it is here that biological and socially derived times meet. The physiology of the body is also temporally organized. We eat, sleep, breathe, use energy, digest, perceive, think, concentrate, communicate, interact and work in rhythmic ways that are tied to the functions of organs, tissues and hormones. Hence, we get tired, indigestion and feel out-of-sorts if we work through the night (Adam 1995). The relationship between biological and social times is a source of many contemporary ethical debates, including the use of medical science to prolong the fertility age of women and the use of cosmetic surgery to overcome the process of ageing.

A second sense in which we can refer to lifetimes is through the timing of one's birth. Mannheim's (1952) concept of generation is significant here. Mannheim was concerned with the collective production and circulation of knowledge and the conditions under which different forms of knowledge flourished. He argued that generations, groups of people born around the same time and experiencing similar social conditions in their formative years, acquire similar forms of knowledge and thus interpret the world in similar ways. The collective cohesion of generations can be found on three levels. The first is the 'generational site'. People born in the same time period experience events at the same phase in their biographical development and experience those events in a similar sequence. The second level is 'generational actuality', where those born in particular time periods share collective interpretations of events and ideas. Third are 'generational units' which account for variations, largely based on more localized interpretations of the same sequence of events, within each generation site. Shared timing of birth and sequential experience of events presents collective groups:

> with a common location in the historical dimension of the social process...
> [which is important because]... participation in the same social and histori-
> cal circumstances... [means that such groups]... coalesce into a natural view
> of the world... [and]... all later experiences then tend to receive their meaning
> from this original set, whether they appear as that set's verification or its nega-
> tion and anti-thesis. (Mannheim 1952: 291–298)

Mannheim's account is subject to strong critique, not least because it is difficult to draw boundaries around generational sites, actualities and units. However, it presents an important contribution to understanding the relationship between lifetimes, the relations between different social groups, and cultural understandings of the social world. In Mannheim's theory, lifetimes are critical to understanding how people relate to one another and the forms of knowledge that bind them together or emphasize their differences.

A further dimension of lifetimes is the life-course, which marks the different stages of life. Before the nineteenth century, the unpredictable length of any individual life meant that the idea of understanding age as a process of 'stages' lacked any substance, and numerical age had limited significance beyond broad categorizations of childhood. It was only once individuals lived predictably into old age that any standardized passage across the life-course could be conceived (Gillis 1996). It was from the 1870s that stages of childhood, adulthood and eventual old age could be understood as 'stages of life'. As Cook (2000) details, between the nineteenth and twentieth centuries, life stages really began to penetrate social life. He identified a range of processes: legislation around child labour; the establishment of educational and charitable institutions; the emergence of medical discourses surrounding physical and psychological development and decay; market segmentation strategies of retailers and manufacturers; and the formation of the welfare state. Critically, when contrasted with Mannheim's concept of generation, time is relevant not in terms of when one is born but to the timings of biographical ages. Life-course amounts to the similarity of experience and knowledge of those who share the same stage of life, and lifetimes follow broadly predictable sequences of events and challenges. While debates have emerged regarding the sequential rigidity of life stages (Hockey and James 2003; Bauman 1992) the point remains that lifetimes refer to a fundamental feature of the relationship between time and society.

The final set of approaches that conceptualize the relationship between time and society are those that focus on socio-temporal rhythms. At the core of these approaches is the premise that time in human societies is socially constructed. Durkheim (1915) described how the rhythms of social life are the very basis for the idea of time itself and that time is a thoroughly modern idea. For Durkheim the notion of time emerges from the regularity of events such as market day, holidays and festivities such Christmas and Easter—all of which can be thought of as events in the day, week, month, year that mark the temporal rhythms of society and our collective understandings of the passage of time: of past times, present times and future times. Elias (1992) formulated this as 'social time', because time is understood and experienced through the intervals that derive from collective social activities and the comprehension of their appropriate 'timing' (Tabboni 2001).

It is, however, Zerubavel's (1979, 1981, 1982) analysis of socio-temporal rhythms that represents the most systematic conceptual analysis of social time. He identifies four major dimensions of the temporal profile of any event or situation. First are *sequential structures*, which refer to the sequences in which events occur. Zerubavel points out that most events are sequenced following culturally sanctioned conventions. Career structures, eating events, rituals (such as a wedding) and even dating display distinct sequential structures and, in most cases, offer a guidance regarding the tempo through which events in the sequence 'should' flow, such as a new relationship can progress 'too fast' or 'too slow' depending on the cultural conventions of different societal contexts. The second dimension is *duration*, which is the length of time for which the event lasts. Again, cultural conventions shape the length of time that any event is expected to last. Zerubavel provides the example of entertainment events such as concerts, opera and cinema tending to have a duration of approximately two hours, and that people feel cheated when an event lasts for a shorter duration and restless if it 'drags on'. Leaving 'too early', doing something for too long (e.g. being engaged for too long), overstaying one's welcome represent examples of cultural conventions that regulate the durations and timings of an event. Third are *standard temporal locations*, which refer to the times when events typically occur within the context of a day, week, month, year, and so on. Eating times, working times, appropriate times to drink alcohol, to sleep, leisure times, times for worship or intimacy are all forms of institutionalized collective timings of events that represent shared understandings of the rhythms of society. The final dimension identified by Zerubavel is *rate of recurrence*, which refers to the frequency with which events occur. Everyday events recur on a 24-hour basis (e.g. eating, sleeping and news broadcasts), or across the weekday and weekend (e.g. work and leisure). Other events occur on annual cycles (such as festivities and national holidays).

It is through these four dimensions that our understandings and lived experiences of time are formed and through which the temporal structures of social life are ordered and regulated. This is made possible through the intricate relationship between clocks, calendars, schedules and timetables, which come to represent and order events into rhythmic patterns. For Zerubavel, social time is rendered meaningful through the temporal ordering of collective social events and activities, and it is that ordering that reproduces and structures the organization of contemporary experiences of everyday life.

The five approaches to temporality presented in this section reflect the broad range of critical social scientific engagements with notions of time and how it relates to social life. Some attempts have been made to synthesize and weave together these different temporal perspectives into a coherent analytical framework, the most comprehensive being Adam's (1998) 'timescapes' perspective. Synthesis is not, however, the objective of the analysis in this book, not least because each of the approaches seeks to address quite different intellectual questions. As already discussed, the substantive entry point of this analysis is the time squeeze. Seeking to explain if contemporary lives are experiences of time scarcity (whether perceived or actual) and examine what processes of social change might have given rise to such experiences represents a critical first step of the analysis. The changing ways in which time is understood, including the rise of scientific measurement of action and motion, are therefore an important part of the argument. So too is consideration of past–present–future societal forms and the temporal framings of succession or continuum between past and future that are commonly employed to explain rates and processes of societal change. At various points throughout the book intercultural comparisons and differentiation between lifetimes (mostly related to age) will form part of the analytical discussion and in most cases used to clarify that temporalities are organized and experienced in varying ways by different social groups. It is, however, with reference to the approach that I have described here as socio-temporal rhythms that this book is principally focused. This is because the core argument that will be developed in the following chapters is that time does not exist outside, or independently from, the organization and performance of social practices.

1.3   Towards a Social Practice Theory of the Socio-Temporal Organization

This book is broadly organized into three parts. The first charts the development of theories that explain the relationship between time and society by considering the rising centrality of clock time in modernity (Chap. 2), how the commodification of time in the context of an emerging consumer culture became synonymous with perceptions of time scarcity (Chap. 3), and accounts that diagnose the acceleration of everyday lives in late modernity (Chap. 4). The second section reviews empirical accounts of everyday temporal experiences, considering the ways in which people organize their time and the rhythms that are produced (Chap. 5), and contrasts that temporal organization with accounts of British everyday lives in the 1930s (Chap. 6). The final section sets out to explain the processes through which temporal rhythms are formed and reproduced (Chap. 7) and to consider the implications of this analysis for contemporary concerns about everyday lives in which time (scarcity and pressure) is often mobilized as both a cause and a barrier to the resolution, of societal problems particularly related to well-being and sustainable consumption. The remainder of this section provides a summary of the book and its core arguments.

Chapter 2 focuses on the significance of clock time in framing understandings and explanations of time and social change. The rising centrality of clock time and its contribution to profound changes in the organization and experience of social life during modernity have led to the dominance of the clock for framing and understanding time in contemporary societies. Such framings present time as an objective unit (of minutes, hours, etc.) that measures human activity as a matter of succession: activities start and end, follow a linear succession and have a before and after—all of which are codified through the objective units of clock time. And the clock, quite literally, comes to objectify time—time is represented and interpreted through the object of the clock with 'time' seen to pass independently from human activity. Framed in this way, a socio-historical account of time and society present the clock as a means of regulating, coordinating and synchronizing economic and social activity. Through these processes, clock time became a standardized mechanism for measuring activity, facilitating the attribution of scientific principles of time management to maximize economic efficiency and as a form of social discipline. Time, in this perspective, became commodified as a decontextualized resource to be valued, exchanged and negotiated. The post-war period of mass consumption signalled new ways in which clock time penetrated into our everyday lives. Time consciousness came to infuse our leisure and consumption practices, with leisure subject to forms of measurement and principles of efficiency, while the growing access to consumption for more members of society meant that people had more opportunities and choices to pursue consumption through expression of lifestyle. Both leisure and consumption became increasingly time-consuming, while the means to facilitate both (i.e. disposable income) required that people work more. As Juliet Schor (1992) has so neatly summarized, by the end of the twentieth century those living in affluent societies were locked into 'work-spend' cycles while those in less affluent societies aspired to this (consumer-lifestyle-oriented) predicament.

Chapter 3 considers the evidence from time diary studies to examine in detail claims of the scarcity that results from working more to consume more. First, time spent in paid and unpaid work is examined across affluent societies with a focus on changes over time. While the data presents many important nuances, it shows little overall evidence of any systematic increase of time spent in paid and unpaid work. General convergence between men and women with respect to the amounts of time devoted to paid and unpaid work (men spending less time in the former and more in the latter, with a reverse trend for women) is revealed, although these trends do not convince of significant gender equity in time use. The more important insight from time diary data is that objective time is not the property of individuals but shared and managed across people, especially in the contexts of personal relationships. Couples distribute activities such as paid and unpaid work between each other, with flexible hours of working emerging as a means for seeking to achieve 'work-life balance' and for juggling the demands of paid and unpaid work. It is argued that these processes essentially extend the logic of objective and rationalized time to the organization and experience of personal life. As Arlie Hochschild (1997) argues, societal responses to the perception of time scarcity, such as flexible working, time-saving domestic technologies and the outsourcing of domestic activities such as childcare, have the effect of commodifying personal life. Relationships with intimate partners, children, family members and friends come to be judged through the quality of time made available to spend with them. These processes only serve to raise cultural standards of comfort, cleanliness and convenience (see Shove 2003) and cultural expectations with respect to the 'qualities' of time that one makes available for those closest to them. The irony is that the main societal responses to perceptions of time scarcity essentially only serve to increase cultural expectations, standards and activities while rationalizing, intensifying and depersonalizing the qualities of our temporal experiences.

Chapter 4 turns attention to debates regarding time pressure that are associated with claims that social lives are an experience of acceleration. Many popular science books diagnose the chronic speeding-up of more or less all aspects of social lives and do so largely through a focus on technological innovations. While such books seem to present the twenty-first century as something of a high point in the speeding-up of societies, concerns with processes of acceleration have been a notable feature of social theory since the nineteenth century. Innovations in travel and communications technologies, particularly the railway and telephony, expanded and accelerated the movement of people, the circulation of goods and the capacity to exchange information. The disorienting effects of speed combined with the new sensory experiences of urban living, in which the spectacle of urban spaces and the anonymity of the crowd offer new opportunities for individuation but in a context of indifference, underpinned modern experiences of constant flux and rapid change. Innovations in travel and information and communications technologies in the post-war period continued, leading David Harvey (1989) to describe a process of time-space compression as the globe effectively shrinks when represented in terms of the time it takes to traverse space whether in person or through communications. These processes of acceleration are captured and summarized in Rosa's (2017) theory of dynamic stabilization, in which the only stable feature of late modern societies is their constant and rapid change. The rate of technological innovations constantly increases, the speed of change outstrips the pace at which social institutions (e.g. the family, occupational structures and forms of governance) can respond, and together everyday lives come to be experienced overwhelmingly as one of speed and time pressure.

While broad theoretical accounts of acceleration contain many interesting and persuasive arguments about the general perception of speed in contemporary societies, the empirical evidence to support claims that everyday lives are an experience of overwhelming time pressure remains inconclusive. Chapter 4 concludes by reviewing the empirical material, much of which is drawn from studies of science and technology and particularly the impacts of digital technologies. Such technologies afford new temporalities (described by Hassan [2003] as 'network time') and forms of instantaneous communications. These technologies offer scope for the intensification of activities in units of time (minutes or hours). However, the empirical evidence demonstrates that technologies such as mobile phones, emails and the internet are embedded in daily life in multiple ways that can be experienced in terms of acceleration and deceleration, of fast and slow, and as offering scope for micro-coordination and sense of greater control over personal activities alongside feelings of being overwhelmed by the sheer range of demands that compete for one's time (Wajcman 2015). Recent time diary evidence also suggests that people in the UK actually feel less 'time pressed' in 2015 than they did in 2000 and that the types of fragmented episodes of activity that would be expected by theories of acceleration are simply not revealed in the data (Sullivan and Gershuny 2018).

The theories explored in Chaps. 2, 3 and 4 represent a wide range of interpretations and understandings of the relationship between time and social change and about how people experience that relationship. At the core, however, remains a conceptualization of time that presents it as an objective and objectified unit. Clearly, this is one important way of analysing temporalities and how they are experienced: clock time matters

and remains fundamental to the ways in which human activities are organized. However, when pieced together with the empirical evidence, theories that conceptualize time in objective terms fail to convincingly explain
why the notion of a time squeeze is so prevalent in descriptions of contemporary everyday lives. Applying a different empirical lens, one which
explores how activities are allocated and scheduled in the context of a day
or week, offers an alternative framework for examining how time is experienced in daily lives. It is this empirical lens that forms the focus of the
second part of this book.

The first step in developing such an empirical approach is to consider
the ways in which people experience time through the organization of
activities from which their daily lives are comprised. Chapter 5 reports on
empirical studies that consider whether people feel time squeezed and if
so, why they feel this is the case. The data revealed an overwhelming sense
of feeling time squeezed, which respondents explained as a consequence
of different examples of 'doing more'. However, first-hand experiences of
the time squeeze in day-to-day lives revealed it to be a consequence of the
challenge of coordinating everyday activities with others and synchronizing the timings of those activities. This challenge of coordination and
synchronization led to everyday temporalities that were captured as experiences of 'hot spots' of intensive activities deemed necessary to create the
possibility of (temporal) 'cold spots' reserved for meaningful practices
with others (often referred to as quality time).

One difficulty with accounts of temporal experiences is the paucity of
data that enables comparison with past lives. Analysing 'day in the life'
diaries from 1937 held in the Mass Observation Archive, Chap. 6 explores
the extent to which diarists described feelings of being time squeezed.
The striking feature of the narratives provided by diarists was the absence
of the challenges of coordination and synchronization that featured so
strongly in the accounts of contemporary temporal experiences. By contrast, past lives featured strong collective timings of daily activities that
resulted from clearly defined institutionally timed events, particularly
start and end times of work, mealtimes but also events such as Sunday
lunch, Monday as wash day and market days. As a consequence, diarists
did not describe any sense of discretion in how activities were allocated
within their day nor a need to coordinate activities with others. One

explanation for this empirical finding is that flexibility in the timings of paid and unpaid work together with a greater variety of options for leisure and consumption has facilitated increasing individualization of temporal experiences, reducing constraints to the allocation of activities in daily lives and undermining shared socio-temporal rhythms. This does not mean that contemporary lives lack temporal rhythms—indeed analysis reveals a temporal ordering of the day in which activities with fixed temporal locations in the day or week, and that required coordination with other participants determined the sequencing of all daily activities in ways that produced discernible temporal rhythms—but that those rhythms are less collectively binding with respect to the timings of activities. The weakening of collectively timed activities does, however, make the task of coordinating daily lives, especially in the context of activities that require the participation of others for their satisfactory performance, more challenging.

The final part of this book turns its attention to developing a theoretical framework for conceptualizing socio-temporal rhythms and explaining how they are formed and reproduced. It does so by introducing social practice theories and their application to the study of time, before considering the implications of such a theoretical perspective for understanding the types of societal problems outlined at the beginning of this chapter. In so doing, a distinct analytical shift is made. In the empirical studies examined in Chaps. 5 and 6, the object of analysis was the ways in which activities were allocated within the context of a day or week and the challenges that people face in negotiating such allocations. In Chaps. 7 and 8, the object of analysis is social practices and the temporalities that can be identified through the ways in which shared practices are organized and performed. Switching the analytical lens from how activities are experienced in time to how practices are organized and the temporalities that emerge from practice performances, it is argued, offers a different perspective on the relationships between time and society.

Chapter 7 begins this task by observing that much social scientific enquiry into phenomena such as collective timings, synchronization and coordination tend to describe them generically as forms of socio-temporal rhythm. Defined as shared social phenomena related to or of time (socio-temporal), theories of rhythms are reviewed to argue that rhythms take circular (recurrent) and linear (sequential) forms that can be observed in the aggregate patterning of the 'times when' (timing) shared social practices are performed across society. Such rhythms can also be observed at multiple scales, from the micro-level rhythms experienced by individuals and households through to the macro-level rhythms of peak hours in energy demand and rush hours. Informed by social practice theory, and illustrated through an empirical study of laundry practices, the chapter argues that socio-temporal rhythms form and reproduce through the organization and performance of social practices. While laundry no longer has the distinct collective timing reflected in accounts of diarists in 1930s Britain where 'Monday was wash day', it remains a practice with discernible circular (e.g. the timings of washing machine use and times when people report doing laundry activities) and linear (e.g. the sequential flow of laundry activities) rhythms. These temporal rhythms were formed out of the organization of laundry practices, which were shaped by shared cultural meanings, skills and competence and the materialities of the practice.

The concluding chapter summarizes the core arguments by reviewing three themes that run throughout the preceding chapters: the dominance of the clock, commodification and acceleration in framing understandings of time; coordination and synchronization of everyday activities and the declining strength of collectively timed events; and the formation and reproduction of socio-temporal rhythms through the organization of practices. In doing so, Chap. 8 considers the contributions that this analysis has advanced to social scientific understandings of time and society. The first is its presentation of further evidence that understanding time necessitates examination of multiple temporalities (especially related to the duration, periodicity, tempo, sequence and synchronization of activities), which moves beyond the measurement of activity distributions in clock time. Second is to establish that consumption and temporalities are indivisible. Consumption does not simply take time (although, of course, this is an important aspect of it) but is also embedded within conventions related to when consumption should happen, with whom, with what degree of frequency, and at what appropriate pace. Third, and drawing parallels from critiques of the methodological individualism that underpins dominant theories of consumption and behaviour change, the analysis of this book demonstrates that temporalities cannot be explained through recourse to the discretionary time allocation choices of individuals. Informed by this analysis, the chapter concludes by returning to contemporary societal problems, particularly sustainable consumption and well-being, in which the time squeeze is often presented as both a cause and a barrier to be overcome. Treating time as an objective variable to be intervened in—by substituting, extending, displacing or resisting the allocation of activities in (clock) time—through policy is argued to be a weak, potentially flawed, response to the capacity of 'temporal thinking' for providing solutions to social problems. Rather, focus on the organization of practices and the socio-temporal rhythms that they shape offers alternative options for addressing major societal issues. Such an approach would place emphasis on the temporal alignment of practices and reinstitution of collectively timed events, offering scope to alleviate the cognitive load of micro-coordinating activities in daily life and to foster new forms of collective consumption.

References

Adam, B. (1989). Feminist Social Theory Needs Time. Reflections on the Relation between Feminist Thought, Social Theory and Time as an Important Parameter in Social Analysis. *Sociological Review, 37*, 458–473.

Adam, B. (1990). *Time and Social Theory*. Cambridge: Polity.

Adam, B. (1995). *Timewatch: The Social Analysis of Time*. London: Polity.

Adam, B. (1998). *Timescapes of Modernity: The Environment and Invisible Hazards*. London: Routledge.

Adam, B. (2004). *Time*. Cambridge: Polity.

Bartlett, R. (2004). *The Hanged Man: A Story of Miracle, Memory, and Colonialism in the Middle Ages*. New Jersey: Princeton University Press.

Bauman, Z. (1992). *Intimations of Postmodernity*. London: Routledge.

Beck, U. & Beck-Gernsheim, E. (2001). *Individualization: Institutionalized Individualism and its Social and Political Conseqeuences*. London: Sage.

Bergmann, W. (1992). The Problem of Time in Sociology: An Overview of the Literature on the State of Theory and Research on the Sociology of Time, 1900–82. *Time & Society, 1*, 81–134.

Bourdieu, P. (1979). *Algeria 1960*. Cambridge: Cambridge University Press.

Colville, R. (2016). *The Great Acceleration: How the World is Getting Faster*. London: Bloomsbury.

Cook, D. (2000). The Rise of 'the Toddler' as Subject and as Merchandising Category in the 1930s. In M. Gottdiener (Ed.), *The New Means of Consumption* (pp. 111–130). Lanham, MD: Rowman & Littlefield.

DEMOS. (1995). *The Time Squeeze*. London: Demos.

Durkheim, E. (1915). *The Elementary Forms of Religious Life: A Study in Religious Sociology* (J. W. Swain, Trans.). London: Allen & Unwin.

Elias, N. (1992). *Time: An Essay*. Oxford: Blackwell.

Evans-Pritchard, E. (1969). *The Neur*. New York: Oxford University Press.

Gershuny, J. (2000). *Changing Times: Work and Leisure in Post-industrial Society*. Oxford: Oxford University Press.

Gershuny, J. (2005). Busyness as the Badge of Honor for the New Superordinate Working Class. *Social Research, 72*(2), 287–314.

Gillis, J. R. (1996). *A World of Their Own Making: Myth, Ritual and the Quest for Family Values*. New York: Basic.

Gleick, J. (1999). *Faster: The Acceleration of Just About Everything*. New York: Abacus.

Harvey, D. (1989). *The Condition of Postmodernity*. Oxford, UK: Blackwell.

Hassan, R. (2003). Network Time and the New Knowledge Epoch. *Time & Society, 12*(2/3), 225–241.

Heidegger, M. (1927). *Being and Time* (J. Stambaugh, Trans.). New York: Harper and Row.

Hewitt, P. (1993). *About Time: The Revolution in Work and Family Life*. Rivers Oram Press.

Hochschild, A. R. (1997). *The Time Bind: When Home Becomes Work and Work Becomes Home*. CA Henry Holt.

Hockey, J., & James, A. (2003). *Social Identities Across the Life Course*. London: Palgrave Macmillan.

Linder, S. B. (1970). *The Harried Leisure Class*. New York: Columbia University Press.

Luhmann, N. (1976). The Future Cannot Begin: Temporal Structures in Modern Society. *Social Research, 43*, 130–152.

Mannheim, K. (1952). The Problem of Generations. In K. Mannheim (Ed.), *Essays on the Sociology of Knowledge*. London: Routledge Kegan & Paul.

Putnam, R. (2000). *Bowling Alone: The Collapse and Revival of American Community*. New York: Simon & Schuster.

Roberts, K. (1976). The Time Famine. In S. Parker (Ed.), *The Sociology of Leisure*. Allen & Unwin.

Robinson, J., & Godbey, G. (1997). *Time for Life: The Surprising Ways That Americans Use Their Time*. Pennsylvania State Press.

Rosa, H. (2017). De-Synchronization, Dynamic Stabilization, Dispositional Squeeze: The Problem of Temporal Mismatch. In J. Wajcman & N. Dodd (Eds.), *The Sociology of Speed: Digital, Organizational, and Social Temporalities* (pp. 25–41). Oxford: Oxford University Press.

Schatzki, T. R. (2010). *The Timespace of Human Activity: On Performance, Society, and History as Interminate Teleological Events*. Plymouth: Lexington Books.

Schor, J. (1992). *The Overworked American: The Unexpected Decline of Leisure*. Basic Books.

Schulte, B. (2015). *Overwhelmed: How to Work, Love and Play When No One Has the Time*. London: Bloomsbury.

Shove, E. (2003). *Comfort, Cleanliness and Convenience: The Social Organization of Normality*. Oxford: Berg.

Southerton, D. (2013). Temporal Rhythms, Habits and Routines: From Consumer Behaviour to the Temporal Ordering of Practices. *Time and Society, 22*(3), 335–355.

Sullivan, O., & Gershuny, J. (2018). Speed-Up Society? Evidence from the UK 2000 and 2015 Time Use Diary Surveys. *Sociology, 52*, 20–38.

Tabboni, S. (2001). The Idea of Social Time in Norbert Elias. *Time & Society, 10*(1), 5–27.

van Tienoven, T. P. (2019). A Multitude of Natural, Social and Individual Time. *Time & Society, 28*(3), 971–994.

Wajcman, J. (2015). *Pressed for Time: The Acceleration of Life in Digital Capitalism*. Chicago: Chicago University Press.

Warde, A., Cheng, S.-L., Olsen, W., & Southerton, D. (2007). Changes in the Practice of Eating: A Comparative Analysis of time-use. *Acta Sociologica, 50*(4), 365–387.

Zerubavel, E. (1979). *Patterns of Time in Hospital Life: A Sociological Perspective*. Chicago, IL: University of Chicago Press.

Zerubavel, E. (1981). *Hidden Rhythms: Schedules and Calendars in Social Life*. Chicago: Chicago University Press.

Zerubavel, E. (1982). The Standardization of Time: A Sociohistorical Perspective. *American Journal of Sociology, 88*, 1–23.

2

The Rise of the Clock: Time Discipline and Consumer Culture

2.1 Introduction

As the introduction to this book outlined, one of the most enduring features of modernity has been the extent to which clock time has come to
pervade social lives. This chapter reviews theoretical accounts that seek to
explain the processes through which time as an abstract unit of measurement of human activities has come to play such a central role in the
organization of societies. It considers the processes through which clock
time increasingly became embedded in economic, social and cultural life
in ways that are suggested to discipline human action. Second, it explores
theories that explain the rising significance of consumption in contemporary societies (often described as consumer culture), and how imperatives
to consume are argued to underpin the work-spend cycles that produce
contemporary experiences of time as being 'squeezed'. The broad-ranging
theories of societal change discussed in this chapter are important because
they represent the basis upon which popular and policy-oriented interpretations of the relationships between time and society are understood
and reproduced. As will be evidenced and argued in subsequent chapters
this is both instructive and problematic. The theoretical framing of time

© The Author(s) 2020
D. Southerton, *Time, Consumption and the Coordination of Everyday Life*,
Consumption and Public Life, https://doi.org/10.1057/978-1-349-60117-2_2

as principally a matter of activity measurement and distribution within the context of a day or week is particularly useful for describing processes of change throughout modernity. It also, however, has a tendency to reduce explanations of temporal experiences to a matter of more or less minutes available to spend on different activities.

2.2   Time Discipline in Industrial Societies

Many accounts that seek to explain the social history of time contrast a notion of 'natural time' consisting of cyclical rhythms of day and night, seasons and biological or 'bodily' rhythms, and clock time as the uniform measurement and coordination of linear (successive) human activities (e.g. Young 1988). As Adam (1995) demonstrates, it is the latter understanding of time that is most commonly associated with temporal experiences in contemporary societies. Innovations, for example, in electrical lighting, communications and mobility technologies (see Chap. 4 for a full discussion) have played an important role in overcoming constraints with respect to where and when human activities are performed and in doing so have standardized clock time as the principal means through which human activity is coordinated, understood and articulated. When the word 'time' is mentioned today, it is most commonly interpreted as a reference to the time of day or duration of an activity.

Perhaps the most influential account as to how clock time came to dominate our understandings of time is presented by E.P. Thompson (1967) in his classic essay 'Time, Work-Discipline and Industrial Capitalism'. Thompson was particularly interested in explaining how the development of industrial societies in the nineteenth and early twentieth centuries led to fundamental changes in the ways in which time was understood and how it shaped experiences of work. Critical to this process was a transition from 'task' to 'time' orientation. Task orientation refers to the organization and understanding of time in terms of the particular tasks being performed: 'the day's tasks... seem to disclose themselves, by the logic of need'. Thompson's contention was that pre-industrial understandings of time were bound together with the tasks at hand (whether harvesting, weaving baskets or tending to livestock). As with

Young's distinction between natural and clock time, Thompson's account of task orientation rests heavily on anthropological accounts of imperatives of necessity in contexts of limited technological organization and divisions of labour. In Thompson's task-oriented societies fence get repaired only when they are broken and baskets weaved only when they are needed (O'Malley 1992).

The rise of time orientation, according to Thompson, had its roots in religion. Puritanism, like the Protestant ethic identified by Weber (1989 [1905]), emphasized predestination and a compulsion to work hard. This mapped neatly onto an emerging idea that societies, and thus individuals, should not waste but save time. Time, like anything else, was subject to Calvinist ideas of thrift—that it was a sin to waste the resources that God has given us. Work, and the time it takes to do it, thus came to be treated with diligence and frugality. Religious orders played an important role in providing the blueprint for time-oriented action. The everyday lives of monks were rigidly organized, with meticulous allocation of predefined sections of time for specific activities—time for prayer, to eat, to work and to study. Zerubavel (1981) identified that monastic time reckoning represents an early historical example of contemporary forms of time reckoning. They featured rigid sequential structuring of activities and events that were allocated fixed durations with a standard temporal location (within the day, week, month or year) and were performed at uniform intervals to create clearly demarcated socio-temporal rhythms.

While religious temporal ordering and the emergence of Protestant valuing of time laid the foundations for time discipline, it was through the onset of mass industrial society that everyday experiences of time were transformed. As industrialization developed, it became increasingly necessary to regulate time so that economic activity could be synchronized. In the past, the way that people knew it was time to go to church was through the ringing of bells (Glennie and Thrift 1996). However, as industrialization developed factories required a far more precise calibration of people and machines in order to maximize efficiency, and innovations in mechanized time devices were critical in this transition. At first, public clocks served the purpose of synchronizing human labour, but as the eighteenth and nineteenth centuries progressed time-pieces in the form of household clocks and then watches took grip. Such time-pieces had the effect of not only ensuring that workers arrived at the factory at a set time, took breaks at the same time and left at the same time, but also coordinated exchange between factories—such that raw materials were delivered at particular times (Landes 1983). The whole factory system began to be regulated by clock time.

For Thompson, the rationalization of time through industrial activity was accompanied by a more pervasive (and arguably pernicious) process in which the internalization of time-oriented action resulted in clock time acting to discipline social life. This is because time discipline required more than just worker's compliance with the start and end times of work. In addition to learning the importance of punctuality, workers also needed to associate their labour and productivity with time. Ticking, ringing and striking clocks were all employed as devices that made workers' aware of the passing of time and labour came to be paid by the hour, week or month. This internalization of clock time had two primary implications. First, it forged a rationalized culture of time as a resource to be utilized and effectively deployed in all aspects of everyday life:

> Puritanism, in its marriage of convenience with industrial capitalism, was the agent which converted people to new valuations of time; which taught children even in their infancy to improve each shining hour; and which saturated peoples' minds with the equation, time is money. (Thompson 1967: 129)

Second, time orientation had the effect of presenting task orientation as simplistic, ineffectual and backward:

> a community in which task-orientation is common appears to show least demarcation between 'work' and 'life'… to men accustomed to labour timed by the clock, this attitude to labour appears to be wasteful and lacking in urgency [sic]. (Thompson 1967: 60)

By the early twentieth century time orientation as a fundamental and unquestionable mode of temporal organization was so firmly established that industrialists turned to scientific studies in efforts to maximize economic productivity. Frederick Taylor's (1911) time and motion studies provide an excellent example. Taylor monitored how workers worked and noticed that much time was wasted between tasks. As a result, he championed the introduction to the production process of a number of efficiency measures. While a range of measures advocated by Taylor as 'Scientific Management' techniques are too numerous to detail here, the central logic was that each task in the production process came to be understood and managed as much in relation to clock time as it was in terms of money. Companies calculate their labour costs in 'man hours' [sic]. Overtime, time-out through illness, holidays and strikes are all understood as extra or lost time. Time becomes decontextualized. It is no longer understood in terms of the natural passage of time but as having an invariable and abstract exchange value. Time becomes a valuable resource tied to the economy and work, something that can be exchanged, saved through efficiency measures and bargained over.

Thompson's account of the shift from task to time orientation has many critics. Most powerful are those that argue it oversimplifies past temporal experiences. O'Malley (1992) suggests that pre-industrial societies did not consist of a primitive hand-to-mouth existence, where tasks were only done out of necessity and in line with natural rhythms. While the seasons, night and day and critical annual events such as the harvest did play an important role in dictating temporal rhythms, task orientation did not lead to a simplified understanding of time. Rather, the meanings of time were culturally derived: 'Fences are not mended, nor baskets, shoes or barrels made, simply because they have broken or worn out' (ibid.: 345) but were embedded in cultural rituals and festivities. Similarly, Glennie and Thrift (1996, 2009) point to a range of time-disciplinary measures in pre-modern economies. Markets were temporally regulated so that trading between wholesalers and stall-owners and between stall-owners and customers took place at different times. If they were not, then customers would attempt to buy direct from wholesalers and the system of trade would collapse. To regulate markets, periods of trade were reserved between specified hours that were marked by the ringing of bells. Task and time orientations are not binary but, instead, represent orientations to time reckoning that exist simultaneously and which are mediated by a range of technological and cultural forms.

A second set of critiques highlight an overemphasis on 'industrial production'. Clock-time discipline could also be found in many domains of daily life. News is reported in the printed press based on the date and time of the news event; the recording of time and dates became fundamental to legal documents and to concepts of justice (e.g. measured through the length of prison sentences as opposed to physical punishments), and in consumption and leisure through the timings of shop opening hours, fetes and fairs (Glennie and Thrift 1996). Glennie and Thrift (2009) also reveal documents from fifteenth-century England that indicate schools were already imposing time discipline through the use of timetables, although the extent to which timetables were followed or enforced or whether it created a norm of time discipline is unclear from the records. By focusing only on industrial production, Thompson's account also ignored the temporal experiences of significant everyday activities; most notably domestic work and caring are ignored, while women's occupational experiences of time management are not considered (Sabelis 2001). Clock time, and its relationship to factories, can be understood as primarily the domain of men's daily experiences (Adam 1990). Finally, Harvey (1999) questions whether Thompson's account, while an important historical study, has much relevance to contemporary working experiences as many jobs require portfolio or project-oriented tasks and employees have discretion over what time of the day, when and even where they conduct their paid work (as will be discussed further in Chap. 3).

Thompson's account overemphasizes the distinction between task and time orientation in both pre-industrial and industrial societies, only considers time in the context of industrial activity and ignores experiences of time that exist outside of the domain of paid labour. It is, therefore, best to view his account as a partial explanation of broad processes of socio-temporal change. Nevertheless, his account of time orientation and discipline demonstrates how clock time—as an objective determinable unit that measures and orders human activity regardless of context, and which has become objectified—came to regulate and organize human activities and framed how those activities are understood and experienced.

2.3   The Commodification of Time, Leisure Society and Consumer Culture

The processes of time discipline identified by Thompson provide a basic introduction to the commodification of time. A central argument of Marx's *Capital* (1976 [1867]) was that an abstract, objective and quantifiable notion of time is a precondition for its use as exchange value and, therefore, for the commodification of labour. Put another way, labour obtains economic value when it can be measured through an abstract, objective and quantifiable notion of time. The proletariat effectively sell their time in the form of labour and the bourgeoisie calculate production costs through the amount of time they need to purchase in order to produce goods and services. It is based on this logic that economic analyses calculate time lost due to illness, injury and strikes as loses of economic productivity. Time is decontextualized and exchanged as units (of hours, days, weeks, etc.) for money that can then be spent on other commodities. Not wasting time and maximizing our economic return for the time we 'spend' further reinforces notions of time discipline. Furthermore, understanding time as a commodity is not constrained to the world of work. Rather, we can also consider how we use or exchange our time for leisure and consumption. This section considers the rise of the leisure society and consumer culture and how each places ever-growing demands on the finite resource of (clock) time.

A distinctive feature of the mid- to late twentieth century was the rise of mass production and consumption (Trentmann 2012). Central to Keynesian economics, the orthodox approach to macroeconomic policies in the post-war period through to the early 1970s, was the pursuit of full employment through state investments in public goods such as welfare, health, education and national infrastructure development. High levels of employment increased taxation income to pay for state investments but also increased disposable incomes that workers could spend on private goods within consumer markets (Keynes 1936). As such, the early post-war period is characterized by gradually increasing wages, the rise of the welfare state and the emergence of mass production and consumption. Keynes anticipated that continued economic productivity would drive, and be driven by, further technological innovation that would mean societies material needs could be supplied with ever-diminishing inputs of human time. Based on this economic rationale, the arrival of a 'leisure society' (Dumazedier 1967) featuring declining hours of paid work and rising levels of consumption and leisure was widely anticipated in the affluent societies of the 1950s and 1960s.

Such proclamations of a leisure society failed to materialize, at least not in the forms envisioned. The 1960s and 1970s witnessed an explosion of mass-produced consumer goods which, together with rising disposable incomes, made the consumption of a huge range of consumer goods—from clothing to domestic furniture, consumer electronics, automobiles and domestic appliances—accessible to the general population. Rather than take all of the gains from growing economic productivity in the form of less work, society instead deployed much of that labour time to produce more consumer goods. If, at the start of the twentieth century, work was essentially necessary for survival, by the end of the century it had become the means for acquiring goods and services and for engaging in an ever-expanding range of leisure pursuits (Bocock 1993).

Linder's (1970) account of the *Harried Leisure Class* represented the first systematic account examining the relationship between everyday experiences of time and the rise of both mass consumption and leisure. Reformulating Veblen's (1899) influential theory of conspicuous consumption, Linder presented the possibility that leisure in affluent mass consumer societies is not particularly leisurely! Veblen's theory stated that in a context of nineteenth-century mass urban living it became increasingly difficult for the elite to symbolically demonstrate their high social status through conspicuous 'abstention from labour' (i.e. through leisure). For Veblen, the American nouveau riche required a new vehicle through which to display their status. This vehicle was conspicuous consumption—a demonstration of wealth through the symbolic display of material abundance.

Linder argued that post-war mass consumption made the means of conspicuous consumption available to the majority of society. In this context Linder proposed that status comes again to be displayed through the conspicuous display of leisure. The marker of high status, however, is not abstention from labour but the amount and range of leisure in which one can engage. The consequence is that leisure becomes less leisurely as people attempt to cram more leisure activities into their daily life. As detailed by Roberts (1976), this includes leisure activities taking on a time-oriented characteristic. He provides the example of dancing, which once required significant amounts of time devoted to practising complicated moves but now often represents sporadic and spontaneous movements that require little investment of time for practice. Another is the jogger and the stopwatch—the pleasure gained from the activity being to beat one's previous time rather than simply taking part in the activity. For Roberts, we perform more leisure activities in our daily lives and those activities are increasingly subject to the regulation and time-disciplining effects of the clock.

It was not simply that leisure became less leisurely. The period from the 1960s to the 1990s also witnessed the emergence of consumer societies in which the range and varieties of consumer goods and services available to the majority of people in affluent societies proliferated. The mass production of the early post-war period had saturated markets with vast numbers of identical goods (Slater 1997). Socially, the corresponding forms of mass consumption offered little scope for personal expression or social differentiation and demand for varieties of goods increased (Trentmann 2012). Two critical processes were set in train: a shift from mass to flexible production techniques and the emergence of consumption as the principal mechanism for the expression and communication of identity.

These economic and societal shifts are closely related to what can be characterized as the shift from Fordist to post-Fordist modes of economic organization. Fordist modes (symbolized by Ford's Model T car—an average car priced for the average American) were characterized by the efficient production of vast numbers of identical or similar consumer goods using time-efficient assembly line techniques and then storing those goods in bulk ready for distribution to consumers. The period of the latter third of the twentieth century, however, witnessed a number of significant changes to the global economy. Innovations in production techniques, supply chains and distribution networks for consumer goods (Slater 1997) facilitated the relocation of production and manufacturing activities to developing nations where labour was cheap. The affluent economies of Europe and North America began to deindustrialize as material processing and manufacturing activities were replaced with service and knowledge-based economic activities (Bell 1976). During this process innovations in production techniques resulted in a rapid shift to post-Fordist modes of economic organization characterized as a 'just-in-time' mode of production. Rather than produce consumer goods in bulk, technological and logistical advances, aided significantly by innovations in information and communications technologies, facilitated systems in which goods could be made to order. The shift from Fordist arrangements of mass production and consumption to post-Fordist arrangements of flexible production systems across the global economy represents a critical process underpinning the rise of consumer culture (Southerton 2011).

During the same period, the significance of consumption in social lives was also transformed. Inspired by the expressive youth lifestyles of the 1960s and 1970s, where distinctive groups forged shared identities around the consumption of music, stylized consumer goods (such as Mopeds) and particular styles of dress (Hebdige 1979), consumption became increasingly important as a means of forming and expressing senses of self and social identities (Featherstone 1991, 1997). The global economic shifts that deindustrialized affluent societies also had the effect of undermining the certainties of class- and gender-based identities (Giddens 1991). The emergent service sector offered employment opportunities to women (often described as the feminization of labour markets) and blurred or complicated conventional demarcations between blue (manual) and white (service) collar occupations. Identities, once associated with one's relationship to production, became more pliable and increasing variations of goods and services offered a means for expressing senses of identity and belonging (Warde 1994). If Fordism could be defined as a regime of mass production and consumption, then post-Fordism represented a regime of flexible production and niche consumption. As consumer culture, a term used to capture the process whereby the consumption of goods and services becomes central to all domains of everyday life, reached its maturity, consumption became the principal mode of social differentiation, undermining conventional social orders of stratification, in which a sense of infinite varieties of consumer lifestyles are available for consumers to assemble into the style of life that most appeals to them (see Warde 2017 for a full discussion).

Consumer culture thus came to be a defining feature of late twentieth-century societies, in which an enormous marketing and advertising industry emerged to offer a range of experts in the form of celebrities and cultural intermediaries (connoisseurs, journalists, retailers and brands) offering help and guidance to the consumer in making the right choices to fit with their desired lifestyle. The implications of consumer culture for contemporary lives have been interpreted as both liberating and constraining. On the one hand, it is celebrated as a liberating process facilitating individuals to embrace commodity culture, to personalize in playful and expressive ways the value of commodities and to find new pleasures in the aesthetic qualities of consumption: 'consumer culture publicity suggests that we all have room for self-improvement and self-expression whatever our age or class origin' and that the means of achieving this is through the 'assemblage of goods, clothes, practices, experiences, appearance and bodily dispositions' (Featherstone 1987: 59). On the other hand, consumer culture is inescapable because even attempting to opt out of consumer culture is in itself an expression of a consumer lifestyle (Bauman 1991; Wernick 1991; see Southerton 2019 for a full discussion).

The rise of consumer culture is at the core of Schor's (1992) highly influential account of *The Overworked American*. Schor points to a simple paradox: Americans were working more at the end of the twentieth century despite the gains made from the phenomenal productivity growth associated with, first, Fordist and, second, post-Fordist economies. Using estimates of hours spent in paid and unpaid work between 1969 and 1987, Schor demonstrated the steady increase of work time. This contrasts with productivity measures (which calculate the goods and services that result from each hour of work) that show American productivity increased in all but five years since 1948. Analysing the productivity dividend, where increased productivity presents the possibility of either more non-work time or more money to facilitate higher levels of consumption, she demonstrates that the latter path has characterized US society in the post–Second World War era. Indeed, by the early 1990s the USA produced in six months the same volume of goods and services that it did in the whole of 1948. Rather than take such productive gains as 'leisure time' (as predicted in the leisure society theory), the average American took more consumption: by the early 1990s the average American owned and consumed more than double the consumer goods and services than did an average American in 1948.

Schor identifies two fundamental processes to explain these trajectories. The first is the logic of production in capitalist economies. She explains the economic benefits for firms of training a limited number of employees who work long hours as opposed to a large number of employees who work limited hours. Second is the emergence of consumer culture and its capacity, through the media and marketing, to ratchet upwards expectations and perceptions of needs and wants. Premised on the basis that people value their consumption relative to others and that a global consumer culture places the lifestyles of the most affluent as the key consumer referent group, 'the average individual needs to earn more money' in order to fund consumer lifestyles (Schor 1998: 123). The overall consequence is that people work more to consume more, which squeezes the time available for leisure and personal life, undermining well-being despite the apparent rise of living standards as measured by material affluence.

Schor's is a powerful and influential argument, not least because it raises serious questions about the measurement of economic growth and welfare (living standards) being based exclusively on the exchange and circulation of money, while ignoring the time use implications of economic growth for well-being (see Gershuny 2000 for a similar argument in relation to European societies). There are, however, two important critiques. First, it is debatable as to whether work time has increased (as will be discussed further in the next chapter). For example, Robinson and Godbey (1997) show that the amount of time Americans spend working has declined over the same time period as Schor shows it as increasing, although, paradoxically, their data reveals that Americans felt more time pressured in 1987 than they did in 1969! In response, Leete and Schor (1994) argue that conventional time-use studies underestimate the amount of paid work because they do not correct for second jobs, industry variations or make adjustments for business cycles. Nevertheless, some caution over the crucial claim that Americans work more is warranted. This is especially as data for European societies consistently reveals a decline in time spent working over the course of the twentieth century (Gershuny 2000).

The second critique relates to the dependence of her theoretical account on emulation as the principal driver of consumption and identity. Schor presents plenty of evidence that consumers desire more consumer goods, underestimate their own material wealth relative to others and aspire to consume at levels enjoyed by the elite (principally celebrities). However, while emulation is certainly relevant to processes of consumption, consumption cannot be reduced to a process of emulation. As the work of Bourdieu (1984) demonstrates, consumption is relational not only in terms of aspirations but also in terms of rejection of the tastes of others. Consumers identify within groups of people who share similar tastes and cultural dispositions, and reject—as extravagant, wasteful and pretentious or vulgar, frugal and unrefined—the consumer lifestyles of other groups whether wealthy or poorer than themselves (see also Lamont 1992 or Bennett et al. 2009). Consequently, the critical mechanism in Schor's account of why people might work more (to emulate the consumption of the wealthy elite) must, at the very least, be questioned with respect to its veracity. If people do work more, it might be due to reasons other than lifestyle status competition.

Despite critiques, Schor presents a provocative commentary on American consumer culture and its capacity to generate time squeeze. Her analysis demonstrates the commodification of both work and leisure time, and presents a generic explanation of how the relationship between paid work and consumption is associated with senses of a time squeeze. Arguably, it matters rather less whether people actually work longer hours; the critical point is the emergence of consumer culture and the diversification of goods and services is associated with pervasive feelings and experiences of time famine (Cross 2005). This is certainly the case in Darier's (1998) account of busyness, which he suggests has become symbolic of a 'full' and 'valued' life. The emerging demands on individuals to narrate their identity through styles of consumption bring with it the requirement of trying new and varied experiences and, he argues, it is this that leads individuals towards the pursuit of more and more cultural practices. There are so many cultural experiences and lifestyles to 'try-out' in the course of searching out and narrating our senses of identity that we feel under pressure to try them all. The notion of the 'bucket list' and examples of commonly found articles in newspapers and magazines describing 'places to visit' or 'dishes to try' all do so through the framing that time is finite and that one is successively moving through 'a life'.

2.4   Conclusion

This chapter has presented an overview of the influential theories that have shaped contemporary understandings of the changing relationship between time and society. It demonstrates that a distinctive feature of modernity has been the rising significance of the objective measurement of motion and activity through abstract and objectified clock-mediated units of time. As a device for maximizing economic productivity, coordinating labour and organizing the circulation of goods, services and people, the clock has come to regulate, standardize and discipline social lives. Thompson's account of how clock time has been internalized through time orientation and Marx's account of time as a commodity reveal the processes through which time has come to be understood as a resource that exists independently from human activity and which can therefore be subjected to principles of management, effective allocation and utility maximization. By the early twentieth century, objective and objectified time was firmly established as the temporal norm that ordered social, economic and cultural life.

The logic of objective time has taken on greater significance in the post-war period as its capacity for organizing and maximizing the efficiencies of production processes and the circulation of goods and services extended beyond the industrial economy. This is most evident in the rise of mass consumption. Time management techniques applied to Fordist mode of mass production resulted in an ever-growing range of consumer goods at relatively cheaper prices bringing consumption to the masses. Some predicted that these changes signalled the dawn of a new leisure society, in which mass production could satisfy consumer needs while reducing the amount of time required to produce those goods. Goods could be produced faster and at lower costs; consumers could therefore consume what they needed for less money thus freeing them to spend less of their time in paid labour. This was not the outcome. Instead, leisure activities became subject to the same principles of time management that Thompson identified with respect to industrial labour as a greater range of leisure activities emerged, and the logic of the clock came to be employed to measure and discipline the performance of leisure activities. Leisure became less leisurely.

Finally, in the latter third of the twentieth century, objective time came to represent a core dimension of understandings of consumer culture. As post-Fordist production methods increase the diversity of consumer goods and consumption becomes increasingly significant in defining senses of identity and lifestyles, awareness of the challenges of 'fitting' consumption desires into the time available in people's everyday lives becomes a focal point of popular anxieties. This argument is captured in Juliet Schor's account of 'work-spend cycles'. In the pursuit of insatiable consumer lifestyles, which are heavily marketed and advertised in consumer societies, people need to work more in order to obtain the income necessary to engage with ever-more consumption (that also takes up units time). By the late twentieth society the logic of maximizing objective units of time by filling it with more work to facilitate more consumption is pervasive. It is this, according to Schor, that causes the contemporary time-squeeze which undermines senses of well-being.

As we will see in the following chapters, the reduction of temporalities to objective understandings of (clock) time does not represent a complete explanation of temporal experiences nor of the range of ways in which time relates to social lives. However, the discussion in this chapter of the dominant social scientific theories of time does demonstrate the centrality of the clock in shaping academic and popular understandings of time and social change. At the heart of these accounts is the premise that time is objective and exists independent of human activity. This understanding of time undoubtedly played an important role in the development of industrial society through principles such as scientific management that increased productivity rates and the standardization of time through the clock that enabled more effective coordination of labour and goods. And it is this objective framing of time that represents the default mode of

analysis for the senses of a time squeeze that have come to represent and
define descriptions of contemporary everyday lives.

References

Adam, B. (1990). *Time and Social Theory*. Cambridge: Polity.
Adam, B. (1995). *Timewatch: The Social Analysis of Time*. London: Polity.
Bauman, Z. (1991). *Modernity and Ambivalence*. Cambridge: Polity Press.
Bell, D. (1976). *The Cultural Contradictions of Capitalism*. New York: Basic Books.
Bennett, T., Savage, M., Silva, E., Warde, A., Gayo-Cal, M., & Wright,
    D. (2009). *Culture, Class, Distinction*. London: Routledge.
Bocock, R. (1993). *Consumption*. London: Routledge.
Bourdieu, P. (1984). *Distinction: A Social Critique of the Judgment of Taste*.
    London: Routledge & Kegan Paul.
Cross, G. (2005). A Right to Be Lazy?: Busyness in Retrospective. *Social Research:
    An International Quarterly, 72*(2), 263–286.
Darier, E. (1998). Time to be Lazy. Work, the Environment and Subjectivities.
    Time & Society, 7(2), 193–208.
Dumazedier, J. (1967). *Toward a Leisure of Society*. New York: Free Press.
Featherstone, M. (1987). Lifestyle and Consumer Culture, *Theory. Culture &
    Society, 4*(1), 55–60.
Featherstone, M. (1991). *Consumer Culture and Postmodernism*. London: Sage.
Featherstone, M. (1997). Lifestyle and Consumer Culture. *Theory, Culture &
    Society, 4*(1), 55–70.
Gershuny, J. (2000). *Changing Times: Work and Leisure in Post-industrial Society*.
    Oxford: Oxford University Press.
Giddens, A. (1991). *Modernity and Self-Identity*. Cambridge: Polity.
Glennie, P., & Thrift, N. (1996). Reworking E.P. Thompson's "Time, Work-
    Discipline and Industrial Capitalism". *Time & Society, 5*(3), 275–299.
Glennie, P., & Thrift, N. (2009). *Shaping the Day: A History of Timekeeping in
    England and Wales 1300–1800*. Oxford: Oxford University Press.
Harvey, M. (1999). Economies of Time: A Framework for Analysing the
    Restructuring of Employment Relations. In A. Felstead & N. Jewson (Eds.),
    Global Trends in Flexible Labour. London: Macmillan.
Hebdige, D. (1979). *Subcultures: The Meaning of Style*. London: Routledge.

Keynes, J. M. (1936). Economic Prospects for our Grandchildren. In D. E. Moggridge (Ed.), *Essays in Persuasion: The Collected Writings of John Maynard Keynes* (Vol. 9, pp. 321–332). London: Macmillan Press.

Lamont, M. (1992). *Money, Morals & Manners: The Culture of the French and American Upper-Middle Class*. London: Chicago Press.

Landes, D. (1983). *Revolution in Time: Clocks and the Making of the Modern World*. Cambridge, MA: Harvard University Press.

Leete, L., & Schor, J. (1994). Assessing the Time-Squeeze Hypothesis: Hours Worked in the United States, 1969–89. *Industrial Relations, 33*(1), 25–43.

Linder, S. B. (1970). *The Harried Leisure Class*. New York: Columbia University Press.

Marx, K. (1976[1867]). *Capital, Vol. I*. Penguin: London.

O'Malley, M. (1992). Time, Work and Task Orientation: A Critique of American Historiography. *Time and Society, 1*(3), 341–358.

Roberts, K. (1976). The Time Famine. In S. Parker (Ed.), *The Sociology of Leisure*. Allen & Unwin.

Robinson, J., & Godbey, G. (1997). *Time for Life: The Surprising Ways That Americans Use Their Time*. Pennsylvania State Press.

Sabelis, I. (2001). Time Management. *Time & Society, 10*(2–3), 387–400.

Schor, J. (1992). *The Overworked American: The Unexpected Decline of Leisure*. Basic Books.

Schor, J. (1998). Work, Free Time and Consumption. Time, Labour and Consumption: Guest Editor's Introduction. *Time & Society, 7*(1), 119–127.

Slater, D. (1997). *Consumer Culture and Modernity*. Cambridge: Polity.

Southerton, D. (2011). Introduction. In D. Southerton (Ed.), *Encyclopedia of Consumer Culture* (pp. xxiix–xxxiv). Thousand Oaks, CA: Sage.

Southerton, D. (2019). Consumer Culture and Personal Life. In V. May & P. Nordqvist (Eds.), *Sociology of Personal Life*. Palgrave Macmillan.

Taylor, F. W. (1911). *The Principles of Scientific Management*. New York: Harper & Brothers. [C2]

Thompson, E. P. (1967). Time, Work-Discipline and Industrial Capitalism: Past and Present, 38: 56–97; repr. in Flinn, m. & Smout, T. (eds.) (1974) *Essays in Social History*, Oxford: Clarendon Press.

Trentmann, F. (Ed.). (2012). *The Oxford Handbook of the History of Consumption*. London: Oxford University Press.

Veblen, T. (1935[1899]). *The Theory of the Leisure Class*. New York: American Library.

Warde, A. (1994). Consumption, Identity-formation and Uncertainty. *Sociology*, *28*(4). https://doi.org/10.1177/0038038594028004005.

Warde, A. (2017). *Consumption: A Sociological Analysis*. London: Palgrave Macmillan.

Weber, M. (1989 [1905]). *The Protestant Ethic and the Spirit of Capitalism*. London: Unwin Hymen. C2

Wernick, A. (1991). *Promotional Culture: Advertising, Ideology and Symbolic Expression*. London: Sage.

Young, M. (1988). *The Metronomic Society: Natural Rhythms and Human Timetables*. London: Thames and Hudson.

Zerubavel, E. (1981). *Hidden Rhythms: Schedules and Calendars in Social Life*. Chicago: Chicago University Press.

3

Time Scarcity: Work, Home and Personal Lives

3.1   Introduction

The dominance of clock time in social scientific theory sets empirical enquiry on a particular pathway. Theoretical accounts present contemporary experiences of time as being a matter of more human activities being 'squeezed' into finite units of (clock-based) time. It is this, so the argument goes, that creates temporal experiences of time scarcity: people simply no longer have enough minutes and hours in their days to fulfil all the activities that they deem necessary to realize a satisfactory everyday life. From such theoretical bases it is no surprise that empirical investigations focus attention on which activities have increased in volume. As we have seen in Chap. 2, some suggest an increase of time devoted to paid work and to consumption, while others focus on leisure.

This chapter examines the empirical evidence that seeks to reveal whether changes in the amount of time devoted to paid and unpaid work, consumption and leisure, and personal relationships reveal any substantive grounds for time scarcity. It demonstrates that, at best, a focus on more or less activities is inconclusive because no simple correlation between the performance of activities and objective time can be

© The Author(s) 2020   43
D. Southerton, *Time, Consumption and the Coordination of Everyday Life*,
Consumption and Public Life, https://doi.org/10.1057/978-1-349-60117-2_3

determined, and that on balance the evidence provides little support for the notion that contemporary lives are more time scarce than were the everyday lives of people in the past.

Objective conceptualizations of time as an abstract commodity that can be exchanged for labour, the pursuit of leisure, consumption and desired styles of life (or lifestyles) also tend to take the individual as the central unit of analysis and seek to examine whether each individual devotes more or less of their time to particular activities. Such a conceptualization fails to fully recognize that the ways in which time is distributed across society are rarely an individualized matter. Activities, and therefore the time required to perform them, are shared across groups of people. This includes households in which partners distribute and share domestic chores, networks of family and friends who offer support, for example, with childcare, workplaces in which colleagues might exchange tasks and social institutions which perform activities that reduce the time demands on individuals (such as schools providing childcare and markets providing services that reduce the time needed for grocery shopping). A key theme of this chapter is therefore how objective time is distributed, negotiated and exchanged in the performance of core everyday activities across social groups at different scales (from the individual, households, workplaces and social institutions).

This chapter also demonstrates that the distribution of activities in and across objective time is not simply a matter of individual discretion. First, as will be shown through debates about work-life balance, the distribution and exchange of time for different kinds of activities (paid, unpaid work, childcare, leisure, etc.) are matters of negotiation and arrangement within and across households and involve different modes of provision (state, market, household, social networks, etc.). For example, some use their economic capital to purchase domestic services in order to reduce the amount of time, as a household or couple, required for the completion of domestic tasks while others may rely on their social capital in the form of extended family or their social networks. Second, what is understood to be appropriate standards for accomplishing practices to a satisfactory level are not static but culturally derived, dynamic and differentiated across social groups. As we will see, while services purchased from markets might reduce the amount of time required, say to wash or iron an item of clothing and clean the home, those markets also play a role in raising standards of cleanliness and, therefore, the frequency with which that item of clothing 'should' or 'needs' to be washed. Finally, the ways in which time and activities are distributed within personal relationships, whether couple or parent-child relationships, are highly emotive. As will be shown, clock time infuses personal relationships with a framing of objective measurement and commodification that undermine (or clash with) established cultural meanings of the satisfactory performance of caring in intimate relationships.

3.2 Time Spent Working and Gendered Divisions of Labour

The domestic division of labour refers to the (unequal) distribution of household tasks performed between men and women. A critical question, which also returns us to the major contentions of Schor's theory of work-spend cycles discussed in Chap. 2, is whether the gendered division of labour is reflected in the time use patterns of men and women. Table 3.1 reports the mean minutes spent in the core categories of

Table 3.1 Change in total minutes per day devoted to paid and unpaid work among UK adults aged 20–60

		1961	2001	2015	Change between 1961 and 2015
Paid work	Men	434	323	309	−125
	Women	183	203	216	+33
	All	307	262	262	−45
Unpaid work	Men	83	146	140	+57
	Women	303	277	249	−54
	All	193	213	195	+2
Total work (paid and unpaid)	Men	517	469	449	−68
	Women	486	480	465	−21
	All	500	475	457	−43
Non-work time	Men	923	971	992	+69
	Women	954	959	975	+21
	All	939	965	983	+43

Source: Adapted from Gershuny (2005) and OECD (2018)

everyday activities for the UK population in 1961, 2001 and 2015. While a crude measure of changing time use, the Table demonstrates that working-age Britons in 2015 spent less time in paid work (45 minutes) and marginally more time in unpaid work (2 minutes) than their counterparts did in 1961. The working-age British population have gained somewhere in the region of 43 minutes of time to devote to non-work activities. The distribution of time remains gendered, women in 2015 spent less time in paid work than men (1 hour 33 minutes less per day) and considerably more in unpaid work (1 hour 49 minutes more per day). Over the period we have seen some convergence: women perform more paid and less unpaid work and men the opposite. Men have gained the most with respect to non-work time, with an increase of over an hour compared to the gain of 21 minutes for women (for a comprehensive analysis of the changing ways in which Briton's use their time, see Gershuny and Sullivan 2019).

While making cross-country comparisons is difficult given variations in the ways in which data is collected, sample selection and demographic variations, the pattern for the UK is broadly repeated across Europe, North America and Australia (see Gershuny 2000 for the most comprehensive cross-country analysis). For instance, Aguiar and Hurst (2009) show that leisure time increased for both American men and women between 1965 and 2005. Broadly, men gained around 5 hours per week of non-work time and women around 3.5 hours, although much of this gain occurred before the mid-1980s. Men have significantly reduced their time in paid work and marginally increased their time in unpaid work including childcare, while women show the reverse trend with increases in paid and decreases in unpaid work, a trend that has stalled somewhat since the mid-1980s.

When various time use studies from different eras are reviewed together, whether focused on a single country (Robinson and Godbey 1997; Fisher et al. 2006; Aguiar and Hurst 2007) or from multiple countries (Gershuny 2009), the results reveal a continuous increase of non-work time in the post-war era. Such aggregation does, however, mask an important trend across occupational types. Gershuny (2011) demonstrates that in the UK, since 1974, both men and women with university-level education have actually seen a marginal increase in the amount of time they spend in paid work, while those with incomplete secondary education have seen a reduction. One explanation for this is Gershuny's (2005) argument that being busy at work has become a 'badge of honour' because it symbolizes occupational success and achievement. Furthermore, those in managerial, professional and technical occupations where levels of intrinsic enjoyment from work are highest have also increased as a proportion of the total time spent in work across the UK population, while those occupations with the lowest levels of intrinsic reward (manual occupations) have decreased. In other words, the UK has seen a rise in the total proportion of work time devoted to occupations with the highest levels of intrinsic enjoyment (with professional, managerial and technical occupations accounting for 39% of total work time in 2001 compared with 17% in 1974) and a decline of manual occupations (from 53% to 31% of total work time over the same period). In the USA, Aguiar and Hurst (2009) similarly show that since 1965, less-educated men and women have experienced substantial leisure increases relative to their more educated counterparts who have experienced little, if any, leisure gains since 1985. And, Gimenez-Nadal and Sevilla-Sanz (2012) reveal the same patterns of those with lower levels of education gaining more non-work time relative to their educated compatriots in their multi-country analysis of time use trends since the 1970s in Australia, Canada, Finland, France, the Netherlands, Norway and the UK. Broad aggregates for the total population reveal less work and more leisure time, but this general trend is less pronounced amongst the highly educated professional middle classes. Whether this is because of the demands of professional occupations (as will be discussed in the following sections) or because, as Gershuny (2011) argues, the highly educated receive greater intrinsic pleasures from their work remains an empirical contention.

Returning to the domestic division of labour, the aggregate data of mean time spent in broad categories of activities reveals the persistence of real gender inequalities but with trajectories that could be read as a narrowing of the gender division of labour. This is precisely the argument put forward by Gershuny et al. (1994) in their theory of 'lagged adaptation'. They argue that as women enter paid work (the traditional cultural role of men) men slowly adjust to take on more unpaid work (domestic labour—the traditional cultural role attributed to women). This is not simply a process of acquiring new competence in performing unfamiliar domestic tasks, but it is also a process where identities based around cultural conceptions of masculinity and femininity are challenged and remade. There is, according to Gershuny et al. (1994: 155), an inevitable 'time-drag' between women entering paid work and changing gender divisions of labour:

> we could only expect it [sex equality] to be complete and painless once all adult members of households were themselves children in households with unchallenged egalitarian models—this is, a very long time into the future.

The crude data presented in Table 3.1 does show some convergence in that women do more paid and less unpaid work than they did in the 1960s and men vice versa, but it also reveals that women now perform a greater volume of total work than men do and have enjoyed only a third of the increase of non-work time that their male counterparts have experienced over the period.

Using the multinational time use survey (MTUS)—a harmonized data set of time diaries from 25 countries conducted since the 1960s—Gershuny (2018) returns to this subject to provide a comprehensive analysis of gendered distributions of time against broad categories of activity. His analysis lends further support to the general trends—with trajectories of convergence in time spent in paid and unpaid work across the sexes, but women still performing over 60% of all unpaid work activities. Greater conversion is demonstrated in the Nordic welfare state countries, followed by the neo-liberal market anglophone countries (UK, USA, Australia) and corporatist states of Western Europe (Belgium, France, Germany, Netherlands and Poland). Data for these countries also demonstrates what Young and Willmott (1973) described as symmetrical relationships, in which the total work within households is distributed equally across men and women although not in an egalitarian form in which men and women perform equal amounts of the same types of work. Gershuny (2018: 12) summarizes this finding as:

> The pattern first identified by Young and Willmott in their pioneering time budget study, of two-and-a-half job heterosexual couples, in which the

man has full time employment, and the woman has a shorter-hours job and takes on a disproportionate share of the unpaid work, is a pretty good summary of what we see in all the 81 national surveys discussed here.

Gershuny offers two explanations for why the combined (paid and unpaid) amount of time that men and women spend in work oscillates around 480 minutes per day in all countries studied. First, the evidence suggests that couples seek, and as we will see later with differing degrees of success, to synchronize their work time in order to spend their non-work time together. The second is that couples distribute their total work time according to principles of 'fair share'. Gershuny also reminds us that symmetrical divisions of labour have continuing and significant gender inequality implications with respect to financial earnings and the independence this affords for the sexes.

Critics of the lagged adaptation theory challenge the notion that mean minutes of time spent in generic categories of activity, especially when based on records of 'primary activities', represent a robust measure of how men and women experience time. When combinations of primary and secondary activities—primary being the activity recorded as the main activity, secondary being activities performed simultaneously—are taken into account the picture changes. Bittman and Wajcman (2000) demonstrate that even though the amount of leisure time enjoyed by men and women in all OECD countries has become roughly equal, this does not result in similar experiences of leisure time. When secondary activities are included in the analysis men appear to enjoy consolidated periods, of say two hours, of leisure while a principal feature of women's leisure is its punctuation with unpaid work, especially childcare. Further empirical evidence is provided by Shaw (1998) who demonstrates that women feel less entitlement to reserve uninterrupted time for themselves and a sense of moral responsibility to be always available for family matters. And, returning to time diary data analysis, Sullivan (1996, 1997) shows that the unpaid work conducted by men is overwhelmingly 'masculine' in character, such as maintaining the home and gardening. Clearer still, analysis of secondary activities reveals that married women multitask to a much greater extent than men do. She shows that married women spent 31 hours 19 minutes per week in combined activities compared with

23 hours and 28 minutes for married men. This is not a natural gendered disposition because single men spent 27 hours and 18 minutes in combined activities compared with 19 hours and 19 minutes for single women. It would appear that women multitask more than men if they are married.

3.3   Flexitime and Work-Life Balance

As we have seen, aggregates of hours and minutes attributed to broad categories of activities provide an important overview of the general trends and trajectories of the distribution of human activity within the 24-hour day. It does not, however, explain how those broad categories of activities have changed during the periods covered by the diaries. In addition to the rising number of women entering paid employment, a significant change in working time arrangements has been the rise of flexible working hours or, to use the terminology employed by organizational studies, the rise of non-standard work time arrangements. In 2011 some 30% of UK workers had access to flexible work time schedules and 23% regularly worked outside of their office, most often from their homes (Chung 2018). In the USA, 14% of those in employment had access to flexible work schedules rising to 30% by 1997 and remaining at that level through to 2004 (McMenamin 2007). And analysis of Belgian time diary data reveals that less than 40% of employees work the 'standard' hours of weekdays only (Minnen et al. 2016).

When considering the rise of flexibility and working non-standard hours, it is important to recognize that these shifts relate to the development of post-Fordist economic arrangements (discussed in Chap. 2) in which the production of goods and services demands non-standard work time arrangements to meet the flexible consumption demands of 'just-in-time' economies. It is in this context that Breedveld (1998) makes the critical distinction between flexibility 'of' and 'for' employees. Breedveld reveals that flexible work in professional, managerial and technical occupations offer flexibility 'for' workers. Such occupations, which comprise of those with high socio-economic status, increasingly offer autonomy over the allocation of tasks within their working day and over which hours of the day are worked. He provides examples of managers taking home routine paperwork and filling in forms while watching TV. By contrast, flexibilization for lower socio-economic status groups in routine manual and clerical jobs demands flexibility 'of' employees, whose work times tend to be controlled by the needs of their employers. They have little autonomy over what hours they work and have to adjust their daily life around the hours of employment required by their employers. It is little surprise that an Australian study revealed that they preferred longer hours of employment working standard weekday shifts than shorter hours imposed rosters that included night-time and weekend work but fewer hours (Baker et al. 2003).

The distinction between flexibility of and for workers does not necessarily correlate to entirely positive or negative outcomes for either set of work time arrangements. Garhammer (1995) reveals how 'flexibility of' working arrangements tend to be organized as predictable and regular shifts with a clear demarcation between times of work and non-work. This contrasts with those who have 'flexibility for' arrangements (i.e. are contracted to work a particular number of hours per week but retain some discretion over when and where those hours are worked), which Garhammer demonstrates as blurring the boundaries between work and non-work times, results in unpredictable times of work and has the effect of undermining collegiality because it individualizes work patterns and intensifies senses of workplace competition.

Ethnographic studies of workplace environments support Garhammer's analysis. For example, Rutherford (2001) revealed how women with 'flexibility for' working arrangements were pitted against one another with respect to career progression, through references and gestures that made it clear that the most committed would progress faster in their company. And the way to demonstrate commitment was to be in the office before and after the boss had left and by working longer hours than their contracts required. Kunda's (2001) study reported a similar situation for men, who worked long working hours as a means of demonstrating commitment to their employers, to their fellow workmates and to indicate to those outside of their working environments that they had a full and demanding (thus high-status) job. A more recent study by Lott and Chung (2016) that examined the German Socio-Economic Panel Study (SOEP) (2003–2011) also revealed that those with 'flexibility for' occupations increase their working hours. Having greater autonomy over one's hours of work results in longer working hours, which is consistent with Gershuny's finding that the professional, managerial and technical occupations have seen moderate increases in work hours relative to those in manual occupations. In other words, those in lower-paid jobs are most likely to experience predictable working arrangements, work comparatively fewer hours and have limited control or autonomy over the timing of work activities. The professional middle classes are likely to have 'flexibility for' working arrangements and work comparatively long hours but have greater autonomy over the allocation of work activities within clock time.

Together, the rise of non-standard working arrangements and dual income households has two important implications for the temporal experiences of work and home life. The first relates to the ways in which the boundaries between work and home are managed. In her study of call-centre workers, Brannen (2005) argues that non-standard working hours can have the effect of undermining such boundaries such that work remains very much in the foreground and family life in the background. From her study she identified two distinct tendencies that employees adopt to manage the relationship between home and work: separators and connectors. Separators work hard to maintain a clear boundary between home and work, including avoidance of discussing work-related matters outside of work and avoiding work-based social events such as Christmas parties. Connecters, on the other hand, were those fully engaged in work, pursuing a career and receiving particular 'identity-value' from their work. These were the people who volunteered to do the office collection, work late by choice and go on training courses outside of standard work hours (such as on the evening) in order to maintain their skill base. In both cases dissatisfaction with life was strong. Separators were alienated from work and fought hard to erect boundaries. Connecters viewed home life as a constraint on work and the boundaries between work and home were constantly up for negotiation, bartering and quarrels between partners. She concluded that while flexible working hours offer benefits in terms of juggling the demands of work and home, it also perpetuates an assumption that individuals can manage or control a better work-life balance simply by having some marginal discretion over the allocation of work time.

The second implication to consider is how dual income households manage and negotiate the impacts of the time spent in paid labour of two adults within a household. Fagan (2001) identifies four ways in which dual income households organize their paid work and domestic obligations: (1) similar start times—both partners work similar hours; (2) sandwich arrangements—one person starts later and finishes earlier than the other; (3) overlapping—one person starts later and finishes later than the other; (4) consecutive—one person starts work after the other has finished. Lesnard (2008) demonstrates that a number of dual income couples with desynchronized work schedules (i.e. sandwich, overlapping or consecutive work time arrangements) have increased in France and the USA such that by the late 1990s some 20% of the times at which French couples were in paid employment was desynchronized. Furthermore, when French couples had control over their times of work 79% opted for synchronized (i.e. with similar start and end times) work patterns. In the UK, Warren's (2003) study using the British Household Panel study estimated that one-third of couples worked split (desynchronized) schedules and that for those couples in manual occupations this estimate rose to 41% which contrasts 24% of couples in professional occupations. A more recent study of UK dual income couples also demonstrates a strong tendency for couples with flexible working arrangements to seek synchronized work schedules (Bryan 2017). These findings are no surprise given that studies continuously reveal that couples who report the most satisfaction in their relationships are those who spend leisure time together (Daly 1996). In addition, the limited number of studies on work time arrangements and friendship patterns also reveal the importance of work schedule synchronicity (Pisarski et al. 2008), with a Danish study showing that shift workers with predictable hours of work were most able to find time to spend with friends and those with flexible working arrangements went to significant lengths in order to manage their work times in order to enable sociability (Pedersen and Lewis 2012).

Answering the question of whether or not people spend more time in work, whether paid or unpaid, opens up a diverse range of critical questions regarding how work time arrangements have changed and what implications these have for the relationship between time spend in and outside of employment. The rise of flexible work and dual income households has offered greater autonomy to those in professional, managerial and technical occupations. It also appears to foster increased workplace competition and longer working hours when compared with other occupational groups and blurs the boundaries between work and home. For those in manual occupations flexibility represents a different set of work time conditions which might offer relatively shorter hours of work but also reduces capacity to synchronize times of work with partners, family and friends. And, the emphasis on synchronization of work and non-work activities in the findings of studies on flexible working times demonstrates that the timings of activities matter as much as the time spent on them. Overall, significant variations of temporal experience underpin aggregated mean minutes of time spent in broad categories of activities that demonstrate an overall general decline in time spend in paid and unpaid work.

3.4   Time for Personal Life

In the late 1990s Arlie Hochschild (1997) explored the relationships between work and personal life through an ethnographic study of a major American corporation. Her conclusions reveal a somewhat prescient analysis of the interactions and implications of paid work, unpaid work, consumer culture and experiences of time. She argued that as hours of paid work increase (what she calls the first shift), time for domestic matters (the second shift) is squeezed, and time devoted to emotional and interpersonal relationships becomes experienced as a 'third shift' subject to time planning and management. This is a process of rationalization because, she argues, the principles of Taylorization (discussed in Chap. 2 with reference to industrial production) have increasingly come to characterize the experience of the second shift. The rise of domestic appliances, essential to reducing the labour involved in the performance of unpaid work, operate by breaking down (or fragmenting) domestic tasks into their component parts and enable their re-sequencing in order to maximize temporal efficiency (see also Shove and Southerton 2000, for an example of the domestic freezer). Washing clothes, for example, fragments into components of sorting items, washing, drying, ironing and then re-sorting for storage, with each component being performed at different times across several days (see Mylan and Southerton 2018 and Chap. 7). Even time spent with family and friends comes to be experienced as a 'third shift', deconstructed into allocated time slots and subject to time management. She sees this as rationalization—as calculated planning of when to spend time with loved ones which, even when the plans come off, corrodes the quality of the time together because it is subject to the principles of time management. It is in this context that the search for 'quality time' has emerged as a major concern, and anxiety, of American family life.

One of the ironies, she suggests, is that modern corporations have responded to workers' senses of alienation associated with Tayloristic time management arrangements. Corporations now provide a range of social activities, including gyms, therapy, book clubs, sports teams, crèche's, work-based 'exchange boards' (for unwanted goods or cheap rental of holiday homes), fetes and so on. This is coupled with shifts towards project- or portfolio-based working, working in teams and more frequent monitoring of and support for career progression. In such contexts, work becomes more rewarding than home, while domestic work and the interpersonal relationships that are conventionally associated with 'home' take the kind of alienating, rationalized and commodified forms of time once associated with the (clock) time discipline of factories highlighted by E.P. Thompson.

For Hochschild such changes in the temporal experiences of everyday life lead to the further commodification of time and of personal lives. She provides the example of the rise of outsourcing in which households purchase domestic services, such as housekeepers, gardeners, childcare, laundry services and pre-prepared and takeaway foods, from the market as opposed to performing the tasks themselves. For Hochschild, the care associated with personal life and intimate relationships (with partners, children and friends) that conventionally represent a critical part of a moral economy of time in which emotion and love represent unquantifiable properties are increasingly handed over to the market and commodified. It is this process of the commodification of the moral economy of time that creates the conditions in which a market culture for managing personal relationships emerges. This market culture presents the activities associated with emotional bonds and connections as open to the principles of market exchange and substitution in order to maximize available amounts of (clock) time for other activities. In the process, perceptions and awareness that time is scarce become increasingly acute as we become more reliant on markets to provision those activities conventionally associated with the moral economy and emotional labour of the household, family and personal relationships (Hochschild 2003).

As with other accounts, such as Schor's work-spend cycles, the evidence from time diaries casts some doubt on Hochschild's argument that the 'first shift' consists of longer working hours, although time diary evidence is clear that women's time spent in paid work has increased significantly across all OECD countries and it is the experience of women that is at the heart of Hochschild's account. Whether work has become more rewarding is equally unclear, although it would seem that there has been an increase in the proportion of occupations within the labour markets of affluent societies that people find more intrinsically rewarding and that those people working in such occupations have increased their work time relative to those working in manual occupations. It is also the case that those in such occupations tend to have greater autonomy over the times when they work and that this may contribute to undermining or blurring the boundaries between work and home. In this respect, Hochschild's analysis of the first shift seems to fit the experience of those, especially women, who work in the ever-expanding professional, managerial and technical occupations of affluent societies.

Hochschild's second contention, regarding the second shift, is worth some further exploration. The innovation and diffusion of domestic appliances is a defining feature of the post-war period, with a range of labour-saving devices entering into the home. In her analysis of the industrialization of domestic work, Schwartz-Cowan (1983) details the range of technologies introduced to homes that reduced the physical demands of domestic tasks and increased the productivity of households.

She also demonstrated how the diffusion of such technologies was accompanied by the development and marketing of domestic science and what Ehrenreich and English (1979) describe as 'scientific motherhood' in which new standards of housework and childcare emerged. Furthermore, this industrialization of the home can be understood as a key feature of the rise of what Gershuny (1978) identified as the self-service economy, in which households purchase technologies in order to service themselves (such as cars and washing machines), thus reducing their use of collective services (such as public transport and launderettes). For Schwartz-Cowan these processes resulted in 'more work for mothers' because while domestic technologies increased household productivity and reduced the physical demands of the work involved, they also exponentially raised standards and expectations in the delivery and outcome of those domestic services.

Further support for Hochschild's arguments about the rationalization of domestic work and Schwartz-Cowan's account or rising domestic service expectations can be found in our study of the diffusion of the freezer in the UK (Shove and Southerton 2000) and research on the meanings and styles of British kitchens (Southerton 2001). A striking feature of the changing British kitchen is its standardization that resulted from the mass manufacturing of kitchen units and the domestic technologies embedded in its design. During the 1970s and 1980s, UK kitchens increasingly came with standardized spaces in which fridges, ovens and eventually dishwashers were to be slotted. By the 1990s those kitchens were designed with such appliances build-in or embedded within kitchen units. One such technology was the freezer, which over the period went from being a device owned by only 3% of UK households to 96%. Accompanied by changes in the retail of domestic food (i.e. the growth of the supermarket) and the rise of dual income households, the freezer has come to play a pivotal role in the food provisioning practices of UK households. Yet the meaning and uses of the freezer also changed during its diffusion, from originally being a device to store novel foods (ice cream), to be a device for domestic economy (by bulk buying food) and then to becoming a convenience device. Once firmly embedded in standardized kitchen units, the freezer, especially when combined with the microwave, enabled the fragmentation of domestic food practices with the tasks of shopping, cooking, preparing and eating food separated and extended over discrete time periods, and the need for the consecutive sequencing of those tasks removed from the practice. The combination of washing machines and tumble dryers offers similar time reordering properties for laundry practices. Such task fragmentation effects also offer scope for new forms of simultaneous performances of domestic tasks, such as cooking while the laundry is washing. Domestic technologies have deconstructed and fragmented the activities required to perform domestic practices, enabling those activities to be separated, delayed and performed in new combinations of simultaneity and which result in the complex scheduling of activities and domestic time management (Southerton 2007).

For Shove (2003), it is the relationship between rising cultural standards and expectations of cleanliness (as identified by Schwartz-Cowan), comfort (such as thermal comfort derived through space heating and cooling) and convenience (as demonstrated by the aforementioned freezer example) that underpins changing patterns of household consumption. In the process, the resource intensity of everyday social practices has escalated in ways that lock people into unsustainable yet entirely normal lifestyles (an issue that will be returned to in Chap. 8). The key point for this discussion, however, is that household technologies and the changing forms of domestic organization associated with them may have reduced the physical labour and increased the productivity of domestic tasks, but they are also associated with the increasing fragmentation of those tasks into discrete activities and escalating standards and expectations of domestic service outcomes. Together, these processes increase the frequency and time management demands of those discrete activities (Shove 2003).

The final component of Hochschild's analysis relates to the commodification of personal life that she describes as coming to resemble a 'third shift' in which increasingly more aspects of everyday life become subject to the principles of time management and commodification. Three bodies of research cast further light on this argument: the rise of outsourcing and domestic labour; consumerism as compensation for senses of time scarcity; and framing the quality of relationships through time management.

The contracting out of domestic work is a growing trend in affluent societies, especially among the professional and managerial classes

(Ehrenreich and Hochschild 2003). This includes services related to home maintenance and cleaning, laundry services and childcare. This is a process of commodification in which services purchased from the market as opposed to being performed as unpaid labour by household members. In other words, households exchange money for time in order to facilitate more rewarding activities for personal relationships. In Hochschild's study, the use of such services is met with anxiety because domestic activities conventionally understood as expressions of care are effectively exchanged for money (i.e. commodified) to facilitate more time to pursue other activities (such as paid work). This is especially the case with childcare, which is conventionally associated with the emotional work invested in parenthood. However, while we see greater outsourcing of domestic work including childcare, time diary data also reveals that both mothers and fathers are spending more time with their children today than they did in the past. Yet again, where we find empirical evidence to support claims that people spend less time in activities (in this case childcare) we also find evidence that people spend more time in related tasks (spending more leisure time with children).

Wajcman (2015) points to changing expectations and cultural understandings of what constitutes proper parenting to explain this apparent contradiction. She highlights empirical studies that suggest the emergence of 'intensive parenting' in which smaller family sizes together with dual income household arrangements have the effect of intensifying the focus on child development. Cook's (2004) fascinating account of the commodification of childhood provides an explanation of the processes underpinning such changing cultural understandings of parenting and childcare. He demonstrates how the categories of childhood and parenthood emerged through the interactions between scientific discourses of 'healthy' child development, the professionalization of home economics, retail markets and marketing that combined to define 'child needs', and in the process raised expectations regarding good parenting (Schor 2004). The concept of intensive parenting is perhaps best illustrated through the work of Lyn Craig and colleagues. First, using time diary data they identify a distinction between 'talk-based' and 'routine physical' care (Craig and Mullan 2011). Talk-based refers to face-to-face parenting interaction including reading, talking, storytelling and playing games, all of which are focused on educational needs. Physical routine care includes a broader range of activities from caring for a child's physical development through to transporting them to school and activities such as sports clubs and music lessons. In addition to demonstrating that fathers do less of both types of childcare than mothers do, they also show that fathers do little of the types of childcare that demand predictable or timetabled schedules. It would seem that fathers fit in childcare at opportune moments. They also show that mothers are present during the majority of the time that fathers devote to childcare (but not vice versa) and reveal in a separate study that Australian fathers spend more of their total childcare time in talk-based activities (Craig et al. 2014). Wajcman (2015) summarizes that the empirical evidence suggests intensive parenting might have increased time spent with children, especially by fathers, but it has only served to reinforce the gendered role of women as household manager and supervisor of domestic activities.

Given this evidence, and that the 'third shift' of time for personal relationships has become increasingly subject to the forces of commodification, it is not surprising that numerous studies discuss how women experience dual burdens as they seek to juggle paid work, the management of domestic tasks and supervision of personal relationships. Thompson's (1996) study of the time pressures faced by American women in dual income households captures these experiences. He provides examples of children eating their breakfast during the car journey to school as mothers tried to juggle getting their children dressed, fed and dropped to school on time and then getting themselves to work. Significantly, these working mothers explained the imperative for such 'juggling' through the importance placed on providing a life for their children that they never had—including giving them opportunities to play a musical instrument, to try out different sports and to have the consumer goods that were denied to them as children. They felt an obligation to work in order to provide a basic consumer lifestyle acceptable to themselves and their children. To alleviate senses of 'guilt' at not being at home for their children after school, they rewarded their children with treats—thus increasing the need to work. In this respect, Thompson's study lends some support to Schor's 'work more to consume more' theory, only the consumption is for children and facilitated by parents.

However, many of the women studied also outsourced many of their domestic tasks: it was not necessarily a lack of time that underpinned their juggling lifestyles but that their paid work meant that they felt they were not in the right place at the right time for their children.

The process of commodification is at the heart of all of these accounts of contemporary temporal experiences. In the terminology of Hochschild, the first shift is at least in part related to the work-spend cycles identified by Schor even if that is focused on the exchange of parents' time to foster the consumption activities of their children. The rise of domestic technologies that facilitate self-servicing and the outsourcing of domestic tasks are examples of how the 'second shift' has become increasingly subject to 'market-based' solutions for domestic management. And the associated marketing of these 'solutions' has led to changing and more time-demanding standards, conventions and expectations surrounding comfort, cleanliness, convenience and 'good' (intensive) parenting. Market solutions to managing such technologies, standards and expectations have also emerged through the proliferation of 'self-help' guides for time management, which effectively individualize the problem as a matter of individual organization and utilization of commodities in the forms of goods and services (Hochschild 2003; Larsson and Sanne 2005). In his study of time management and family life, Daly (1996) identifies four processes that commodify personal lives. First, he shows that the core discourse of domestic time management advice is to 'take control over your life' through time planning systems (e.g. rotas) that enable the time-efficient use of domestic technologies. Second, he shows how such discourses reproduce norms that commodify time by emphasizing an exchange, or trading, of tasks through the advice of establishing rules like 'work before you play'. Third, children's time was always presented as 'valuable' investments in the development of their 'human capital' (acquisition of knowledge, skills and credentials) and was therefore a necessary and wise 'investment'. Finally, fourth was the effective planning of time to spend with intimate partners. Citing studies of intimate relationships, Daly concludes by suggesting that even sexual intercourse has become commodified as an activity to be scheduled, rationed, controlled and exchanged (with other time-consuming activities).

3.5   Conclusion

This chapter has examined the empirical evidence that seeks to explain why contemporary societies are often characterized as an experience of time scarcity. In doing so, it has discussed a wide range of studies that employ a conceptualization of objective time into which more or less everyday activities are allocated. In this framing, time scarcity is presented in zero-sum terms, in which more activities of one kind means less clock time for other activities. Many of the studies reviewed, however, avoid the risks of methodological individualism by recognizing that the activities of daily life are shared and distributed across groups or networks of people and across different modes of provision whether through households, markets or social institutions.

The evidence from time diary data lends little support to the straightforward notion that people spend more time in work (paid and unpaid) than they did in the past and consequently experience a time scarcity for non-work activities. However, the evidence is nuanced in that it shows different socio-economic groups have varied experiences of relative increases or decreases of time spent in paid or unpaid work. Women spend more time in paid work than they did in the past. Those in professional and managerial occupations have seen their paid work decline at a much lower rate than those in routine manual or clerical occupations. Whether or not this is a matter of discretion is difficult to discern. The professional and managerial classes reveal greater levels of work satisfaction and achievement, have experienced greater flexibility and autonomy in their work time arrangements and appear to embrace the status offered by their employment. Yet, these same workers face increased workplace competition that appears to generate a demand to work longer hours than other socio-economic groups. By contrast, routine manual and clerical workers have seen the greatest decline in time spent working and appear to gain some benefits from predictable hours of work with respect to patterns of sociability, but they also experience less work satisfaction and significantly lower levels of autonomy in their work time arrangements. When examined as couples, the evidence also shows that changing work time arrangements have increased levels of desynchronization across all social groups, and particularly those in routine manual and clerical occupations, despite the ideal being for partners to synchronize their working times in order that they can enjoy their non-work times together.

The empirical evidence presented from time diary analysis also appears to suggest some convergence between the sexes with respect to the amount of time spent in paid and unpaid work. Again, when scrutinized in detail, the data reveals that women disproportionately retain responsibility for the management and supervision of unpaid domestic work and experience dual burdens of juggling home and work while their leisure time is more likely to be fragmented and interrupted than men. Both mothers and fathers are spending more time in childcare activities, although women again take responsibility for the more regular and routine activities. So, while the evidence suggests convergence of time spend in work across the sexes, the detailed evidence focused on the ways in which those activities are organized and performed within time seems to lend support to the general arguments that time scarcity is experienced more acutely by women when compared with men.

One particular difficulty of empirically investigating time scarcity as conceptualized in terms of more or less activities allocated within clock time is that the form and meanings of activities change over time. As the discussion of emergent work time arrangements in the form of flexible hours and rise of project- or portfolio-based work tasks implies, workplace activities are dynamic and change in form and meaning. The discussion of domestic technologies and changing cultural understandings of cleanliness, comfort, convenience and parenting represent further examples of how the form and meanings of activities change over time. Domestic technologies might reduce the physical labour involved in the performance of domestic tasks, but they also fragment those tasks and render them subject to the principles of scientific time management. In doing so, the marketing of these technologies plays a pivotal role in raising expectations and standards. In such contexts not only does unpaid work not decline at the rate that might be expected by the diffusion of domestic technologies but the ways in which domestic work is performed change. This says very little about time scarcity but does suggest that the temporalities of everyday domestic life are very different from those of the past (a subject that will be returned to in Chap. 6).

In many respects the analysis of this chapter raises more questions than it answers. The most significant insights presented are that activities are shared and distributed across social groups and that activities are dynamic; they change in terms of their socio-cultural meanings and with respect to the ways in which they are performed. This is demonstrated by the discussion of personal relationships, intensive parenting and the search for quality time that appears to have emerged in the context of anxieties about a substantive time squeeze. And this line of enquiry poses a different set of questions in the context of a lack of evidence for substantive forms of time scarcity: are the ways in which we perform and experience everyday activities accelerating, and is the time squeeze more a condition of the pressures that result from the speed at which we perform activities? In other words, is the time squeeze more a condition related to the speed (or tempos) at which activities are performed as opposed to the scarcity of time in which to perform those activities?

References

Aguiar, M., & Hurst, E. (2007). Measuring Trends in Leisure: The Allocation of Time Over Five Decades. *Quarterly Journal of Economics, 122*, 969–1006.

Aguiar, M., & Hurst, E. (2009). Summary of Trends in American Time Allocation: 1965–2005. *Social Indicators Research, 93*, 57–64.

Baker, A., Roach, G., Ferguson, S., & Dawson, D. (2003). The Impact of Different Rosters on Employee Work and Non-Work. *Time & Society, 12*(2–3), 315–332.

Bittman, M., & Wajcman, J. (2000). The Rush Hour; the Character of Leisure Time and Gender Equity. *Social Forces, 79*(1), 165–189.

Brannen, J. (2005). Time and the Negotiation of Work-family Boundaries: Autonomy or Illusion. *Time & Society, 14*(1), 113–131.

Breedveld, K. (1998). The Double Myth of Flexibilization: trends in scattered work hours, and differences in time sovereignty. *Time & Society, 7*(1), 129–143.

Bryan, M. (2017). Flexible Working in the UK and its Impact on Couples' Time Coordination. *Review of Economics of the Household, 15*(4), 1415–1437.

Chung, H. (2018). *Gender, Flexibility Stigma, and the Perceived Negative Consequences of Flexible Working in the UK.* Social Indicators Research, Online First.

Cook, D. (2004). *The Commodification of Childhood: The Children's Clothing Industry and the Rise of the Child Consumer.* Duke University Press.

Craig, L., & Mullan, K. (2011). How Mothers and Fathers Share Childcare: A Cross-national Time-use Comparison. *American Sociological Review, 76*(6), 834–861.

Craig, L., Powell, A., & Smyth, C. (2014). Towards Intensive Parenting? Changes in the Composition and Determinants of Mothers and Fathers' Time with Children 1992–2006. *British Journal of Sociology, 65*(3), 555–579.

Daly, K. (1996). *Families and Time: Keeping Pace in a Hurried Culture.* London: Sage.

Ehrenreich, B., & English, D. (1979). *For Her Own Good: 150 Years of the Experts' Advice to Women.* London: Pluto Press.

Ehrenreich, B., & Hochschild, A. (Eds.). (2003). *Global Women: Nannies, Maids, and Sex Workers in the New Economy.* New York: Metropolitan Boons.

Fagan, C. (2001). Time, Money and the Gender Order. Work Orientations and Working-Time Preferences, Gender. *Work and Organizations, 8*(3), 239–267.

Fisher, K., Egerton, M., Gershuny, J., & Robinson, J. P. (2006). Gender Convergence in the American Heritage Time Use Study (AHTUS). *Social Indicators Research, 82*, 1–33.

Garhammer, M. (1995). Changes in Working Hours in Germany. *Time & Society, 4*(2), 167–203.

Gershuny, J. (1978). *After Industrial Society? The Emerging Self-service Economy.* London: Macmillan.

Gershuny, J. (2000). *Changing Times: Work and Leisure in Post-industrial Society.* Oxford: Oxford University Press.

Gershuny, J. (2005). Busyness as the Badge of Honor for the New Superordinate Working Class. *Social Research, 72*(2), 287–314.

Gershuny, J. (2009). Veblen in Reverse: Evidence from the Multinational Time-use Archive. *Social Indicators Research, 93*, 37–45.

Gershuny, J. (2011). Increasing Paid Work Time? A New Puzzle for Multinational Time-diary Research. *Social Indicators Research, 101*, 207–213.

Gershuny, J. (2018). *Gender Symmetry, Gender Convergence and Historical Work-time Invariance in 24 Countries.* Centre for Time Use Research, Working Paper 2: 1–16.

Gershuny, J., & Sullivan, O. (2019). *What We Really Do All Day: Insights from the Centre for Time Use Research.* Milton Keynes: Pelican Books.

Gershuny, J., Godwin, M. & Jones, S. (1994). The Domestic Division of Labor: A Process of Lagged Adaptation? In M. Anderson, F. Bechhofer, & J. Gershuny (Eds.), *The Social and Political Economy of the Household*. Oxford: Oxford University Press.

Gimenez-Nadal, J. I., & Sevilla-Sanz, A. (2012). Trends in Time Allocation: A Cross-country Analysis. *European Economic Review, 56*(6), 1338–1359.

Hochschild, A. (2003). *The Commercialization of Intimate Life*. Berkeley: University of California Press.

Hochschild, A. R. (1997). *The Time Bind: When Home Becomes Work and Work Becomes Home*. CA Henry Holt.

Kunda, G. (2001). *Scenes from a Marriage: Work, Family and Time in Corporate Drama*. Paper Presented to the International Conference on Spacing and Timing, November, Palermo, Italy.

Larsson, J., & Sanne, C. (2005). Self-help Books on Avoiding Time Shortage. *Time & Society, 14*(2/3), 213–230.

Lesnard, L. (2008). Off-scheduling Within Dual-earner Couples: An Unequal and Negative Externality for Family Time. *American Journal of Sociology, 114*, 447–490.

Lott, Y., & Chung, H. (2016). Gender Discrepancies in the Outcomes of Schedule Control on Overtime Hours and Income in Germany. *European Sociological Review, 32*(6), 752–765.

McMenamin, T. (2007). A Time to Work: Recent Trends in Shift Work and Flexible Schedules. *Monthly Labour Review, 130*, 3–15.

Minnen, J., Glorieux, I., & Pieter van Tienoven, T. (2016). Who Works When? Towards a Typology of Weekly Work Patterns in Belgium. *Time & Society, 25*(3), 652–675.

Mylan, J., & Southerton, D. (2018). The Social Ordering of an Everyday Practice: The Case of Laundry. *Sociology, 25*(6), 1134–1151.

Organisation for Economic Co-operation and Development. (2018). 'Time Use Portal', https://stats.oecd.org/Index.aspx?DataSetCode=TIME_USE

Pedersen, V., & Lewis, S. (2012). Flexible Friends? FLEXIBLE Working Time Arrangements, Blurred Work-life Boundaries and Friendship. *Work, Employment and Society, 26*(3), 464–480.

Pisarski, A., Lawrence, S. A., Bohle, P., & Brook, C. (2008). Organizational Influences on the Work Life Conflict and Health of Shiftworkers. *Applied Ergonomics, 39*(5), 580–588.

Robinson, J., & Godbey, G. (1997). *Time for Life: The Surprising Ways That Americans Use Their Time*. Pennsylvania State Press.

Rutherford, S. (2001). Are You Going Home Already?: The Long Hours Culture, Women Managers and Patriarchal Closure. *Time and Society, 10*(2/3), 259–276.

Schor, J. (2004). *Born To Buy: The Commercialized Child and the New Consumer Culture*. New York: Scribner.

Schwartz-Cowan, R. (1983). *More Work for Mother: The Ironies of Household Technology from the Open Hearth to the Microwave*. London: Basic Books.

Shaw, J. (1998). "Feeling a List Coming on": Gender and the Pace of Life. *Time & Society, 7*(2), 383–396.

Shove, E. (2003). *Comfort, Cleanliness and Convenience: The Social Organization of Normality*. Oxford: Berg.

Shove, E., & Southerton, D. (2000). Defrosting the Freezer: From Novelty to Convenience. A Story of Normalization. *Journal of Material Culture, 5*(3), 301–319.

Southerton, D. (2001). Consuming Kitchens: Taste, Context and Identity Formation. *Journal of Consumer Culture, 1*(2), 179–204.

Southerton, D. (2007). Time Pressure, Technology and Gender: The Conditioning of Temporal Experiences in the UK. In J. Scott & J. Nolan (Eds.), *Equal Opportunities International, Special Edition on Technology and Gender Inequalities, 26*(2), 113–128.

Sullivan, O. (1996). The Enjoyment of Activities; Do Couples Affect Each Others' Well-being? *Social Indicators Research, 38*(1), 81–102.

Sullivan, O. (1997). Time Waits for No (wo)men: An Investigation of the Gendered Experience of Domestic Time. *Sociology, 31*(2), 221–240.

Thompson, C. (1996). Caring Consumers: Gendered Consumption Meanings and the Juggling Lifestyle. *Journal of Consumer Research, 22*, 388–407.

Wajcman, J. (2015). *Pressed for Time: The Acceleration of Life in Digital Capitalism*. Chicago: Chicago University Press.

Warren, T. (2003). Class- and Gender-based Working Time? Time Poverty and the Division of Domestic Labour. *Sociology, 37*(4), 733–752.

Young, M., & Willmott, P. (1973). *The Symmetrical Family: Study of Work and Leisure in the London Region*. London: RKP.

4

Time Pressure: Innovation, Acceleration and the Speeding-Up of Everyday Life

4.1 Introduction

The idea that contemporary lives are lived at ever-greater speeds is one that captures popular imaginations. Speed, it would seem, is pretty much everywhere. The most recent popular social science endeavour in the great discourse of speed is Robert Colville's (2016) book *The Great Acceleration*. Amongst his claims as to why pretty much everything is getting faster is that the growth of urban living correlates with people moving faster on account that an increase in the volume and density of social interactions compel us all to increase the rates at which we perform activities. Our lifestyles accelerate because we have an ever-expanding range of consumption choices, everyone around us is racing to enjoy those choices and we all get carried along in a mass social movement of speed. Epitomized by the logic of the digital economy where 'every millisecond counts', information, opinions, cultural insights, political debates, production methods and consumer goods swirl around us at ever-faster speeds offering an enrichment of opportunities and cultural experiences so long as people take advantage of all the technologies that facilitate the speed-up of our lives. Colville's prognosis follows on from a stream of

© The Author(s) 2020
D. Southerton, *Time, Consumption and the Coordination of Everyday Life*,
Consumption and Public Life, https://doi.org/10.1057/978-1-349-60117-2_4

popular accounts about the ever-quickening pace of societal change and everyday lives. Gleick's (1999) aptly titled book *Faster: The Acceleration of Just About Everything* presented an earlier contribution to our modern fascination with speed. Gleick presented a now-familiar account of how the internalization of time discipline together with the ever-increasing precision of clock time measurement and the constant innovation and marketing of goods and services that promise speed and convenience means that our (over)valuing of time leads us to seek to do everything faster, including love, speech, politics, work, TV and leisure. Athletes seem to run faster, computers compute faster, and even our neighbours seem to move in and out of their homes faster. Clock time is an accelerant that leads to us to speed-up, multitask and cut corners, and in our rush we lose the capacity to appreciate or savour the world and the people around us. It would seem, as Schulte (2015) diagnoses in another lament of this popular condition, that we are *Overwhelmed* by the speed of the societies in which we live. The time squeeze, according to this set of theories, is less a matter of time scarcity and more of a feeling of being under time pressure.

This chapter examines theories of social acceleration. It begins by returning to the nineteenth and early twentieth centuries and classic social theories of modernity. It charts theoretical accounts of acceleration through processes of industrial capitalism, urbanization and the rise of the money economy. Technological innovations in transport and communications technologies are presented first in the context of the faster movement of people and goods through space and, second, in the context of instantaneous global connectivity. The resultant time-space compressions, distantiation and rise of networked connectivity are theorized to have fundamentally changed the ways in which social lives are organized and temporalities experienced. It is in the work of Helmut Rosa that a comprehensive explanation of societal acceleration is advanced. Section 4.3 examines, in detail, Rosa's argument that the late modern period is defined by acceleration across the interrelated domains of technology, societal change and everyday life. The dynamics of speed have become so ubiquitous in late modern societies that constant acceleration has come to represent the principal form of stability. However, social systems of acceleration are at odds with ecological and psychosomatic systems as well as with the remaining traditional subsystems of society such as political democracy and the money economy. It is these contradictions that underpin the major societal challenges of our time in the form of climate change and human well-being, while the societal structures of our political and economic systems established in modernity remain too slow to deal with these challenges.

Accounts of acceleration represent a persuasive case, although this may be because our preoccupation with speed leads us to search for it in our analyses of social life (Virilio 2001). Considering a number of empirical studies that examine the impacts of information and communications technologies (ICTs), especially email and mobile phones, on our work and personal lives presents a rather different picture of how people experience the processes that are typically evoked in diagnoses of a condition of acceleration. Empirical studies do demonstrate some experiences of time intensification and provide some evidence of the fragmentation of activities that are claimed to be hallmarks of an accelerated society. However, those empirical studies also demonstrate that temporal experiences are multiple and nuanced. Where there is apparent speed, intensity and compulsion, there is also meaningful interpersonal connections, experiences of slow and degrees of autonomy. Evidences from time diary studies also cast doubt on whether people increasingly feel rushed due to the speeding-up of all that surrounds them and shows very little evidence of the features of acceleration that are described in theoretical accounts of the condition.

This chapter concludes by reflecting on the common threads that diagnose theories of acceleration. These threads are remarkably consistent in terms of the identification of technological innovations leading to the constant acceleration of pretty much all aspects of social lives. This is the case from the mid-nineteenth century onwards. Of course, it could well be that technologies continuously accelerate human activities and with it experiences of a faster tempo of our daily activities, although the empirical evidence does little to support such a broad claim. It is certainly the case that theories of acceleration are principally focused on technological capacities, on the fact that technologies do enable faster movement through space and instantaneous communications in time. However, and as the work of Judy Wajcman (2015) demonstrates, such technological changes always evolve in relation to societal changes in which acceleration and speed is not always the dominant feature. As such, the chapter concludes by again questioning whether the default conceptualization of temporal experiences—in zero-sum terms with a focus on the concentration of human activities and interactions within objective units of time—found in theoretical prognosis of acceleration offers limited scope for explanation beyond recognition that the tempo of daily activities is constantly changing.

4.2   Modernity: Speeding-up the Circulation of People and Goods and Compressing Time and Space

The impression that contemporary societies are experiences of speed is not as recent a phenomenon as the persuasive writings of Gleick, Colville or Schultz suggest. Commentaries on the acceleration of societies emerged in the mid-nineteenth century alongside capitalist industrialization and urbanization. This section begins with a brief discussion of what is often regarded as a first wave of acceleration theories in which urbanization together with technological developments in transport and communications were identified as having profound implications for everyday experiences of time and space. For scholars such as Simmel (1971 [1903]), it was these processes that gave rise to immediacy, simultaneity and presentism as dominant temporal experiences of modern life (see Wajcman 2015). However, it was further technological developments in the speed of travel and telecommunications during the twentieth century that led to a second wave of theories that identified processes of time-space compression as the defining feature of accelerating societies. While such accounts of acceleration have come to dominate contemporary (popular) discourses of time and societal change, critics of this general thesis point to its technological-determinism, homogenizing tendencies with respect to the temporal experiences of different social groups and its lack of acknowledgement of the significance of 'slow' tempos.

For Thrift and May (2001) two critical technological developments—in transport and in communications—underpinned the acceleratory effects of the nineteenth century, which Marx (1996 [1848]) described as a process of the 'annihilation of space by time'. Throughout this period the time required to travel between places rapidly diminished as a result of, first, the rapid expansion of stagecoach networks and, second, the development of railways. Not only did the time required to travel between cities and towns radically diminish but the speed of transportation within places increased through the development of road networks, tram systems and underground railways. Similarly, communications networks developed and expanded rapidly throughout the same period through postal services, the telegraph system and telephone cabling networks. These technologies of speed were accessible to, and used by, an ever-expanding number of people. For example, Thrift (1994) reports that 333.6 million railway journeys were undertaken in 1870, the majority were taken by third-class passengers, and that an infrastructure of almost 22,000 miles of wire had been developed between 1830 and 1863, that transmitted around 6 million messages per year from 3381 connection points. Innovations in global telecommunications also meant that distant events could be experienced, or at least understood, soon after those events had taken place. For the first time local populations could hear about events within a time frame when action could be taken to influence those events (Adam 1990). Together, these technological developments had significant implications for how people understood and experienced the relationship between space and time (Kern 1983) such that the speed of travel and communication resulted in 'both a progressive shrinking of the world and its simultaneous enlargement as people become aware of events in ever more distant parts of the world' (Thrift and May 2001: 8).

The profound impacts of these nineteenth-century acceleratory processes can be found in the changing ways that people experienced the tempos of everyday activities. Literary commentaries of the period, such as Charles Dickens's *Hard Times* and Marcel Proust's *A la Recherche du temps perdu* (In Search of Lost Time), describe the sensory disorientation of high-speed rail travel as passengers came to terms with the experience of landscapes whirring past as train sped through urban and rural landscapes. Experiences of the speed and transitory nature of social changes represent a core theme running through Simmel's accounts of individualization processes at the end of the nineteenth century. In *The Philosophy of Money* (2004) Simmel draws explicit parallels between money and clock time, both of which have come to take on abstract forms as modes of exchange. In the case of money, its abstract form depersonalizes processes of exchange because its meaning is indifferent to context. As a consequence, the value of money can only be released in its circulation through the core activities of production, distribution and consumption of commodities such that the realization and accumulation of value in a money economy rests on the acceleration of these core activities. This process has two implications. First, as we have seen in Chap. 2, a means of accelerating the production, distribution and consumption of commodities is the measurement and effective management of these activities through the application of clock time. Second, the dynamics of the money economy contributed to an increased circulation of people and things, creating what Wajcman (2015: 51) describes as 'a transitory constellation of relations in which everything is in flux'. For Simmel, these processes of accelerated economic activity created a 'feverish' modern culture (Simmel 1991: 27).

It is in his account of modern urban life that Simmel (1971 [1903]) develops his description of a 'feverish' culture. In *The Metropolis and Mental Life*, Simmel presents everyday lives in cities as an emergent time consciousness based on immediacy and simultaneity. The increasingly rapid circulation of commodities associated with the money economy renders the metropolis a site in which a dizzying array of 'stimulations, interests, fillings in of time and consciousness are offered' (quoted in Frisby and Featherstone 1997: 15). Alongside such spectacles, urban spaces also offer anonymity amongst the crowd, and when contrasted with the slow rhythm and dense personal connections that characterized rural life, the city becomes a space in which self-expression of lifestyles and identities can be explored through culture, art and fashion. This condition creates a paradox. On the one hand, individuals are free to explore cultural experiences and experiment with their lifestyles, but on the other, in a money economy underpinned by indifference and the anonymity of urban life, it becomes impossible to determine if any individual lifestyle (and therefore identity) has shared meaning (Gronow 1997). In this context, the capacity of fashion to simultaneously offer scope for individual expression and shared meaning makes is a principle cultural vehicle for managing this paradox. However, in doing so fashion, as with the money economy, also becomes subject to constant flux and diversity.

The sense of constant flux in the money economy and urban life of the late nineteenth century had profound effects on experiences and understandings of time. On the one hand, time takes the same abstract, formless, depersonalized and indifferent characteristics as money. On the other, the rapid circulation of fashion, of economic activity and of spectacle and stimulations fosters sensory overload and a permanent state of transience which breeds an indifference (or blasé outlook) to the distinctions of modern life. This transience undermines any stable basis upon which the passing of time can be understood, leading to what Dodd and Wajcman (2017: 16) describe as a 'permanent "now time"' characterized by the 'eternal presentness' of the money economy and the immediacy and perpetual flux of urban cultural life.

It is in the latter third of the twentieth century that the second wave of theories of acceleration has come to represent a dominant discursive characterization of contemporary societies. This is most evident in the work of David Harvey (1989), which proposes that neo-liberal capitalist societies have been transformed through a 'post-modern condition' in which time and space has been compressed. Continuing the processes of acceleration that emerged in the nineteenth century, Harvey demonstrates how technological innovations in travel and information technologies have led to a shrinking of the world into a 'global village' as the time it takes to traverse space diminishes. Aeroplanes, high-speed rail links and advances in automobile technologies mean that people and goods can travel at ever-greater speeds and ever-diminishing economic costs, significantly reducing the time it takes to travel through space. The limitations of space for the purposes of communication have been obliterated by innovations in information and communications technologies. This collapse or radical restructuring of conventional constraints and relationships between time and space has the impact of making everything closer. This includes the circulation of goods and services, cultural ideas and experiences, connections with and understanding of different cultural groups, the immediacy of events that play out across the globe which emphasizes the interconnections of global systems (of finance, politics, inequality, production, etc.) and the need for their governance. Time-space compression not only connects people across the globe in their economic, cultural, social and political experiences but it also globalizes the logic of capitalism and further accelerates the circulation of goods, services, people, ideas and cultural experiences.

According to Giddens (1990), while time-space compression might produce a global village with respect to movement and communications, it also serves to further 'distantiate' (or separate) cultural understandings and experiences of time from space. The same processes identified by Harvey, particularly related to communications technologies, distribution infrastructures, travel networks and global institutions of political and economic governance, have the simultaneous effect of stretching social systems and their relations across time and space. Social relations that were once rooted in localized spaces—such as those related to place and interest communities, family networks, friendships, employment and social class—become dislocated from time and space. The emergence of the global middle class or elite (Massey 1994) is often cited as an illustration of these processes in which members have more in common and shared interest with people who live across the globe than they do with their neighbours. The global reach of consumer markets also provides the capacity for shared lifestyles everywhere and at any time (Featherstone 1997).

If the dominant feature of the first wave of acceleration was the capacity of clock time as an abstract unit that measures and manages social and economic activity, then the dominant feature of the second wave is the 'information age' of electronic communication technologies. For Castells (1996, 1998), the information age is best described as a network society in which global 'flows' of information, images, commodities, people and money are dispersed and distributed across digitalized networks. Digital networks enable immediate access to, and transfer of, information across its nodes, leading to the emergence of 'instantaneous time' (Urry 2000) and a 'detemporalised present' (Leccardi 2007). Furthermore, the asynchronous technologies of the digital age also mean that the ways in which activities are coordinated and synchronized in time are fundamentally altered. Email and social media are commonly cited examples because communication no longer depends on the scheduling of (synchronous) conversations but fragments the timings of those communication exchanges into multiple discrete actions that can be performed at any time. This fragmentation of activities and capacity for instantaneity exacerbates senses of speed because time in a network society is little more than 'inconceivably brief instants' (Wajcman 2015: 19).

More recent reflections, particularly in the context of continuing innovations in digital technologies, on the informational flows and instantaneity of network societies have led to claims that clock time is being replaced by network time as the dominant temporal mode (Hassan 2003, 2005). Rather than speculate that the information flows of networks produce 'instantaneous time', Hassan argues that network time should be conceptualized as 'digitally compressed clock time' that enables 'connected asynchronicity'. Digital technologies and ICTs do not dispense with clock time (Agger 1989) but create digital environments with their own temporal norms and standards (Hassan 2003). Such environments offer greater variation, differentiation and pluralities of the times when networked activities happen and also the tempos through which those activities are experienced, because they facilitate 'context-created temporal experience... [that] is disconnected from the local clock time of users' (Hassan and Purser 2007: 52). Whether through social media, internet chat forums or video-gaming communities (Majamäki and Hellman 2016), users within these networked virtual communities utilize the asynchronicity of digital technologies to create their own intense communities that interact across the globe and its time zones in ways that form their own networked times (Johnson and Keane 2017). The constant connectivity and instantaneity of the network society is presented as offering new opportunities and freedoms for groups to form and colonize their own network-based times of interaction beyond the constraints imposed by conventions of localized clock times (Agger 2011).

However interpreted, the rise of information and digital technologies are widely presented as the drivers of a further acceleration of temporal experiences. Time-space compression and distantiation are processes held to both shrink and stretch interconnectivities and social relations across the globe. New forms of instantaneous flows of information, communication and connectivity are held to fragment time and create experiences of acceleration. For Virilio (2001) this 'cult of speed' represents a continuation of the association of speed with progress, the irony of which is that progress generates major societal challenges for which urgent societal responses are needed. Climate change provides an excellent example. The drive for ever-faster capitalist accumulation, economic growth, circulation and acquisition of goods is also the driver of climate change, and the response to this challenge is a call for greater speed in responding to this problem: acceleration is inescapable. This fixation on speed also diverts popular and intellectual attention away from the many instances of slow. Returning to an earlier example, the sensory disorientation associated with 'high-speed' rail travel of the mid-nineteenth century might demonstrate the effects of faster travel, but as Schivelbusch (1986) has observed the development and diffusion of the railway changed how people understood other modes of travel with horseback riding and walking emerging as 'leisure activities' valued for the sensory and aesthetic experiences of slowness (see also Parkins and Craig 2006). Virilio lists a number of contradictions in accounts of speed: the more that people travel the more time people spend in static traffic jams and waiting in queues, and that in a society of instant communications people spend more time inactive and stationary in front of screens. Such juxtapositions of fast and slow, fluid and static, will be further explored in the next section of this chapter.

It is also worth noting two further, fundamental, critiques of the acceleration thesis that are articulated most forcefully by Thrift and May (2001). First, these accounts are techno-centric, verging on techno-deterministic, in that the start and end point of these theories are fixed within the technological developments of transport and communications. Other technological developments, such as electric lighting, have had equally as profound effects on the organization of daily life by essentially extending the times (by overcoming the darkness of night) and spaces (e.g. cities) of human activity. Secondly, the periodization of the changes related to clock time and the coordination and circulation of people and goods overestimates the degree of abrupt social change. In their account of time-keeping in England and Wales, Glennie and Thrift (2009) demonstrate how time measurement instruments and timetabling techniques are broad descriptions of long-term processes of socio-temporal development that can be traced back to the fifteenth century (see Chap. 2 for a discussion). The argument that temporal acceleration is a distinctive and disruptive feature of modernity ignores the many different forms of timekeeping that have evolved throughout the enlightenment period.

4.3 Accelerated Societies, Dynamic Stabilization and Desynchronization

The most comprehensive account of an accelerating society is presented by Helmut Rosa (2003, 2013 [2005]; 2017, 2019 [2016]). He argues that theories of 'acceleration' consider temporalities implicitly as a secondary focus, or assumed consequence, of technological changes that have increased the speed through which things, people and communications circulate. This is important, but for Rosa represents only a partial explanation of the forms of acceleration in contemporary societies. In addition to technological acceleration, Rosa places equal emphasis on accelerations in the domains of societal change and of the pace of everyday life. He argues that it is the interrelationships between each of these three domains that shape contemporary experiences of speed and time pressure and which produce an underpinning and foundational condition of dynamic stabilization in contemporary societies that results in critical forms of desynchronization between environmental, social and psychological systems.

At the core of technological accelerations are the speeding-up of communications, travel and modes of production. To this Rosa adds the speed with which technological innovations occur. For example, for someone living in the 1930s the idea of a colour TV would seem unthinkable—by the 1970s colour TVs were found in most Western homes. By contrast, in the 1980s the idea of mobile phones and the internet appeared as a sci-fi invention and in the late 1990s the claim that people would purchase large quantities of goods over the internet was ridiculed (Rutter and Southerton 2000). And it is not just technological innovations in electronic goods such as nano-technologies, artificial intelligence and digital data, but also biotechnologies. Technologies accelerate human actions but have also accelerated with respect to the rate and speed with which those innovations diffuse around societies.

The second domain of acceleration identified by Rosa is the increasing rates of change in the institutions and organizational structures of society. He provides the family and occupations as examples. Other than a steady decline in the average number of children per family the ideal-typical structure of the family based on a married couple raising children remained relatively stable during the course of modernity. This structure was based on a form of generational turnover, with sons tending to follow the occupations of their father and daughters of their mothers. Extended families tended to live in the same local area offering mutual support and a steady intergenerational turnover as elder generations were replaced by younger ones. Today, this intergenerational turnover has been torn asunder. High divorce rates mean that the family life-cycle may last only a few years. The family form is fluid and in constant flux. Children rarely follow the occupations or even the values of their parents, and grandparents are increasingly less likely to live close to their grandchildren. The internal coherence of the family is gone, lost to accelerated forms of social change in the very fabric of what constitutes that family. Rosa's account of occupational structures presents a similar, and well-rehearsed, story. Jobs and occupations are rarely 'for life' and people frequently change jobs and careers during their lifetime; they increasingly work in varieties of settings and are often required to relocate or work at ever-greater distances away from their homes. For Rosa, these are examples of how the social institutions that organize societies are increasingly fluid and the pace at which they are changing has accelerated throughout the twentieth and early twenty-first centuries.

The final domain of *acceleration is the pace of daily life*. For Rosa, technological innovations logically speed-up (or reduce) the amount of time taken to complete daily tasks and therefore should reduce senses of time pressure 'unless the background conditions of our lives change, too' (Rosa 2017: 25). Technologies allow us to do things faster, to cook faster, move faster, clean our homes faster, contact friends and family, reply to queries at work and so on. This, however, effectively creates a culture of speed—we eat faster, drink faster and talk faster. The increasing fluidity of social institutions that result from societal accelerations also acts to increase the number of 'legitimate claims' that can be made on people's time budgets. The discourse of 'work-life balance' (discussed in Chap. 3) represents an example of the difficulties that people face in completing with any satisfactory level of performance, the range of tasks expected in an accelerated society—whether that relates to the welfare and care of children and wider family members and friends, fulfilling work tasks and meeting career aspirations, managing and maintaining a home or taking care of one's own health and well-being. All of these claims to one's time emanate from particular contexts of social life and are legitimate within the particularities of those contexts. The multiplication of contexts that result from societal acceleration also leads to a multiplication of claims on one's time, while technological acceleration offers, at least in theory, the potential to meet those claims. One example of the consequence of these interrelated forms of acceleration is the disappearance of leisure time in the sense of it once being characterized as a time for when: 'the day's work is done... an inner attitude, a disposition toward the world in which, for the time being, there are no valid claims made on us, and no claim toward the world we have ourselves, that demand for any kind of action' (ibid.: 28).

Acceleration is therefore the core and unifying feature of late modern societies to the extent that constant and rapid change comes to represent a 'mode of dynamic stabilization'. Societal progress (often represented as economic growth), innovation and acceleration become the foundations of stability. This can be clearly observed in the foundational institutional structures of society. Economies are premised on growth that demands the acceleration of innovation, production and consumption. Science and knowledge represent an incessant demand for new discoveries, new knowledge and new findings. The legal system is no longer defined by the need to restore and preserve laws but as a perennial task of legislation to be improved and adjusted incessantly. Even art is now defined through the constant search for innovation and originality. Finally, politics is increasingly defined by competing claims to 'progress' through accelerated growth and innovation. Rosa (2017: 35, original emphasis) thus summarizes his theory of societal acceleration as follows:

acceleration can be defined as *quantitative growth* or *increase in quantity of per unit of time*... Thus, in the realm of transport, e.g. acceleration figures as an increase of kilometers covered per hour, with respect to communication, it might refer to the number of signs transmitted per microsecond, and in production, acceleration refers to the material output per hour, day, month, or year... accelerated *social change* can be interpreted as instances of this form of acceleration, too: if people change jobs or partners at higher rates, this amounts to an increase in the average number of jobs or spouses (or newspapers, or bank accounts, or cars, or telephone-numbers, etc.) per lifetime... Finally, the acceleration of the pace of life... amounts to an increase in the number of episodes of experience or action per unit of time (be it a day, a month, a year, or a lifetime)... [These are] three aspects of the same underlying phenomenon, which perhaps is best grasped by the term of "dynamization".

In essence, processes of growth, acceleration and innovation create a condition of dynamic stabilization, in which the volume of activities and tasks continually increase per unit of time, but those units of time cannot be expanded.

The mode of dynamic stabilization that underpins social acceleration is, for Rosa, at the very heart of the major societal challenges of the twenty-first century. Employing the conceptual language of 'systems-thinking', Rosa argues that major societal challenges are a consequence of the desynchronization that emerges between the fast social systems of an acceleration society and the slow tempos embedded in other systems. Rosa locates social systems (which are accelerating) between the eco-system (climate, nature and the environment) and the psychosomatic systems of individuals. As discussed in Chap. 1, and to be explored further in Chap. 8, the relationship between time, climate change and environmental degradation is a relatively straightforward example of Rosa's claims to the desynchronization between social and eco-systems. The acceleration of processes of production and consumption (which deplete natural resources), of technological innovations (that increase the speed of production and consumption processes) and of the pace of daily life (which becomes increasingly resource-intensive in order to perform 'legitimate claims' on one's time) is such that the earth's eco-systems simply cannot cope. Rosa also highlights evidence and argumentation from the World Health Organization to demonstrate that 'depression and burnout' are amongst the fastest growing health problems across the globe to demonstrate desynchronization between the social and psycho-somatic systems.

Yet even within the social system, acceleration causes desynchronization between social groups and, more significantly, between subsystems. In contemporary society those groups that suffer from social exclusion and isolation are those who have few direct claims on their time and limited access to the technologies of speed (e.g. the long-term unemployed and the elderly). A 'crisis of democracy' and the 2008 financial crisis are provided as two further examples of desynchronization with societal subsystems. Scheuerman (2003; see also Rosa and Scheuerman 2009), for example, argues that democratic political systems, which are built around the notion of deliberation and consensus, are unable to adequately meet the challenges created by an accelerated society. Put simply, the speed of events and communications mean that the critical political issues of any one moment have moved on before politicians have been able to meet in their Assemblies, Parliaments or Senates to deliberate. The second example is the 2008 financial crisis, which Rosa attributes to the desynchronization between the virtual and real (material) economy, and between financial markets and the speed at which governmental regulation processes could respond to changes in those markets. The basis for this claim rests on how financial markets, in their pursuit of ever-faster forms of capital accumulation, came to focus their activities on the 'buying and selling' of virtual products (e.g. financial products such as subprime loans) in which the transaction processes could be accelerated and profits gained in microseconds (see also MacKenzie 2017). This financial system collapsed when the 'virtual' market of financial products became desynchronized with the economic value of the 'real' or material economy (in this case the value of homes in the USA).

Rosa's theory of acceleration represents a totalizing account of the critical processes that underpin late modern societies, which are characterized as fluid, unstable and chaotic not just because the pace of acceleration outstrips the capacity for the foundational institutions of society to cope but also because the very dynamism of continuous acceleration comes to represent, or be, the stable form of societal organization. This has profound implications for how societies respond to major societal challenges, which themselves are the consequence of desynchronization between the rates of change possible between eco, social and psychosomatic systems, and between subsystems within societies. This means that to reduce acceleration to a matter principally borne from technologies of speed, such as communications and travel (as was the case with accounts of time-space compression and distantiation), is to ignore the full range of processes of acceleration and desynchronization that have come to represent the normal, everyday lives of all those people not socially excluded from the dynamic stabilization that characterizes accelerated societies.

4.4   Information and Communications Technologies: Empirical Studies of Intensification, Fragmentation and Acceleration of the Pace of Daily Life

While theories of speed place different degrees of emphasis on the extent to which acceleration is principally a consequence of technological advances or whether technological innovations interact with other societal domains to generate temporal experiences of fast societies and fast lives, they all nevertheless rely on an inextricable relationship between technologies and time. The empirical evidence of the speeding-up of movement through space as a consequence of high-speed travel and information technologies that enable the complex coordination of the circulation of goods around the globe is reasonably self-evident. The first circumnavigation of the globe began in 1519, took three years and most of the crew, including the captain Ferdinand Magellan, died during the voyage. In 1992, Concorde circumnavigated the globe in just under 33 hours. Of course, contradictions abound. As Wajcman (2015) shows, people use faster modes of transport to travel more kilometres on an average day than they did in the past, but while we might travel longer distances than our grandparents, the amount of time we spend travelling has hardly changed. And while modes of transport have the capacity to move at faster speed, they are often stationary in traffic, held up on lines or with passengers waiting to board them. These forms of congestion—of people and vehicles—mean that it took a similar amount of time to cross Los Angeles or London at 5 pm in 2018 as it did in 1900!

The key empirical observation of all acceleration theories is, however, that the speed of ICTs and their capacity for instantaneous connectivity and networking across time and space have the effect of intensifying and fragmenting activities within and across 'units of' time. By the early 2000s American industries become 5.5 times more ICT-intensive than they were in 1995, according to Rainie and Wellman (2012). Surveys reveal that between 2000 and 2011 internet access at work increased from 37% to 76% of full-time American employees, with the mean amount of time spent on the internet at work doubling from 4.6 hours per week in 2000 to 9.2 hours in 2010 (Center for the Digital Future 2013). As we have seen in Chap. 3, there is a little noticeable effect of the diffusion of ICTs in workplaces when it comes to the amount of total time people spend working. However, and consistent with Rosa's account of acceleration and Hassan's account of network time, the impact of ICTs on experiences of time is more likely to be revealed through the intensification of working times. Green (2006), for example, suggests there is a correlation between ICT diffusion and labour productivity, arguing that ICTs enable greater micro-coordination of work tasks because of the speed at which information can be exchanged and schedules adjusted. ICTs facilitate working to tight deadlines but also offer scope for discretion and initiative from workers which results in greater employee engagement with work tasks.

Two communication technologies have received the most empirical attention due to their capacities for instantaneous connectivity: email and the mobile phone. Email, Wajcman (2015) suggests, has become symbolic of speed and its associated negative connotations of increasing the intensity of workplace experiences. Barley et al.'s (2011) study of knowledge workers illustrates this argument. They found that almost half of the knowledge workers they studied associated email with a loss of control and fear of falling behind or missing information. The more time they spent on email, the more overloaded with work they felt. However, and somewhat paradoxically, they also found that using email helped alleviate their anxieties and the more emails that they sent, the more they felt they could cope with their workload. Barley et al. suggest that work-place cultures have developed a 'norm of responsiveness', which makes the build-up of emails a cause of anxiety and feelings of being overloaded, while the answering of emails becomes the means by which to alleviate that anxiety. Furthermore, the study also highlights the importance of recognizing that email is only one part of the daily flow of communications that occur within workplaces, showing that it is when workers spend significant parts of their day in synchronous meetings (whether in person or over the phone) that senses of overload in the workplace are at their greatest. Email gets the blame, but this is because of its asynchronous qualities (i.e. not requiring co-presence) which mean it is the form of communication and work-based task that is often left until last with the impending end of the workday looming.

The empirical evidence of the fragmentary effects of ICTs is equally nuanced and inconclusive. In their study of the headquarters of a multinational telecommunications company in Australia, Wajcman and Rose (2011) detail the frequency and durations of work-task episodes and the degree to which they are experienced as fragmented because of interruption or disruption. They found that the working day did consist of a large number of short duration (less than 10 minutes) tasks consistent with theories of fast-paced and intensive working practices. However, interruptions or disruptions that fragment work-based tasks were only caused by ICTs on a minority of occasions and the vast majority were initiated by face-to-face communications with work colleagues. Constant connectivity through ICTs did not interrupt or fragment work-based practices and, as with Barley et al.'s study, the asynchronous character of communications through ICTs such as email and text messaging gave workers a degree of control and autonomy over the temporal location of particular work tasks within their working day. Wajcman and Rose also detected a hierarchical structure to communication modes within the organizational culture, with email communications lowest in the hierarchy of importance and of needing an urgent response, followed by landline phone calls and text messages with direct calls on a mobile phone being most perceived as important and urgent. In summarizing this and other empirical studies of the impacts of workplace ICTs, Wajcman (2015) explains that multimodal communications, organizational cultures and multidimensional time practices (i.e. synchronous and asynchronous communications) interact to create new rhythms of work that generate temporal experiences of fast and slow, with urgent and optional responses, and which both represent new temporal demands that afford different forms of autonomy and constraint within the workplace.

Theories of the networked and accelerated society do not only apply to the impact of ICTs in workplaces but also within personal lives. Again, the theoretical prognosis is that ICTs invade, interrupt, punctuate and raise expectations of constant and instantaneous connectivity that intensify and fragment our personal and domestic lives in ways that increase the pace of daily life and create senses of time pressure. In this context it is mobile phones that have been the focus of empirical studies (e.g. see Agar 2003; Goggin 2012; Green and Haddon 2009; Couldrey 2012). Chesley (2005), for example, suggests that amongst American professional and managerial couples the mobile phone has led to greater work-family permeability, which in turn relates to lower overall satisfaction with family life. Furthermore, such permeability is gendered with men more likely to have their home life interrupted by the use of their mobile phone for work and women more likely to receive family-related calls at work. Other studies, however, question the extent to which ICTs like mobile phones invade personal lives. Bittman et al. (2009) reveal from a nationally representative sample of Australian employees that 75% of calls and almost 90% of text messages sent or received from mobile devices are from friends and family. Work-related calls, which accounted for 21% of all calls, overwhelmingly occurred during standard working hours with only 3% of all work-related calls occurring between 7 pm to midnight. Furthermore, survey respondents described the benefits of mobile phones in terms of coordinating personal relationships, whether that was to arrange sociable activities or adjust the schedules of household members to facilitate collection or delivery of children at various activities (Wajcman et al. 2008). And a US study demonstrates that work-based connectivity after hours did not increase feelings of work–home life conflict, although high volumes of hours at work did (Adkins and Premeaux 2014). Far from disrupting or undermining personal relationships, the mobile phone is a technology that enables 'micro-coordination' of friends and family, offering scope for flexibility and contingency in the interpersonal scheduling of activities (Wajcman 2015).

Time diary data presents a further source of empirical evidence that, while limited in its capacity to provide nuanced insights into experiences of acceleration, offers further empirical clues into the veracity of key theoretical claims. Using the latest UK time diary survey, Sullivan and Gershuny (2018; see also Gershuny and Sullivan 2019) examine whether there has been any discernible increase between 2000 and 2015 in the fragmentation of daily activities (measured through the number and duration of events per day) and the intensity of activities per unit of time (measured through multitasking). In addition, they examined whether any increases in fragmentation and intensity relate to survey respondents reporting of 'feeling rushed' and their perceived use of ICTs. The results are instructive. They find no increase in the number of events per day and actually a slight decline for all socio-economic groups, although women's time remained more fragmented than men's. Women also multitask (defined as the proportion of waking time doing two or more activities simultaneously) more than men, although the degree to which they multitask has slightly declined over the period and men's has slightly increased, while the professional and managerial classes multitask more than members of other socio-economic groups do. Women's time is also more fragmented than men's (more events and more events of shorter durations), but again there is marginal difference between the two years. And while women report feeling rushed more than men in both years, there is a significant decline in reporting of feeling rushed for men and women in both the professional and the intermediate socio-economic groups, and only a marginal or no decline for women and men respectively in routine occupations. ICT usage has no statistically significant effect on fragmentation of events, intensification of activities per event or reported feelings of being rushed. They conclude that there is little evidence that people in the UK are experiencing any form of generalized speeding-up of their daily lives, that ICTs do not correlate with any increased intensification or fragmentation of activities per unit of time, and that where we see variations in the degrees to which people feel rushed this is a consequence of the volume of time spent in 'constrained activities' of paid and unpaid work (see Chap. 3).

4.5 Conclusion

All theories of societal acceleration rest on the speeding-up of the pace with which people, goods, financial transactions, information and communications circulate across space and over time. From this perspective, technological advances have literally shrunk the globe. Connected to these technology-driven processes are continuous concerns about the dizzying effects that such changes have on the pace of people's everyday lives and their temporal experiences. Immediacy, instantaneity and connectivity with others from across the globe, the diversification of goods, services and cultural experiences that can be accessed and consumed faster and in greater quantities than at any time in the past, and the economic demands that mean people work in increasingly intensive ways represent the dominant prognosis of such theories. With the rhetoric of speed established, it is not too difficult to consider the obvious temporal mismatch between societal acceleration and major societal challenges that appear to 'creep' in the background, such as climate change and concerns about human well-being, and conclude that it is the acceleration of everything that is to blame.

Given that it is the speed-enhancing effects of technological innovations, especially of ICTs, that are at the core of these theories it is only correct that empirical studies of how people experience these technologies are given due consideration. Wajcman's (2015) account of acceleration and digital capitalism is particularly important in this respect. Her cautionary analysis, based on an exhaustive survey of empirical studies many of which are reported in this chapter, is that the ways in which people experience and understand technologies are shaped by a range of societal factors, which include inequalities (particularly in relation to gender), organizational cultures, interpersonal relationships, the changing materialities of workplaces and domestic homes, and changing forms of employment. Privileging the technological over these other societal factors is a failure to fully consider how the social and the technological are mutually constituted and experienced in context specific ways. From Wajcman's analysis, temporal experiences of speed, of intensive activities, of interruptions, fragmentation and instantaneity can be identified in the empirical evidence alongside an equally significant weight of evidence that people and social groups adjust, improvise, reinterpret, slowdown and coordinate in ways that create multiple temporal experiences. Acceleration, for Wajcman, is only ever a partial explanation for the relationship between technologies, society and temporalities.

Finally, it is also worth briefly reflecting on the conceptualization of time in theories of acceleration. Rosa's definition of acceleration as essentially the consequence of increased activities per unit of time captures the singular conceptual form of temporality in all theories of acceleration. This is a conceptualization of objective time, of time as little more than a measurable unit in which successive activities are allocated and performed. As such, the conceptual foundation underpinning acceleration theories effectively represents temporalities in zero-sum terms: the experience of time is the accumulation of units of activity within fixed and finite units of measurable time. Whether that time is measured in conventional terms as seconds, minutes and hours or in terms of synchronicity and asynchronicity, the conceptual framing essentially remains a calculation of the elastic volume of human activity, whether in terms of connections, communications, transactions or tasks, and the inelasticity of (clock) time. An increasing volume of identifiable and measurable activities in objective time means that those activities have to happen faster, and in so doing generate feelings of time pressure. As will be discussed in Chap. 7, such conceptualizations of objective time represent only one way of theorizing the temporal organization of everyday lives.

References

Adam, B. (1990). *Time and Social Theory*. Cambridge: Polity.
Adkins, C., & Premeaux, S. (2014). The Use of Communication Technology to Manage Work-Home Boundaries. *Journal of Behavioral & Applied Management, 15*(2), 82–100.
Agar, J. (2003). *Constant Touch: A Global History of the Mobile Phone*. Cambridge: Icon Books.
Agger, B. (1989). *Fast Capitalism*. Urbana: University of Illinois Press.

Agger, B. (2011). iTime: Labor and Life in a Smartphone Era. *Time & Society, 20*(1), 119–136.

Barley, S., Meyerson, D., & Gordal, S. (2011). Email as a Source and Symbol of Stress. *Organizational Studies, 22*(4), 887–906.

Bittman, M., Brown, J. & Wajcman, J. (2009). The Mobile Phone, Perpetual Contact and Time Pressure. *Work, Employment & Society, 23,* 673–679.

Castells, M. (1996). *The Information Age: Economy, Society and Culture, Vol.1: The Rise of the Network Society.* Oxford: Blackwell.

Castells, M. (1998). *The Information Age: Economy, Society and Culture, Vol.3: End of Millennium.* Oxford: Blackwell.

Center for the Digital Future. (2013). *The Digital Future Project 2013— Surveying the Digital Future Year Eleven.* Los Angeles: University of Southern California.

Chesley, N. (2005). Blurring Boundaries? Linking Technology Use, Spillover, Individual Distress, and Family Satisfaction. *Journal of Marriage and the Family, 67,* 1237–1248.

Colville, R. (2016). *The Great Acceleration: How the World is Getting Faster.* London: Bloomsbury.

Couldrey, N. (2012). *Media, Society, World: Social Theory and Digital Media Practice.* Cambridge: Polity Press.

Dodd, N., & Wajcman, J. (2017). Simmel and Benjamin: Early Theorists of the Acceleration Society. In J. Wajcman & N. Dodd (Eds.), *The Sociology of Speed: Digital, Organizational, and Social Temporalities* (pp. 13–24). Oxford: Oxford University Press.

Featherstone, M. (1997). Lifestyle and Consumer Culture. *Theory, Culture & Society, 4*(1), 55–70.

Frisby, D., & Featherstone, M. (Eds.). (1997). *Simmel on Culture: Selected Writings.* London: Sage.

Gershuny, J., & Sullivan, O. (2019). *What We Really Do All Day: Insights from the Centre for Time Use Research.* Milton Keynes: Pelican Books.

Giddens, A. (1990). *The Consequences of Modernity.* Cambridge: Polity.

Gleick, J. (1999). *Faster: The Acceleration of Just About Everything.* New York: Abacus.

Glennie, P., & Thrift, N. (2009). *Shaping the Day: A History of Timekeeping in England and Wales 1300–1800.* Oxford: Oxford University Press.

Goggin, G. (2012). *New Technologies and the Media.* New York: Palgrave Macmillan.

Green, F. (2006). *Demanding Work: The Paradox of Job Quality in the Affluent Economy.* Princeton: Princeton University Press.

Green, N., & Haddon, L. (2009). *Mobile Communications: An Introduction to the New Media.* Oxford: Berg.

Gronow, J. (1997). *Sociology of Taste.* London: Routledge.

Harvey, D. (1989). *The Condition of Postmodernity.* Oxford, UK: Blackwell.

Hassan, R. (2003). Network Time and the New Knowledge Epoch. *Time & Society, 12*(2/3), 225–241.

Hassan, R. (2005). Timescapes of the Network Society. *Fast Capitalism* 1(1). Retrieved from http://www.uta.edu/huma/agger/fastcapitalism/1_1/hassan.html.

Hassan, R., & Purser, R. E. (2007). *24/7: Time and Temporality in the Network Society.* Stanford, CA: Stanford Business Books.

Johnson, N., & Keane, H. (2017). Internet Addiction? Temporality and life Online in the Networked Society. *Time & Society, 26*(3), 267–285.

Kern, S. (1983). *The Culture of Time and Space 1880–1918.* Cambridge, MA: Harvard University Press.

Leccardi, C. (2007). New Temporal Perspectives in the "High-Speed Society". In R. Hassan & R. E. Purser (Eds.), *24/7: Time and Temporality in the Network Society* (pp. 25–36). Stanford, CA: Stanford Business Books.

MacKenzie, D. (2017). Capital's Geodesic: Chicago, New Jersey, and the Material Sociology of Speed. In J. Wajcman & N. Dodd (Eds.), *The Sociology of Speed: Digital, Organizational, and Social Temporalities* (pp. 55–71). Oxford: Oxford University Press.

Majamäki, M., & Hellman, M. (2016). "When Sense of Time Disappears"—Or does it? Online Video Gamers' Time Management and Time Apprehension. *Time & Society, 25*(2), 355–373.

Marx, K. (1996[1848]). *The Communist Manifesto.* London: Pluto Press.

Massey, D. (1994). A Global Sense of Place. In D. Massey (Ed.), *Space, Place and Gender* (pp. 146–156). Cambridge, UK: Polity Press.

Parkins, W., & Craig, G. (2006). *Slow Living.* Oxford: Berg.

Rainie, L., & Wellman, B. (2012). *Networked: The New Social Operating System.* Cambridge, MA: MIT Press.

Rosa, H. (2003). Social Acceleration: Ethical and Political Consequences of a Desynchronized High-speed Society. *Constellations, 10*(1), 3–33.

Rosa, H. (2013 [2005]). *Social Acceleration: A New Theory of Modernity.* New York, NY: Columbia University Press.

Rosa, H. (2017). De-Synchronization, Dynamic Stabilization, Dispositional Squeeze: The Problem of Temporal Mismatch. In J. Wajcman & N. Dodd

(Eds.), *The Sociology of Speed: Digital, Organizational, and Social Temporalities* (pp. 25–41). Oxford: Oxford University Press.

Rosa, H. (2019 [2016]). *Resonance. A Sociology of Our Relationship to the World* (J. Wagner, Trans.). Cambridge: Polity.

Rosa, H., & Scheuerman, W. E. (Eds.). (2009). *High-speed Society: Social Acceleration, Power, and Modernity*. University Park: Pennsylvania State University Press.

Rutter, J., & Southerton, D. (2000). E-commerce: Delivering the Goods? *Consumer Policy Review, 10*(3), 139–144.

Scheuerman, W. (2003). Speed, States, and Social Theory: A Response to Hartmut Rosa. *Constellations, 10*(1), 42–48.

Schivelbusch, W. (1986). *The Railway Journey: The Industrialization of Time and Space in the Nineteenth Century*. Leamington Spa: Berg.

Schulte, B. (2015). *Overwhelmed: How to Work, Love and Play When No One Has the Time*. London: Bloomsbury.

Simmel, G. (1971[1903]). The Metropolis and Mental Life. In D. Levine (ed.), *On Individuality and Social Form*. Chicago, IL: Chicago University Press.

Simmel, G. (1991). Money in Modern Culture. *Theory, Culture and Society, 8*, 17–31.

Sullivan, O., & Gershuny, J. (2018). Speed-Up Society? Evidence from the UK 2000 and 2015 Time Use Diary Surveys. *Sociology, 52*, 20–38.

Thrift, N. (1994). Inhuman Geographies: Landscapes of Speed, Light and Power. In P. Cloke, M. Doel, D. Matless, M. Phillips, & N. Thrift (Eds.), *Writing the Rural: Five Cultural Geographies* (pp. 191–248). London: Paul Chapman.

Thrift, N., & May, T. (2001). *Timespace: Geographies of Temporality*. London: Routledge.

Urry, J. (2000). *Sociology Beyond Societies*. London: Routledge.

Virilio, P. (2001). Speed-Space: Interview with Chris Dercon. In J. Armitage (Ed.), *Virilio Live: Selected Interviews*. London: Sage.

Wajcman, J. (2015). *Pressed for Time: The Acceleration of Life in Digital Capitalism*. Chicago: Chicago University Press.

Wajcman, J., Bittman, M., & Brown, J. (2008). Families without Borders: Mobile Phones, Connectedness and Work-Home Divisions. *Sociology, 42*, 635–652.

Wajcman, J., & Rose, E. (2011). Constant Connectivity: Rethinking Interruptions at Work. *Organization Studies, 32*(7), 941–962.

5

Temporalities of Harriedness

5.1   Introduction

This book opened with a discussion of the prevalence of claims that contemporary lives are experiences of a time squeeze. The processes leading to time discipline identified in Chap. 2 together with processes of technological change and senses of the acceleration of everyday life discussed in Chap. 4 represent theories of how fundamental societal change has affected how time is understood and experienced. These theoretical accounts emphasized how, over the course of modernity, time as an objective unit for measuring motion and accounting for, or managing, human action has come to dominate conceptualizations of temporality. In the broadest terms, these accounts create a social history in which the measurement of time has become ever-closely entwined with economic productivity, a unit for measuring value that has been rationalized and standardized across the globe. In the process, clock time has come to act as a disciplining device and taken on a commodity form that defines time as a scarce resource to be effectively allocated and efficiently utilized. It is this search for utility maximization that underpins the technological changes that are widely held to generate a condition of societal acceleration.

© The Author(s) 2020   **95**
D. Southerton, *Time, Consumption and the Coordination of Everyday Life*,
Consumption and Public Life, https://doi.org/10.1057/978-1-349-60117-2_5

Chapters 3 and 4, however, also reveal the paucity of empirical evidence that supports, at least with the same degree of conviction as that advanced by the theories, the claims that people experience a substantive time squeeze in their everyday lives. Much of that empirical evidence either seeks to examine time scarcity in terms by measuring the minutes recorded by time diary respondents to account for their daily activities or seeks to reveal time pressures that result from the fragmentation of specific sets of activities, such as ICT use, and the experiences of intensification that results from capacities and expectations to fit more activities into units of time. This chapter explores empirical research that focused directly on people's interpretations as to whether society is time squeezed, why they felt this to be the case and their temporal experiences of everyday life. It makes a preliminary qualitative distinction between two different temporal conditions: time scarcity and pressure, conceptualized here as feelings of harriedness. Time scarcity is the more familiar term employed in both popular and academic debates, which focuses on how much time people have available to perform different categories of activity and implies capacities to exchange those activities (such as paid and unpaid work, leisure and consumption) between and across units of objective time.

Harriedness, by contrast, is a phrase that intimates at the qualities and subjective experiences of time that people encounter in their daily lives. This might relate to time scarcity but is not equivalent to it. Not having enough time for leisure might make someone feel harried, but equally one person might experience their leisure as harried while another, with the same volume of minutes available for that activity, might not. Hence, Bittman and Wajcman's (2000) finding reported in Chap. 3 that mothers and fathers might spend similar amount of time in leisure activities but their experiences are qualitatively distinct. Literally, the verb harried means "to harass" and "to worry" (Oxford English Dictionary [OED]). Its first recorded usage in 893 AD referred to "predatory raids or incursions". It was not until 1205 AD that its meaning came to resemble something similar to its contemporary usage. Still associated with invasion, harried referred to the 'over-running' of a place or territory. By the fourteenth century the term was associated with 'harassing (a person)', and in the sixteenth century its meaning expanded: 'to goad, torment, harass; to worry mentally' (OED). However, since Linder appropriated the term to describe the 'harried leisure class', its contemporary meaning has come to be associated more directly with an anxiety about the satisfactory performance of activities within objective units of time. Satisfactory performance implies a degree of subjective interpretation or expectation regarding different qualitative experiences of activities and the temporal conditions associated with their conduct. Harriedness therefore does not require time scarcity but, rather, reflects degrees of anxiety regarding the temporalities of everyday practice performances.

This chapter revisits an earlier study conducted in 2000, which consisted of in-depth interviews about temporal experiences with 26 people aged between 24 and 55, who lived in a suburb of Bristol in England (which I will refer to as the 'Bristol study'). This study is interesting because its core focus was on respondents' interpretations of the time squeeze and their everyday temporal experiences (the methodology and findings are discussed by Southerton [2003], although for this discussion the original interview data was reanalysed and therefore contains insights not previously reported). The interviews began by asking whether respondents felt that people today were more pressed for time than people were in the past. Given that all respondents immediately and unequivocally believed this to be the case, respondents were then asked why they felt this to be the case. The next section provides a summary of their responses, which were grouped together under three themes (consumer culture, lifestyle and status; interpersonal relationships; and moral economies of time). While respondents were unanimous that people are more time squeezed today and were clear in their diagnoses as to why this is the case, it was somewhat surprising that when it came to descriptions of their own day-to-day temporal experiences, respondents were far more ambivalent about time pressure. Section 5.3 explores their daily temporal experiences, supplemented with data from another earlier study conducted with Mark Tomlinson using Health and Lifestyle Survey (HALs) data from 1985 and 1992 (Southerton and Tomlinson 2005), to reveal that instances of time scarcity were limited but associated with moments where the volume of activities that demanded performance within designated parts of the day was intensified, while fleeting senses of harriedness (time pressure) were related to the ways in which everyday activities were coordinated and allocated within their daily lives. In conclusion, it is argued that the temporal conditions related to the volume, coordination and allocation of activities in daily lives underpin experiences of conditions that respondents equated with a time squeeze.

5.2   Feeling Pressed for Time: Popular Perceptions of the Causes of Time Scarcity

As already revealed, respondents of the Bristol study, without hesitation, described contemporary societies as an experience of increasing feelings of being pressed for time. The question asked was 'do you think people are busier or more time pressed today than, say, were people 10 or even 20 years ago?' Some examples of the responses included the following: '*absolutely*' (Michael, aged 30); '*God yes!*' (Fiona, aged 40); '*I don't think there is any question*' (Louise, aged 24); '*no doubt, I don't remember things like "burn out" even existing when I was a kid*' (Arthur, aged 55). Such responses were consistent with survey evidence from the same period, for example, the UK Health and Lifestyle Survey (HALs) revealed that 86% of respondents reported feeling 'pressed for time' in 1992 (Southerton and Tomlinson 2005). This section examines the qualifications and explanations as to why respondents so clearly felt that people today are more time pressed than people from the past. Three overarching themes emerged from respondents' diagnoses of the predicament: consumer culture, lifestyle and social status; personal relationships; and the moral economies of time.

Consistent with Juliet Schor's 'work more to consume more' thesis was the claim that the pursuit of social status and lifestyle aspirations, whether through consumerism or work, led to an overwhelming demand on finite volumes of time. This theme was identified by all respondents of the Bristol study as the principal cause of time pressure. Seeking to 'keep up' or to have a lifestyle or a standard of life comparable to others within one's social networks featured prominently, as illustrated by Suzanne (aged 32): '*it is very much like everybody's trying to get better than the other one—a better car or this sort of thing… And that puts pressure on people to do more in their work or fit more into their life in general*. This narrative also emphasized an expectation that lifestyle, or the accumulation of material goods, should always be on the rise throughout the life-course. For example, Mary (aged 52) described how

> *between friends, when one gets a new house you start to feel like you're getting left behind, like you should have a three-bed by now or a car or, it's like anything. At the moment everyone's getting computers and we're like, 'should we get one'.*

All respondents also advanced the view that people were placed under greater pressure from the media and marketing with respect to ever-rising expectations of what constitutes a normal level of consumerism and consumer experiences. Bradley (aged 34) summarized the commonly held view that

> *the media give this impression that everyone… is going to the cinema once a week, they go down to the night-club, or they go to the wine bar three days a week, or they play squash, they play badminton, they are a member of the bridge club, and everyone is doing it… So you feel that you should be, not necessarily that we've got to do it, but that you should have tried more and more things just because you can.*

For Bradley, the media circulates expectations of lifestyle choices that create a pressure to sample options in order to make the 'right choices' and this meant that people spend increasingly more of their time either consuming or thinking about and researching the forms of consumption that they '*should be doing*' in order that they '*don't miss out*'.

While identified as a root cause of the time squeeze, consumer culture was not viewed in entirely negative terms by respondents. The range of cultural experiences it offered was provided as an example of how contemporary lives had, overall, progressed from those experienced in the past by offering people with greater varieties of consumption and choice. Samantha (aged 39) explained that:

*I think people spent much more time doing the boring things in the past...
whereas now they have got more choice of leisure things and they are not spending the whole of Monday doing the washing or whatever, so the boring things
probably take up less time but then there is more choice of interesting things to do.*

Mass Observation Archive data reporting that people in 1950s Britain
found Sundays particularly boring (Mass Observation 2009) might offer
some support to Samantha's claim. And many respondents commented
that consumer culture had been responsible for removing some of the
drudgery and time associated with the performance of domestic tasks:

*it's a bit of a trade-off I suppose. We spend much more of our time buying things
and wanting things and trying to earn the money so that we can, but also we
don't have to go to the supermarket all the time because we have things like
fridges and freezers, and cars, washing machines and even like going to the
cinema where we can watch movies at home now, they all save us time as well.*
(Kathryn, aged 34)

Recognition that consumption might actually save time was also found
through references to pre-prepared food, as described by Arthur, '*nowadays it's all convenience foods, so I don't believe that the average modern family spends anywhere near as much time cooking as they used to*', while
Amanda (aged 35) explained how fast-fashion meant that the need to
spend time repairing clothes is a thing of the past: '*It's like Primark, it's
good because I don't do any repairing of clothes and that like my mum does
but it does mean I am shopping all the time, which I like doing don't get me
wrong but its like, I need a new top and I'm off to Cribbs* [a local shopping
Mall] *again*'.

While all respondents identified consumer culture as the principal
cause of the time squeeze they qualified their claims by identifying ways
in which consumerism might also reduce the amount of time for activities that were usually associated with activities of daily life deemed nei-
ther particularly exciting nor enjoyable.

Concern with social status was not only reserved for the domain of
consumption but also discussed in the context of career aspirations. Sarah
(aged 42) provided the most succinct illustration of the view shared by all

respondents that '*people used to have a job for life you know, but now we pursue careers and being successful gives you a sense of self-worth and social status… its why people sort of give more of themselves to their work*'. The belief that people work more was also found in the view that workplace competition had intensified. Steven (aged 43), for example, claimed that '*since the 80s the workplace has become more cut-throat, people put in more because they want a successful career and because jobs are so insecure nowadays*'. Consistent with ethnographic studies of long-hour workplace cultures (e.g. Kunda 2001; Rutherford 2001), respondents of the Bristol study were clear that the perception of working more was not simply in order to obtain an income necessary to fully participate in consumer culture. In this respect, some support for Gershuny's (2005) claim that being busy at work is a 'badge of honour', was neatly captured with Bob's (aged 52) rather blunt statement: '*if you're not busy with your work you clearly don't have a very important job*'. Finally, a number of respondents also identified how changing forms of work affect the time spent in this activity. Robert (aged 38) explained that:

> *many jobs nowadays involve working on projects, gone are the days when you clock in and out, down tools… and when you're on a project you wanna get it finished and you have deadlines and so on, so people are working late and taking work home with them. I know I do.*

Not only did respondents of the Bristol study unanimously state that contemporary society is an experience of a time squeeze, they immediately identified time scarcity as the symptom of the demands placed upon people by consumption and employment, both of which they felt required more of people's available minutes and hours. In doing so, respondents framed their narratives through the concept of objective time and the prominent accounts that have been developed in the academic literature. They did provide some variations to popular themes, recognizing that consumer culture offers varieties of cultural experiences and choices, that it has reduced the time required for everyday activities that they felt were less enjoyable, and that workplace temporal demands can, in some instances, be tied to positive identity-related factors. However, the consistency between their immediate diagnoses of the problem and those contained within the most prominent academic arguments was striking.

The second theme identified by respondents of the Bristol study is related to the demands of maintaining satisfactory interpersonal relationships. Consistent with Hochschild's (1997) and Thompson's (1996) accounts of working mothers in the USA and studies of child-centred time-use by Craig and colleagues (Craig and Mullan 2011; Craig et al. 2014), an important extension of the working more to consume more diagnosis was that parents worked longer hours to increase the consumption opportunities for their children. Suzanne explained how '*for them* [her friends' children] *there is so much to do, stuff we never had and you have to, or you feel you have to, give them the opportunity. Like Lucy* [her niece] *does gym club, ballet and swimming and she's only four*'. Steven pointed out that, in ways similar to the time demands of status consumption for adults, he was acutely aware of his child 'missing out':

> *we both value being able to give our children what perhaps we didn't have. It's important. Alexandra has her violin lessons and horse riding and it's important to her because her friends also go to these clubs and we don't want her to miss out.*

Dual incomes were therefore regarded as critical to maintain standards of living for those who had children, with Deborah (aged 29) explaining that '*his money pays the bills and mine's for the extras for her* [their daughter]'. Mark (aged 39) was even more explicit about the need for a 'second' household income; '*Chloe doesn't just work for the money but we would have to economize drastically if she quit and that means they* [the children] *do without*'.

As discussed in Chap. 3, studies by Warren (2003), Brannen (2005) and Lesnard (2008) also suggest that managing the work schedules of dual income couples is a particularly difficult temporal challenge. Charlotte (aged 28) offered a first-hand account of the problems faced: '*it's difficult because I rush to get to work, rush to finish work and rush to get home, then rush to get her ready for bed so that she can see Mike when he gets home and I do our tea*'. Meanwhile Bob, rather negatively, shared his observations of his neighbour: '*she leaves with the kids in tow before the dad because she needs to get them to nursery or whatever so that she can get to work and it's always a mad rush, always some commotion you know the kids aren't ready, they have some toast in their hands'*. Together, such narratives of obligations to children's consumption and the family burdens of dual income households all, again, evoked to explain time pressure as a consequence of substantive increases in the volume of activities that need to be squeezed into daily life.

The final prominent narrative given by respondents from the Bristol study referred to acute awareness that (clock) time was a resource to be utilized effectively and efficiently and provided contemporary empirical evidence of the internalization of time discipline identified by E.P. Thompson (see Chap. 2). Elizabeth (aged 43) captured this concern:

> *I find that if I come down and sit down and switch the television on it is very easy to sit and stare at it all evening and then think at the end of the evening that I could have done this, that and the other and then think that you have wasted the whole of the time.*

Sarah added: '*I value time and I think of it as a very important commodity which would be scandalous to waste, it's so easy to just fritter it away'*. Utilizing time was presented as a form of moral economy, something that individuals needed to be conscious of. It echoed through the earlier 'attributes' of time pressure with respect to the desire to experience varieties of consumption and the fear of children 'missing out' on cultural activities, and it was most evocatively expressed by James (aged 30): '*Life is short, you have to live it and not waste your time. And I think we're just more conscious of this today and want to live life to the max'*.

The moral economy of time was not only discussed in terms of efficiency and avoidance of wasting time on activities that were deemed of little value. Returning to comments regarding how consumer technologies, such as domestic technologies, had afforded greater autonomy in how people choose to use their time, some respondents hinted at how this meant that the moral economy of time was ever-present. Take the following exchange between the married couple Bob and Mary as an example:

just look at all the gadgets and appliances we have now that saves us time or at least gives us more flexibility. My mum used to spend all day doing the washing, with one of those top-filled machines attached to the kitchen tap. It used to take her an hour just to get it set up! Once you'd got it out you'd darn well do the lot. Now, you do it when it suits you, so yeah we have much more freedom in terms of when we do things. (Bob)

You would say that as you never do it!!! You're right though, I can do the washing at any time but that means I am always thinking about when's the best time to do a wash. (Mary)

In this response to her husband, Mary was quick to imply that greater autonomy over when domestic tasks are performed also meant that the time management of those tasks is ever-present in her day-to-day life, and lends support to the weight of evidence that demonstrates that women take principal responsibility for the management of domestic tasks (Sullivan 1997; Shaw 1998). In doing so, her remarks also support accounts of how domestic technologies fragment domestic tasks, yet also increase cultural standards of cleanliness (discussed in Chap. 3 in relation to the work of Schwartz-Cowan 1983 and Shove 2003). A further self-deprecating comment from Audrey (aged 42) also emphasized an ambivalent relationship between the valuing of time relative to domestic tasks that represent expressions of care:

I hate the ironing, it's a waste of time in my eyes… Jenny [her friend] looks down on me because I don't iron Jeremy's (her son) school uniform and makes comments like that I would rather chat on the phone, 'cause I do like a chat you know!

While a relatively light-hearted comment about a friend who is clearly very close to her, Audrey later exclaimed that '*it is about the choices we make, and some people just spend too much of their time on pointless tasks and then moan endlessly about not having any time—like Jenny and her ironing* [laughs]!' Moral economies of time were evoked by respondents to emphasize the importance of utilizing time effectively, to point out that how we use time is about moral evaluations of everyday activities, and that micro-time management decisions were ever-present in their day-to-day lives.

When asked why they felt that contemporary lives are experienced as a time squeeze, the respondents of the Bristol study presented explanations closely associated with the core claims of popular academic theories. Time scarcity was associated with more consumption and more work. This was partly explained as driven by social status related to consumer lifestyles, career progression and workplace competition, all of which connect with a desire to provide the consumer goods and experiences deemed necessary for an appropriate standard of life. Respondents' explanations viewed time in objective terms, and consequently how time was 'used' was presented in relation to a moral economy of time: as choices about how to utilize time in the pursuit of activities. In doing so, the internalization of time discipline described by E.P. Thompson (see Chap. 2) is evident in respondents' understandings of (clock) time.

5.3   Harriedness: Volume, Coordination and Allocation of Practices

It is worth re-stating that the themes narrated by respondents of the Bristol study were responses to two relatively simple questions at the start of an interview: 'do you think that people today are more pressed for time than were people in the past' and 'why do you think this is the case?' Respondents immediately replied yes to the first question and their responses to the second are summarized within the three overarching themes discussed earlier. The interviews then asked respondents to 'talk through' their previous weekday and weekend, which they did in rich detail, before being asked if they felt the days discussed were typical of their everyday life and whether they felt time pressed during those days. Given their unanimous view that contemporary society is an experience of time pressure, it was somewhat surprising that all respondents did not describe their own day-to-day lives as an experience of time pressure. At most, they felt periods of 'harriedness' during their days but no overwhelming sense of time scarcity was narrated. This section discusses respondents' descriptions of their daily life and seeks to address this apparent discrepancy between the fundamental view that everyday life is time pressured and the lack or corroboration of this statement when describing their own everyday lives.

When discussing the temporalities of their previous weekday and weekend, respondents tended to describe the 'qualities' of their temporal experience. Reisch's (2001) account of 'time wealth' suggests four dimensions are typically evoked when people describe qualities of their temporal experiences. First is the chronometric dimension, which means having the right amount of time to perform the activities that individuals hold as important to a meaningful life. Second is the chronologic dimension or having available time for activities at the right time of the day, week or season. Third, she identifies a sovereignty dimension, which relates to having autonomy over the allocation of activities within time (control over time). Finally, she identifies the dimension of synchronization or time that fits with the activities of family and friends. Describing these dimensions as different varieties of time wealth, Reisch argues that experiences of the qualities of time are varied and not constrained only to the chronometric dimension that tends to dominate accounts of time scarcity. In their reflections on why contemporary society is an experience of increased time pressure, the respondents of the Bristol study focused on the chronometric dimension. However, glimpses of the other dimensions were apparent in their intimations of having control over time (time sovereignty), as in the case of Mary's response to Bob regarding doing the laundry, or the importance of synchronicity, such as Charlotte's description of rushing to get her daughter ready for bed so she can spend time with her father upon his return from work. When it came to descriptions of their everyday temporal experiences, respondents rarely touched on the chronometric dimension and instead drew upon the other three. They did so by discussing the strategies (or deliberate actions taken) that they put in place to manage the temporal organization of their daily activities, and in doing so three mechanisms emerged that accounted for their experiences of moments of time squeeze. These mechanisms can be described as the volume activities (contained within designated time periods and similar to Reisch's chronometric dimension), coordination (of people and activities, and similar to Reisch's synchronization dimension) and the allocation of activities into particular times of the day or week (similar to Reisch's sovereignty dimension).

Volumes of Activities

The mechanism of volume refers to instances where strategies were put in place to reduce the number of activities that respondents felt needed to be performed within designated periods of time. In some cases, this amounted to strategies that reduced the duration of minutes required to perform an activity or adjusting the activities periodicity, for example, reducing the frequency of cooking food from scratch. Such strategies were entirely focused on the volume of paid and unpaid work activities as opposed to activities related to personal care, leisure or consumption. When mentioned by respondents, these strategies took three forms: reliance on labour-saving devices, use of services (outsourcing) and some attempts to reduce paid work.

Labour-saving technologies were only discussed in passing and, as was indicated in the earlier presented quotations from Samantha and Bob, were only described in the past tense as something that has helped reduce durations of (clock) time necessary to complete domestic chores. As Fiona observed, *'things like washing machines and so on, well they don't really save any time now do they. I mean, they did compared with the distant past'*. Beyond these observations that domestic technologies had historically reduced the duration of time required to complete domestic activities, there was very little mention of other technologies that had such an effect. Instead, greater emphasis was placed on the use of services, both unpaid and paid, as an essential strategy for managing the volume of activities in their daily lives. Informal networks, especially familial, were particularly important for those who had a local support network. Cindy, for example, explained how her *'mum helps with Chloe* [her daughter] *and sometimes does the ironing for me, and she cleans my oven as well, but its Dad who does quite a bit like he mows the lawn for us and does some odd jobs and that, it keeps him busy… and we've come a bit too reliant on it really'*. Others used laundry and gardening services, although the use of paid post-preschool childcare was often frowned upon, as demonstrated by

Amanda's observation of senior work colleagues: *'there's nothing wrong with it, but they have nannies and things and you can't tell me that they deal with all the demands of their children, someone else does that while they sit in their offices'*. Other services, particularly prepared hot food, were frequently mentioned as a strategy for reducing the volume of unpaid work:

> *We depend a bit too much on the Chinese down the road to be honest, but when we're running late or just exhausted from the day it's just a way of getting another job off the list.* (Samantha)
>
> *I don't need an excuse for one, but Claire* [his wife] *doesn't like them as they are not the healthiest way to eat. Anyway, it used to be a treat but it's become more of a way to get dinner done especially if we have both had a long day.* (James)
>
> *We usually get a takeaway on a Friday night, it's a hangover from when the kids were teenagers and Friday night was the start of the weekend.* (Mary)

As hinted by Mary, and in most cases, the use of takeaway services were described not simply as a matter of reducing the time required to complete an activity but also as a marker of a rhythm or routine in the temporalities of the working week (an observation that will be returned to below).

Finally mentioned were occasional references to attempts to reduce the time devoted to paid work. Kathryn, Kevin (aged 43) and Charlotte employed the strategy of working from home one or two days a week to reduce commuting time, although Bradley commented that he found this strategy counter-productive: *'I tried working from home but I find it hard to keep home and work apart anyway and found that working from home I just worked for longer'*. In other cases, 4 of 14 women who were in paid work explained how they had reduced their employed hours to make more time for activities associated with their children. For example, Sarah described:

> *I used to do 25 hours a week but found that when they get to senior school there is just so much still to do on the home front and John* [her husband] *got a new job and more money so we decided to just reduce my hours so I could get house stuff done so we get a bit more time for ourselves and the kids at the weekend, not that it has worked out that way!*

In Cindy's case, the decision to leave paid work had offered instant rewards: '*at first it was lovely but now I am just busy before and after School and weekends are still manic. So instead of us rushing around all the time I am bored and then rushed, bored and then rushed* [laughs]'. In these cases, explicit strategies to reduce the volume of activities contained within a period of time (such as a week) did not appear to have the desired effect with respect to freeing time for other, presumably more desirable, activities.

Nevertheless, the volume of activities contained within a day or week does relate to feelings of time scarcity. This is demonstrated in the HALs data analysis where, when controlling for all variables, levels of paid employment and gender increased the extent to which survey respondents felt 'pressed for time'. Being a parent also increased senses of feeling pressed for time, although this was mostly for fathers of young children (under the age of 5) and mothers of children aged (6–11). The HALs data also revealed that respondents who reported performing a wider range of consumption activities reported feeling more pressed for time than those with fewer consumption interests, although the data contains no evidence that those with a wide range of interests spent any more minutes in those activities than did those people with fewer interests. It would seem that having a greater volume of consumption activities, whether or not those people devote more or less time to those activities, increases feelings of time pressure. Overall, taking the HALs data together with the relatively limited narratives of strategies to reduce volume of activities in time suggests that there is a generic relationship between the volume of activities that people perform in their everyday life and experiences or feelings of time pressure.

Temporal Coordination: Sequencing Activities and Synchronizing Networks

The second mechanism identified in respondents' time management strategies is coordination, which refers to the sequencing and synchronization of people and/or activities. The challenge, as presented by respondents was to develop strategies for coordinating multiple activities together with the people with whom they wanted to perform those activities. This took a number of forms, most prominent being attempts to align the personal schedules of household members and others within their social networks to synchronize particular activities, but also included adhering to routine patterns of activity and imposing rules and boundaries to protect particular parts of the day from the intrusion of unwanted activities or interruptions.

Strategies to align personal schedules represented a response to the experience, vocalized by all respondents, that household members and social networks faced different, individualized, socio-temporal demands within their everyday lives. For example, respondents of the Bristol study reported how partners who finished work at unpredictable times, friends and family who turned up unexpectedly and work colleagues who finished at different times of the day due to flexible working hours, all generated difficulties for respondents' scheduling of their daily activities. Often tensions were created by the successful imposition of personal routines by others upon the schedules of respondents. For example, Kevin described how his boss finished work early while he started work late (both accommodating the needs of their family). Consequently, his day was compressed by needing to meet the daily deadlines imposed on him by his boss's schedule.

A wide range of tactics were employed in seeking to align personal schedules and synchronize the activities of members of one's social network. The most prominent were shared diaries and scheduling systems. Amanda explained the ritual of scheduling that she and her partner followed every Sunday morning:

We get a cup of coffee, take a deep breath, and get out the diaries. First we go through the week ahead, see what we've both got on, and then try and organise ourselves. So, who is doing the school run, parents evening or whatever, the shopping, laundry, all the mundane stuff really… if we get it right we have a chance of some kind of weekend! So, once we've done the week ahead we then do a more general look forward for the next few weeks or even months, just so we can anticipate and think ahead.

Other households had calendars positioned in different places, most often on fridge doors, although Deborah used a chalkboard containing tasks for the next day that she extracted from her diary every evening, which she described as containing '*the masterplan for the week. I just make sure it's clear where everyone will be and so no one forgets anything*'. A large chalkboard in Suzanne's kitchen was divided into two sections, with a list of activities and their timings for herself and partner and a list of activities to remind the children of activities in their day. Not all households had such conspicuous displays of household coordination, with two having a 'standing rota' that marked turns for basic household activities and noted when any household member has an event that would disrupt the household routine. Only three respondents did not mention the use of such coordination devices, one of whom lived alone and the other two were single parents of relatively young children.

To manage the alignment of personal schedules, a range of technologies were described as being critical in order to anticipate potential disruptions and respond to those that emerge. Mobile phones and the use of traffic updates were important: '*the local traffic updates are really important for Darren* [her partner], *he can check on his drive home from work and let me know an eta, that way I can time things like dinner and kids homework*' (Kathryn). Others talked of devices that allowed them to ensure activities were in motion so that schedules were not under risk from disruptions, as Michael (aged 30) explained in his use of the slow cooker: '*I do all the cooking, and unless I know I will have a quiet work day and that I will definitely be home on time I use the slow cooker. Bang it all in before I leave in the morning and it's all ready for when everyone else is*'. Other examples included timing functions on washing machines and tumble dryers in order to synchronize the completion of clothes washing upon waking up or the drying of the laundry for the return home from work (see Chap. 7 for a discussion of the socio-temporal ordering of laundry practices), timing functions on ovens and the use of video recorders for television programmes that were out of sync with the coordinated personal schedules of any given day.

While respondents described, in great detail, the range of devices that helped them to coordinate the shared activities of their household, many also recognized the significance of daily and weekly routines. Some respondents imposed temporal constraints on personal schedules in the form of immovable periodic (daily, weekly or monthly) tasks. Sarah explained how she '*must*' vacuum the entire house daily and iron once every other day, both '*had to be done*' in the morning before work, '*otherwise I'd never stay on top of things*'. Weekly garden tidying, every Sunday, was a necessary task for Bob, and Steven could not start the day '*without reading the paper*'. All represent self-defined obligations, with a high degree of periodic rigidity. In these cases, commitment to conventional social-temporal structures, like mealtimes, bedtime and TV schedules, were used to organize and institutionalize collective schedules around practice performed with high degrees of regularity. To be effective, such strategies required normative policing, as Mary very clearly articulated using the example of when her husband's work colleague phoned outside of office hours and disrupted their evening routine:

> *he'd phone in the evening and be on for a good hour or so… And I used to get quite cross because to my mind when you get home is when you come home, it's our time and I take a very dim view of it being interrupted… it just means our evening is messed-up because, like, the washing-up's not done and we have to dash about so that we, if we want to sit down and watch something. Well, in the end we stopped answering it.*

In another case James explained how fixed temporalities made daily life both predictable and manageable:

> *I start at 8, have lunch at 12, go home at 5, we always have dinner by half 6, wash up, have a chat about the day with Claire and perhaps about the next day, watch some tele and go to bed about half 10, and then start all over again… the only time I'm pushed is if a new Fitter books something in before lunch when there's not enough time to do the job, and if they keep doing that they get sacked!*

Cases such as Mary and James point to a high degree of reliance on others' normative compliance with rigid socio-temporal structures. In both cases, those described as 'breaking' temporal normative conventions were implied to be 'deviant' and were removed from their networks.

Interacting within networks where all followed rigid timings for shared activities was presented as a strategy that reduced instances of being harried for people like Mary and James.

Recognizing and adhering to routines also required the imposition of temporal boundaries around particular sets of activities. School drop-off and pick-up times, mealtimes and divisions between daytime and evenings, between days or parts of the day for housework (morning and evenings) and between times at work designated for breaks (such as mid-morning and mid-afternoon) and those as 'times' for productivity all acted as institutionalized temporal boundaries. The degree to which such institutionalized boundaries were welcomed varied across respondents depending on the extent to which they felt obligated to coordinate their activities with others. For some, capacity to coordinate people and activities in time was particularly challenging in contexts where the respondent had responsibility for the coordination of their social networks. This was especially the case for those with young children, who had occupations that required many appointments with colleagues or clients and for those who sought to organize social activities within friendship groups. To be successful in coordinating people and activities high degrees of self-discipline were required: '*I think "right I'll do this this and this before lunch" and then half an hour before lunch I've still got two things to do and have spent most the morning chatting!*' (Joanne, aged 25). In other cases, the strict imposition of socio-temporal boundaries was to be limited to avoid everyday lives becoming too 'regimented'. Cindy provided a neat example by comparing herself with a neighbour's style of coordinating the activities and people within her household:

I'm amazed at what she gets done and it works for her, everything is so, I don't know, her house is always clean, her kids well groomed you know the type. But it wouldn't work for us, I like to do things spontaneously.

Regardless of the degrees to which respondents could or wanted to impose or follow routines and abide by the timings of institutionalized temporal boundaries, when it came to reflecting on their everyday temporal experiences it was the coordination or people and activities that featured most prominently in their narratives of temporal experience.

Our analysis of the HALs data also provides some strong support for the claim that the challenge of coordination is at the core of feelings of time pressure. The survey data revealed that, when controlling for all variables, those who worked flexible hours felt more pressed for time than those who worked shifts. This suggests that those with fixed patterns of working hours appear less likely to need to coordinate their personal schedules in the ways that those with greater flexibility might. Interestingly, the data also reveals that socializing had no effect on whether people reported feeling more or less pressed for time, but that socializing by arrangement did increase being pressed for time, lending further support to the notion that the need to coordinate activities and people enhances experiences of time pressure.

Allocating Time

The final mechanism identified in the narratives of respondents from the Bristol study refers to the allocation of time for the performance of particular types of activities. Strategies associated with this mechanism took four forms: multitasking of domestic activities, allocating time to meet the needs of others, maintaining standards of performance within allocated times, and allocating quality time.

Multitasking, or the kinds of juggling described in Thompson's (1996) study of working mothers discussed in Chap. 3, was a prominent description of daily activities especially for working mothers. It was not, however, presented as a matter of the volume of activities that required completion but that many activities tended to 'fall together' all at once. As Samantha explained, multitasking is about senses of *'being overwhelmed with things that need doing and rushing around to get them all done'*. In all narratives of multitasking the sense of juggling a number of activities simultaneously derived from those activities being allocated within a designated slot of time often with a fixed institutional event or self-imposed scheduling acting as a clear temporal boundary for that period of time. Cindy presented an example that was typical of accounts of multitasking:

I find the mornings very very hectic what with trying to feed her, get her dressed, to get myself dressed and get her out the door in time to get her to school. Like this evening she got back from school, we had about one hour and then she had to go to gym club and I was like, that's not enough time, she needs to eat her tea and you would think an hour is plenty but, so I find myself stressed all the time by trying to get her to places for the time she needs to be there.

Other cases involved lunchtime, work-based meetings and social events acting to demarcate temporal boundaries between activities. Furthermore, this was not a narrative restricted to women or dual income households but was presented by all respondents as a dominant feature of times in their day when they felt harried.

A second feature of narratives that highlight the mechanism of time allocation were the consequences of the need to meet with the personal scheduling and coordination of activities imposed upon the respondent by other people, especially friends and family. As Suzanne explained, visiting friends and family, which they did every other weekend, meant the:

loss of a whole weekend, so I have to get everything done by Friday or there is a pile of ironing to do on Sunday night, as well as washing from the weekend and just the other stuff you need to do to get ready for a week's work.

In other cases friends and family were described as being less busy and thus expected the respondent to 'make time' for particular practices. Ashley (aged 31) recounted one example:

because he [his brother] *works typical hours he thinks I can meet up for a drink at 5 or a Sunday lunch time you know. If I don't he thinks I'm avoiding him, that my job is more important than he is… So I will try and meet up and I either rush everything to get it finished before I leave or know it's waiting for me the next morning.*

At issue here is the lack of social proximity and imbalance of temporal densities within social networks. In order to meet the coordinated activities within networks, respondents allocated other activities within their day into particular time frames so as to meet the scheduling demands imposed upon them.

Third, the allocation of particular time frames for the performance of activities raised a number of temporal anxieties related to competency (or meeting certain standards). In a work-based context, Elizabeth described:

for me I suppose the pressure of time is when I'm feeling like I've got three things to do all at the same time and I am worried that I am not doing any of them properly.

In a very different observation, Bradley revealed what he perceived to be the root of his partner's experiences of harriedness when he stated to her that:

you spend half the day cleaning one room, because it's like you know, like dusting everywhere, it's almost like in, the sort of, prior to regimental inspection. Whereas I am sure that other people don't clean to that extreme and, so you use the time or create the time that creates the pressures.

As in the case of Sarah who described the need to vacuum her house every morning or Bob's weekly garden tidying, the process of allocating activities within designated time frames raised anxieties about the competent performance. These are concerns about achieving appropriate and usually subjective standards of outcome for any particular activity—whether related to qualities of cleanliness, care or simply '*doing the best job possible*' (Cindy). It was in this context that Mary, Elizabeth, Charlotte, James and Darren each repeated the same phrase of constantly feeling like they were 'having to cut corners' in order to complete tasks within the allocated time frame. The alternative, as explained by Audrey, was '*if you don't get it done it ends up eating into your evening and then you feel stressed, tired and miserable!*' Allocating time frames for the completion of set activities created expectations of outcome and deadlines for the completion of daily activities which created feelings of being harried.

The final strategy that respondents narrated for managing the temporalities of their daily lives was attempts to allocate 'quality time'. Allocating times of the day and week that are free from 'work' activities and in which the main focus was spending times together with significant others was prominent across all of the interviews. The following list of quotations provides some illustrations:

> *In the main we like to have dinner by half past 5 at the latest. And then in the evenings, I mean it's one of the house rules to have everything cleared away by 7 even if that means somebody has to rush to do their job. So we have eaten, washed up, put away and then we are free. And then it's our potter time.* (Mary)
>   *we keep Sundays free as like our quality time but it does make Saturday's a bit hectic, like we try and get everything done so that Sunday is free, so we can spend proper time together.* (Steven)
>   *It's weird in that I will rush to get everything done so I can chill out in the evening then I get bored, but I still do it. I suppose it's good to have nothing to do otherwise you'd get stressed.* (James)

While some accounts described allocating temporal space for the self, as in the case of James, the overwhelming majority of discussions about quality time was focused on creating time frames for spending time with other people, usually family or close friends. Furthermore, as with Kremer-Sadlik and Paugh's (2007) study of American working families, the search for quality time was not exclusively focused on leisure activities but also included household chores such as grocery shopping, with the critical factor in whether that was experienced as 'quality time' being that the activities were performed together with significant others without haste, interruption or high degrees of activity planning beyond making or having the time in which these activities could happen with a degree of spontaneity. In this respect allocating times is closely related to the earlier mechanism of coordinating people and activities and represents purposive strategies employed by all respondents that sought to organize temporalities of togetherness.

Summary: Hot and Cold Spots of Daily Activities

Taken together, the three mechanisms that emerged from the respondents' descriptions of their everyday temporal experiences suggest that feelings of harriedness and time scarcity are momentary experiences as opposed to an ongoing or ever-present condition. While respondents described strategies for reducing the volume of activities, narratives describing a sense of being overwhelmed by the sheer volume of activities within their everyday lives were largely absent from the descriptions to the weekdays and weekends. Instead, it was the mechanisms of coordinating activities and people and allocating times for those activities that dominated respondents' reflections on the temporalities of their everyday lives. In this respect, narratives of feeling harried (feeling harassed and worried about time) captured moments containing a density of activities and network coordination that were experienced as 'hot spots'. Often, hot spots were relatively predictable periods of the day which immediately preceded institutionally timed events, such as meal and school times, which acted to mark relatively fixed boundaries between different types of activities within the temporal organization of the day. However, the experience of hot spots was also countered by the allocation of time for cold spots of activity, which were variously described as '*quality time*', '*potter time*', '*chill time*' and '*bonding time*' (for a similar analysis focused on 'self-time', see Holmes 2018). Respondents scheduled hot spots as practical arrangements that permit the generation of cold spots or block time released from necessary tasks and reserved for more 'meaningful' social activities.

Hot and cold spots represented attempts to gain personal control (or Reisch's dimension of temporal sovereignty) over the temporal organization of daily life. One major challenge facing such attempts was that due to the need to coordinate activities and people within allocated (or scheduled) time frames, the scope for success depended heavily on the alignment of activities, people and time frames. And the interviews were littered with examples of just how difficult this proved to be. In the following quotation notice how Sarah's carefully prepared family day out became an experience of harriedness:

> *We started off early on Saturday and I did the cleaning on Friday night, just to free Saturday up… So, we've done breakfast and the bathing, and we went swimming, and took a picnic so we had that, and then went on an adventure trail at Bowood. And because we had to get there by twelve to make it worthwhile we had to leave swimming with enough time to spare. Then we had to*

find somewhere for the picnic and it just went on like that. God I needed a day off after that day off!

Scheduled cold spots often rapidly turned into experiences of hot spots and the related senses of harriedness that respondents were seeking to avoid.

Reisch's chronologic and synchronization dimensions of temporal experience are also evident in respondents' accounts of the mechanisms of coordination and allocation. Having 'time' for activities at the right time was at the core of attempts to coordinate personal schedules and allocate moments of hot and cold spots. Equally, the dimension of synchronizing activities to fit with those of others is clearly evident. What is more significant about the narratives of the respondents from the Bristol study is that these temporal dimensions were always dependent on the same attempts by others to coordinate activities and people within allocated time frames, and these temporal dimensions became problematic, or experiences of harriedness, because of the difficulty of temporal alignment across schedules. The Bristol study is an example of individuals seeking to micro-coordinate activities and aligning them with those of others who face the same challenges of micro-coordination of everyday activities.

5.4   Conclusion

This chapter has provided a close examination of a study that explored how people in Bristol, England, perceived whether contemporary societies suffer from time scarcity, why they thought this was the case and how they described the temporalities of their day-to-day lives. The study was conducted in 2000 and does not represent an analysis of everyday temporal experiences in the current period, and it is useful to note the discussion in Chap. 4 of the UK 2015 time diary survey that reports a decline of feeling 'pressed for time' when compared with data from 2000 (Sullivan and Gershuny 2018). The Bristol study is reported at length because it remains one of the few empirical accounts that explicitly addresses people's temporal experiences (as opposed to the many studies reported in

Chaps. 3 and 4 that have examined temporal experiences in specific contexts, focused on the use of particular technologies or sought to measure activities in the number of minutes devoted to them). In doing so it offers conceptual tools for examining the temporalities of everyday life and the mechanisms that underpin experiences of harriedness.

The chapter began by reporting the unanimous perception that contemporary societies are an experience of time scarcity. In explaining why they felt this to be the case, respondents provided remarkably consistent accounts of working and consuming more in the pursuit of status-driven lifestyles, the demands of interpersonal relationships and the moral economy of time based on its efficient and purposeful utilization. These narratives were presented in abstract terms, reflecting general observations about societal change rather than directly referring to their own temporal experiences. When it came to descriptions about their temporal experiences of the previous weekday and weekend, very few references to time scarcity were narrated. Instead, the focus was on moments during the day or week when they experienced a feeling of being harried. Three mechanisms of harriedness were revealed in these narratives.

The mechanism of 'volume' was the nearest that respondents came to describing time scarcity in the conventional sense that the absolute number of activities necessary to be performed within a period of time, such as a day, cumulatively exceeded the amount of (clock) time available. Respondents employed strategies including the use of domestic technologies that promised to save time, taking advantage of services either bought from the market (as in the case of takeaway foods or domestic services) or sourced from within their social networks, and in some cases taking measures to reduce their hours of paid work. The mechanism of coordination of activities and people featured more prominently in respondents' accounts of their temporal experiences. Significant efforts at the micro-coordination of personal schedules, especially within households, were described, together with the importance of maintaining daily and weekly routines and establishing temporal boundaries to enforce those routines. Finally, the mechanism of allocating times for the performance of particular activities represented attempts to impose control over the timings of when activities were performed and often led to experiences of multitasking, managing times for social-izing with others, and anxiety in maintaining competent standards of activity performance, and focused around creating temporal space within the day and week for 'quality time'.

Based on the reflections of their everyday lives, time pressure for those interviewed in the Bristol study represented moments of harriedness con-tained within particular times of their daily lives. In many cases moments of harriedness had a degree of predictability as a consequence of their alignment with institutionally timed events, particularly the start and end times of school and work, mealtimes and the period leading into the evening where all people sought to experience a form of quality time. The metaphor of hot and cold spots of activity reflects this ebb and flow in that people described rushing to complete activities within designated hot spots of activity in order to create the temporal space for cold spots of meaningful non-work activities usually or preferably performed with sig-nificant others. Not all hot spots were tied to institutionally timed events but were allocated within particular periods of the day or week. Completing housework on a Saturday to leave Sunday free from domes-tic or paid work was commonly described by respondents. Frequently, however, respondents' efforts to coordinate activities and people to fit within their allocated times for hot and cold spots met with failure because of a lack of alignment between their own schedules and those of others. Individualized attempts at the micro-coordination of activities and people both underpinned a sense of control and autonomy over the temporalities of everyday life and rendered that micro-coordination even more challenging as its success was dependent on close temporal align-ment with the activities of other people.

References

Bittman, M., & Wajcman, J. (2000). The Rush Hour; the Character of Leisure Time and Gender Equity. *Social Forces, 79*(1), 165–189.
Brannen, J. (2005). Time and the Negotiation of Work-family Boundaries: Autonomy or Illusion. *Time & Society, 14*(1), 113–131.

Craig, L., & Mullan, K. (2011). How Mothers and Fathers Share Childcare: A Cross-national Time-use Comparison. *American Sociological Review, 76*(6), 834–861.

Craig, L., Powell, A., & Smyth, C. (2014). Towards Intensive Parenting? Changes in the Composition and Determinants of Mothers and Fathers' Time with Children 1992–2006. *British Journal of Sociology, 65*(3), 555–579.

Gershuny, J. (2005). Busyness as the Badge of Honor for the New Superordinate Working Class. *Social Research, 72*(2), 287–314.

Hochschild, A. R. (1997). *The Time Bind: When Home Becomes Work and Work Becomes Home.* CA Henry Holt.

Holmes, H. (2018). Self-time: The Importance of Temporal Experience within Practice. *Time & Society, 27*(2), 176–194.

Kremer-Sadlik, T., & Paugh, A. L. (2007). Everyday Moments: Finding 'Quality time' in American Working Families. *Time & Society, 16*(2–3), 287–308.

Kunda, G. (2001). *Scenes from a Marriage: Work, Family and Time in Corporate Drama.* Paper Presented to the International Conference on Spacing and Timing, November, Palermo, Italy.

Lesnard, L. (2008). Off-scheduling Within Dual-earner Couples: An Unequal and Negative Externality for Family Time. *American Journal of Sociology, 114,* 447–490.

Mass Observation Archive. (2009). *Meet Yourself on Sunday.* London: Bloomsbury House.

Reisch, L. (2001). Time and Wealth: The Role of Time and Temporalities for Sustainable Patterns of Consumption. *Time and Society, 10*(2/3), 387–405.

Rutherford, S. (2001). Are You Going Home Already?: The Long Hours Culture, Women Managers and Patriarchal Closure. *Time and Society, 10*(2/3), 259–276.

Schwartz-Cowan, R. (1983). *More Work for Mother: The Ironies of Household Technology from the Open Hearth to the Microwave.* London: Basic Books.

Shaw, J. (1998). "Feeling a List Coming on": Gender and the Pace of Life. *Time & Society, 7*(2), 383–396.

Shove, E. (2003). *Comfort, Cleanliness and Convenience: The Social Organization of Normality.* Oxford: Berg.

Southerton, D. (2003). 'Squeezing Time': Allocating Practices, Co-ordinating Networks and Scheduling Society. *Time & Society, 12*(1), 5–25.

Southerton, D., & Tomlinson, M. (2005). "Pressed for Time"—the Differential Impacts of a "Time Squeeze". *Sociological Review, 53*(2), 215–239.

Sullivan, O. (1997). Time Waits for No (wo)men: An Investigation of the Gendered Experience of Domestic Time. *Sociology, 31*(2), 221–240.

Sullivan, O., & Gershuny, J. (2018). Speed-Up Society? Evidence from the UK 2000 and 2015 Time Use Diary Surveys. *Sociology, 52*, 20–38.

Thompson, C. (1996). Caring Consumers: Gendered Consumption Meanings and the Juggling Lifestyle. *Journal of Consumer Research, 22*, 388–407.

Warren, T. (2003). Class- and Gender-based Working Time? Time Poverty and the Division of Domestic Labour. *Sociology, 37*(4), 733–752.

6

Past Times: The Contrasting Timings of Everyday Activities

6.1   Introduction

The analysis of Chap. 5 demonstrated that experiences of the time squeeze are a consequence of the challenges of coordinating and scheduling activities in the context of everyday lives. This raises two critical questions. First, and especially given that most accounts present the time squeeze as an emergent phenomenon, is whether the challenges of coordination and scheduling are particular to contemporary societies. Second, especially given arguments presented both in social scientific theories (Chaps. 2 and 4) and through the diagnoses of those interviewed for the Bristol study (Chap. 5), which suggest time pressure is a consequence of greater varieties of consumption and flexibility over the timings of work activities, is whether processes of individualization in the allocations of activities in time underpin the challenge of coordinating everyday lives. To address these questions, this chapter begins by analysing 'day in the life' diaries from 1937 to gain an impression of the timings and temporal experiences of everyday activities of the past and contrasts insights from diaries with those gained from the interviews of the Bristol study. Demonstrating that the diaries of 1937 did reveal 'strong' collective timings of activities, the

© The Author(s) 2020
D. Southerton, *Time, Consumption and the Coordination of Everyday Life*,
Consumption and Public Life, https://doi.org/10.1057/978-1-349-60117-2_6

chapter then reanalyses the temporal dimensions of everyday activities from the Bristol study to reveal an 'ordering' of activities based on their differential temporal characteristics. While contemporary lives are subject to much weaker collective timings of activities, the temporalities of everyday life retain a temporal order.

6.2   The Mass Observation Archive

Any analysis of societal change is always partial because of the difficulty of identifying reliable comparative data. One source of data is time diaries, which provide a reliable source of data regarding the amount of time people spend in particular activities, and that data has been collected in most affluent nations since the mid-1960s. However, what is recorded as different activities varies over time, as does how people interpret those activities (say, as a primary or secondary activity). And as was demonstrated in Chap. 3, the survey analysis presents little evidence to strongly support the claim that people are working more whether in paid or unpaid labour, yet surveys do reveal that most people feel today's society is more pressed for time than those of the past. The analysis of the Bristol study provided some explanation for this apparent paradox. It suggests that the time squeeze is less a matter of working more or a general increase of the volume of activities condensed into finite amounts of (clock) time but a condition that is manifest in experiences of harriedness that are associated with the challenge of coordinating personal schedules (of activities) with other people, who also share this challenge of coordination. The felt need to align personal schedules to create temporal space for the alignment of meaningful practices (often described as quality time) led respondents to allocate times for different types of activity that produced experiences of hot (harried) and cold (quality time) spots within the temporal organization of their days and week. To empirically examine whether this challenge of coordination is a contemporary phenomenon, qualitative data from past lives is needed. Fortunately, the Mass Observation Study collected qualitative accounts, in the form of descriptive diaries, of 'a day in the life' of British people in 1937.

The Mass Observation project is a social scientific research organization established in 1937 with the aim of creating an '*Anthropology of Ourselves*'. The original studies comprised a national panel of volunteers who responded on a regular basis to questionnaires and directives (Sheridan 2009; Hall 2015). On the coronation of King George VI (May 12, 1937) the first 'day in the life diaries' were collected as a directive to volunteers. Diarists were then asked to repeat the diary format on every 12th day of the month thereafter until the outbreak of the Second World War. Five hundred people recorded diaries, although because the sample was based on volunteers it was not nationally representative nor did every volunteer provide a diary for each month of the study.

The diaries analysed were collected on two days in 1937: Saturday, June 12, and Monday, July 12. This enabled broad comparison with the interview data from the Bristol study in which respondents recounted their previous weekday and weekend (see Southerton 2009, for a full discussion of the methodology). Fourteen female diarists were selected on the basis of the legibility of their diaries and completed descriptions of their experiences on both days. Detailed socio-demographic variables of diarists were not collected to the degree that is common practice in contemporary social scientific research, but the diary entries did reveal age (3 were aged between 20 and 29, 7 between 30 and 39; 3 between 40 and 49 and 1 was aged between 50 and 59), that 3 diarists worked in full-time jobs with 11 described themselves as 'housewives' with various forms of part-time paid work, 10 were married and 9 had children and 5 described themselves as working class while the remaining 9 identified as middle class.

As implied, collection and analysis of the Mass Observation Archive diaries sought to offer a degree of comparison with the interview data from the Bristol study with respect to the range and organization of activities within a given day. The two data sets offer an indication of similarities and differences in temporal organization and experiences across the two time periods. The basis for comparability is that diarists were asked to record what they did and how they felt (their mood) on that particular day. In the diaries, this resulted in variations of the way the day was recorded. In some cases, diarists recorded their day in the form of a time diary (e.g. 7.00 am got out of bed; 7.10 am made cup of tea), others wrote a paragraph outlining the rhythm of their day and their feelings as the day progressed. In this respect, diarists in 1937 were asked similar initial questions as were the interviewees of the Bristol study. However, and by contrast, the interviews conducted for the Bristol study provided scope to explore and discuss the temporal organization of daily lives and how they were experienced by respondents in considerably greater detail.

Given data limitations, the analysis that follows is not a systematic comparison because the diaries largely offer a glimpse into the temporal experiences of daily lives in 1937. Nevertheless, such glimpses are useful for gaining insights into the temporal organization of past lives. To offer a degree of conceptual consistency in the analysis of both sets of data, a social practice theoretical perspective was employed. Social practice theory (see Chap. 7 for a more detailed discussion) takes practices, as opposed to the beliefs and motives of individual actors, as the central unit of analysis. Operationalized for the purposes of diary and interview data analysis, this meant that the activities that people reported were taken as the principal object of analysis and examined in terms of the temporal dimensions that diarists and interview respondents described when recounting their day. Fine's (1996) five temporal dimensions, which he employed to analyse the temporalities of professional kitchens, were employed to interrogate diarists' and respondents' descriptions of the 'durations' of time associated with an activity; indications of the perceived 'tempo' of the described activity; whether the activity was 'synchronized' with other people or activities; the extent to which the frequency (or 'periodicity') of activity performance could be determined; and the 'sequences' in which activities were performed (see Southerton 2006 for a full discussion of the analytical advantages of examining the temporal dimensions of practices). The level of detail recovered from the interview data regarding each temporal dimension was, as would be expected, far greater for the Bristol study interviews.

6.3   1937: 'A Day in the Life'

The Mass Observation Archive provides a useful summary of all leisure activities described by the 63 diarists from Saturday, June 12, 1937. Seventy activities were described in total, the most popular being activities related to the 'garden and home' (10), 9 went on 'visits or outings', 8 described 'reading' and the same number enjoyed 'listening to the radio', while 7 watched and 5 played sports. Other activities included going to 'theatre' (5), the 'pub' (5), 'country walks' (4), 'religious activities' (3), 'cinema' (3) and 'fetes' or 'school events' (3). Despite it appearing that, on average, each diarist enjoyed a leisure activity on Saturday, and that 8 of the 14 sampled diarists stated Saturday to be a *'day of leisure'*, when leisure activities are read within context, it becomes clear that leisure was allocated around a variety of paid and unpaid work practices. As with the types of accounts described by respondents of the Bristol study in Chap. 5, the written narratives of Mass Observation diarists presented an experience of a seamless range of interconnected and overlapping activities dispersed throughout their reported day. Mrs Beken's (a married housewife with four children who lived in Kent and whose husband was a farm labourer) complete diary for Saturday, June 12 (1937), provided a particularly good example.

5.45: Woke by birds
5.55: Alarm clock rings and husband gets up to make tea—gas means no waiting about. I wonder whether I look fat and think about how much husband hates his job. After cup of tea make husband's lunch.
6.40: See him [husband] *off to work.*
6.50: Eldest son wakes up followed by the twins. Arrange flowers and send youngest back to their room to keep them out the way while I do house jobs but, better let come done and not whine, say I.
7.05: Sent Norman, my 9 year old son, to get milk from the dairy.
7.45: Start ironing. Must sandwich this in somehow with all the other jobs to do.
8.20: Eldest son goes to work.
8.30: Finished flowers, in between ironing and cutting bread and jam.
10.00: General tidying upstairs.

11.00: Clean dining room.

11.30: More ironing. Friend comes with fried fish for lunch, she [her neighbour] *has made the last few years bearable.*

12.20: Himself [her husband] *comes home and demands his tea—but he does help with tidying.*

1.05: Eldest son comes but I forgot he has to be back at work for two so had to rush some fried fish to the table and bread and jam for his afters. Tell him he can have pudding for tea. He says "O.K". Good job he's good tempered. Gives me his wages.

1.45: Family sit down for lunch.

2.20: Clear away lunch and husband washes up. I tidy dining room. Hectic scramble to wash twins. Wash and dress the children in best clothes.

3.10: Mother arrives.

4.00: Wash and change my clothes. Send Norman to get biscuits for tea as I have no time for scones as planned. Husband goes to local town.

5.30: Clear up tea, mother washes up and then asks for clothing that needs mending.

7.00: Put son's friend on bus to take him home and put twins to bed.

8.00: Fly along to little general shop for last minute shopping. Meet him [her husband] *coming back from Bromley on bike.*

9.30: Mother goes to bed, followed by Norman.

10.00: Go to pub with husband for one drink. Get home and have supper at same time as eldest son arrives home.

Mrs Beken's use of language such as '*must sandwich in*' and '*hectic scramble*' resemble the descriptions provided by respondents of the Bristol study to capture senses of harriedness (reported in Chap. 5). However, by comparison, diarist descriptions of the temporal organization of everyday activities presented little sense of autonomy or control over the temporal dimensions (duration, tempo, periodicity, synchronization or sequence) of those activities. This could, of course, be an artefact of the data and the diary format of the 1937 narratives. However, all diary entries were ordered around institutionalized temporal events, such as shared times of paid work. Mrs Beken's diary entry for Monday, July 12, reflected an almost identical temporal organization that was dictated by the (paid) work times of her husband and eldest son. All respondents described their Monday, July 12, through reference to the timings of paid work and eight did so for Saturday, June 12, 1937.

The impression that institutionalized events acted to order the day was reinforced by the dominance of mealtimes. Mrs Beken's aforementioned diary entry provided a typical example. Without fail, breakfast was taken after getting up in the morning (usually between 7 and 8 on a weekday) and lunch was eaten between 12.00 and 12.40 on the Monday and between 12.30 and 2.00 for all Saturday diarists. Lunch was an important meal, with husbands and children returning from work or school in order to dine together. Evening meals were a less significant event in 1937 than was the case for respondents of the Bristol study where it acted as the main meal of the day and was presented as the only opportunity for eating together. Rather, diarists reported '*tea*' (light snacks) in the late afternoon of '*bread, apple and cheese*' or '*bread, butter and banana*', and then a similar '*supper*' taken later in the early evening. There were no discussions of eating together on the evening in the weekday diaries, rather each individual member of the household grabbed their pre-prepared (by the diarist) convenience food (e.g. apple, bread, cheese) and ate alone. Eating a cooked meal (rather than snacks) required much planning and preparation, including the timing of when to '*lay the kitchen fire*', which for Mrs Friend (a married housewife aged 32, living in Norbury with no children) was best done to coincide with '*doing the Laundry*' as the kitchen was warm and clothes could be '*dried if the weather turns bad*'. For Mrs Friend, '*laying the kitchen fire*' led to the synchronization of a set of domestic activities, in addition to the laundry. Monday was '*bath day*', '*laundry day*' and also used to produce a stew (with Sunday's leftover meat). Other examples of institutionalized events including 'market days', which represented designated days of the week for which people such as Mrs Elliot (a married housewife aged 48 with children living in Burnley) described the importance of arriving early '*before all the decent stock goes*'. Such material constraints to the timing and coordination of domestic practices, such as cooking, eating and laundry, appeared to have a profound impact on the temporal organization of days in 1937 with Monday widely regarded as the weekly 'wash day' for UK households (see OldandInteresting 2019 for a history of laundry and also 1900s.org.uk).

It was perhaps for this reason that the diarists from 1937 made no mention of the use of coordination or scheduling devices such as shared diaries, calendars or notice boards in the kitchen that featured so prominently in the Bristol study. Rather, it appeared that coordinating devices were not required because fixed institutional events such as meal and work times, or Monday as wash day, acted to order the temporalities of daily practices such that coordination was embedded in the collective timings of when particular activities were performed. In all these ways, time was not negotiated between couples or within social networks in the same sense as they were for respondents of the Bristol study: in 1937 the temporal organization of everyday activities was not presented as malleable or matters of individual discretion. This is not to say that the diarists of 1937 did not plan or make notes about tasks that needed to be completed. Mrs Cotton (28 years old, married with a young child, housewife and elocutionist, living in Brighton) described in her Saturday diary how she '*planned the week-end menu*' and ordered '*everything required up to Monday's breakfast*'. At 12.30 pm on the same day, Mrs Hodson (38 years old, married housewife with one child, living in Marlow) began cooking the Sunday lunch of roast mutton, commenting that '*most working class people cook the joint on Sunday, but I cook on Saturday to lessen the work next day*'. While planning activities was identifiable in 1937 diaries, there was little sense of the need to purposefully coordinate the personal schedules and activities with those of members of households or wider social networks.

Again, it is important to remember that diarists were not directly asked to comment on how they organized their day and did not have the opportunities to expand on their experiences to the extent that interview respondents could. However, the impression that activities required less individualized temporal coordination in 1937 was further indicated by the absence of phrases such as 'quality' or 'family' time in the 1937 diaries, although some comments did imply the significance of togetherness. In Mrs Hodson's Saturday diary, she mentioned for a second time the importance of preparing Sunday lunch a day in advance, explaining that '*I like to make Sunday a day of leisure more or less. I particularly want to be as free as possible this Sunday, as my husband will be off duty, which is unusual*'. Mrs Cotton described how, having made her list of groceries,

Saturday morning presented the opportunity for the family to spend some time together, and she went '*straight down to the town front* [she lived in Brighton], *we went for a Donkey ride, stopped at a café for ice cream and returned home for 12.45*'. After lunch the afternoon was then spent '*idling on the roof, where I sunbathed, the child played and my husband did his stamps (his hobby)*'. While no diarist spoke directly of 'family time' or 'quality time', the importance of spending time together as a family remained clear even if not explicitly articulated.

There were, as might be expected, a range of shared temporal experiences across the two data sets, most notably related to the demands of child-related activities. The challenges of childcare were as present in the 1937 diaries as they were in the narratives of the Bristol study (especially amongst women). For example, Mrs Cotton lamented about how her daughter '*interrupted mostly every minute for help in brick building*'. Several mothers spoke of the rush to get children ready for school, and Mrs Beken commented on the difficulties of caring for children in school holidays: '*the woman next door has had to keep all 5 children off school due to whooping cough.... The school holidays start in 2 weeks and she is really struggling with controlling and looking after all 7*'. Other than the 'whooping cough' and sheer number of children, such challenges of childcare appear consistent across the two studies. With the exception of Mrs Cotton's mention of donkey riding, however, the child-centred leisure and consumption activities that featured so prominently in the narratives of respondents from the Bristol study were almost entirely absent from the 1937 diaries. Rather, children's activities within the day were described either in relation to schooling or as household helpers, as was the case with Mrs Beken's Saturday diary entry in which she '*Sent Norman, my 9 year old son, to get milk from the dairy*' at 7 am and by 4 pm Norman is off to buy some biscuits. It was only Mrs Cotton's mention of '*donkey riding*' in her Saturday diary that indicated any coordination measures for episodes of child-parent leisure activities.

A further contrast with the narratives presented by respondents of the Bristol study was the absence of shared leisure between partners. Eight of the women stated that on the evening their husband '*read*', some listened to the '*wireless*', Mr Cotton '*did his stamps*'; others went out after '*tea*' to '*the pub*' or a '*Union meeting*'. The diarists described how they '*did their letters'*, '*read'*, '*listened to the wireless'*, although implied they did so alone, had '*tea'* with their mother or either visited or was visited by a '*neighbour'*. Mr and Mrs Cotton did spend some time together during the Saturday daytime; two other couples went for a drink in the local pub on Saturday evening, and one couple went out for a business meal with the husband's '*French acquaintances'*. It was only in one diary (Mrs Hodson) that a description was given of the purposeful coordination of activities to facilitate time to spend together with a partner. Compared with the interviews of 2000, where every couple spoke in great detail of the need to make time to spend with one's partner and took measures to achieve this objective, spending leisure time together in 1937 appeared less frequent and taken for granted. This may well be because many diarists wrote of strained relationships with their husbands, but outside of mealtimes there was very little indication of a concern or purposeful efforts to make time to spend together with a partner (consistent with Bott's [1957] analysis of conjugal relationships in the 1950s Britain).

While the diaries from 1937 provide only a brief insight into the temporalities of everyday life, those brief insights do suggest three significant differences from the daily temporal experiences of those interviewed in the Bristol study. The first was that the temporal organization of daily life in 1937 reflected clearly defined institutionally timed events. This was most clear from the temporal organizing effect of work and mealtimes. However, it was in the material constraints and cultural conventions of connected domestic practices that the institutionalization of practice temporalities appeared particularly strong. That Monday was wash day was a consequence of the cultural significance of Sunday lunch, with Monday being the day to make a stew from the leftovers of the most significant meal of the week, and while the stove was making the stew it afforded the opportunity to heat water for washing and provided a hot room for drying. The second was that such institutionally timed events acted to organize everyday practices as collectively timed events and therefore any discussion of alternative options and autonomy regarding the timing, duration and tempo of activities was almost entirely absent from diarists' descriptions of their days (there was no indication of choice as to the timing of such activities). Finally, while spending time together as a family, with children and between partners was described in diaries, there was no emphasis on the significance of 'quality time' in the sense described by respondents of the Bristol study. Child-centred leisure (especially of the sort reported by Craig et al. [2014] as 'intensive parenting'), time for activities with one's partner or descriptions of arrangements to socialize were almost entirely absent. While the Mass Observation diary data can only offer partial insights into the daily lives of people from 1937, the diaries do suggest that past daily lives were experiences of relatively strongly defined collective timings of activities and as such the scope or need for personal scheduling and coordination of activities with other people appeared far less challenging than was the case for respondents of the Bristol study.

6.4   The Temporal Organization of Everyday Activities

The narratives of respondents from the Bristol study presented in Chap. 5 together with day in the life diaries from 1937 imply that the collective timings of many contemporary everyday activities are weaker or less binding than was the case in the past. Times of work (paid and unpaid), eating and leisure featured heavily across the 1937 diaries to represent constraints on not only the timing of activities but also their periodicity (or frequency), synchronization, sequence and tempo. Put another way, the moments 'when' everyday activities were performed appear to have been shared and aligned across social groups to a much greater extent in 1937 than they are today. This alignment of 'moments when' activities were performed contrasts with the hot and cold spots of everyday experiences described by respondents of the Bristol study, in which the moments when activities happened were described specifically in the context of coordination of personal schedules within households or social networks. The hot and cold spots of respondents in the Bristol study did not align with those of other respondents to the degree of collective coherence that was implied in the analysis of the 1937 diaries and which led to clearly demarcated collective temporal organization of activities centred around mealtimes, work times or even Monday as 'wash day'.

As we have seen in the preceding chapters, there are many explanations presented that could account for what appears to be an undermining of the collective timings of everyday activities. Examples include accounts of consumerism, the expansion of consumer choices and the ease of gaining access to consumption experiences that are facilitated by post-Fordist arrangements and 24/7 economic activities, especially related to shopping (see Chap. 2). The rise of dual income households, service economies and flexible working hours (Chap. 3) could also be presented as societal changes that undermine the collective timing of activities. Technological innovations, especially in information, communications and mobility, have been widely identified as offering greater autonomy over the times at which people perform activities, the duration of those activities (or the time required to complete them), their tempo and frequency and offer greater flexibility in the sequencing of activities as was demonstrated by the example of the freezer (see Chaps. 3 and 4). Each of these explanations begins with the premise that contemporary societies are experiences of more activities contained within units of clock time and that it is this increase of activities that both offers greater choice in daily lives and demands more individualized temporal arrangement of those activities as a means of managing or coping with the sheer variety and flexibility of activities available. This implies that the temporal organization of everyday life has become more individualized, with people having greater control and autonomy regarding how they allocate activities within the context of a day, week or month, but the corresponding erosion of the collective timing of when those activities are performed results in the felt need for greater micro-coordination of activities with those people who co-participate.

The erosion of the collective timing of activities is further supported by analysis of the temporalities of eating. Using time diaries, our comparative analysis of the timings of eating events in Spain and the UK demonstrated a clear distinction in the degrees to which eating events represented collective timings of eating activities (Southerton et al. 2012a). Figure 6.1 shows the percentages of people eating or drinking as the main activity between half past six in the morning and one o'clock at night. Breakfast times in both countries share a certain synchronicity, but for the rest of the day patterns of eating times vary significantly. The British appear to

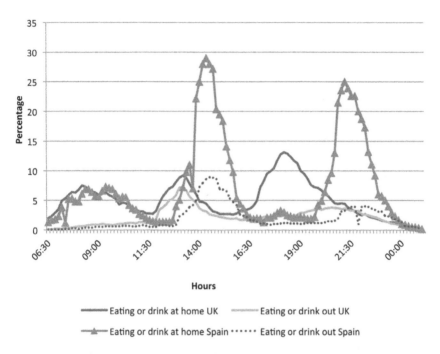

Fig. 6.1 Population percentage (16–65) eating throughout the day (at home and out). (Source: Own elaboration from the United Kingdom Time Use Survey, 2000, and Encuesta Nacional de Uso del Tiempo en 2002 [see Southerton et al. 2012a])

spread meals throughout the day, while Spaniards concentrate them between 1.30 pm and 4 pm (lunch) and between 8 pm and 11 pm (dinner). In the Spanish case this makes for important peaks of individuals eating at the same time (in the periods 2.00–2.30 pm and 9.00–9.30 pm), peaks that are not clearly defined in the UK. People in Spain have fixed mealtimes and as a consequence meals continue to function as a form of collective temporal rhythm in which a large proportion of the population are performing the activity simultaneously. Eating divided the day into clear parts: working time before lunch, a long break for lunch, working time after lunch, and time after work to rest and eat at the end of the day. People mostly return home for lunch at midday and for dinner at the end of the working day. There is a clear correlation between economies of time based around routine working hours and social times based around the collective timings of eating events. This contrasts with the UK, which shows a flatter line with far less pronounced peaks for participation at particular times and relatively shorter periods for lunch (12–2 pm) and dinner (5–8 pm). Whereas in Spain about 40% of the population were eating at 2.50 in the afternoon, and about 30% at 9.30 in the evening, in Britain at no time of the day were so many as 20% of the population so engaged. The temporal pattern of eating events in Spain is similar to that of France, in which over half the French population were eating lunch at 1 pm in 2010 and a third were eating breakfast at 8 am and their evening meal at 8 pm (de Saint Pol and Ricroch 2012). Whether individuals have fixed routines in Britain is not clear, but meal timing forms a much weaker collective temporal rhythm of British daily lives.

While it might be the case that, at least in Britain, there is evidence that the strength of collectively timed activities has been weakened, this is not to say that such timings are no longer significant. In a study of the patterning of UK 'snacking' practices, Warde and Yates (2017) show that snacking has a surprisingly common and predictable schedule across all socio-demographic groups. Based on a survey of 2784 respondents that completed food diaries, it is revealed that the majority of snacks are taken at three points of the day (between 10 am and 11 am and around 3 pm and 9 pm) and half of all snacks taken are done so in the company of others. Furthermore, as Chap. 5 revealed, the interview data from the Bristol study did not reveal strong collectivized timings of eating activities across respondents but did reveal that institutionally timed events such as meal, work and school times played an important role in guiding the broad allocation of activities in relation to a partitioning of parts of the day. It is therefore worth revisiting the Bristol study one further time to examine the temporal dimensions of the practices that respondents described, often in the contexts of hot and cold spots of activity, in order to examine if and how those practices were organized or ordered within the context of a day. Doing so offers some further basis for comparison between the 1937 'day in the life' diaries held at the Mass Observation Archive and the weekdays and weekends described by the respondents of the Bristol study.

Reanalysing the interview data from the Bristol study using Fine's five temporal dimensions (periodicity, tempo, synchronization, duration and sequence) revealed that everyday activities place different temporal demands on their practitioners (see Southerton 2006 for a full discussion). The extent to whether activities required a fixed temporal location within the day, coordination for the purpose of co-presence or participation of others, and the extent to which they are positioned within sequences of activities determined the degrees of autonomy that respondents felt they had when allocating those activities within the context of a day. As a consequence, the temporal organization of everyday life can be understood as a matter of the micro-coordination of activities that each contains different temporal characteristics in order to be performed in a satisfactory way. To explain this conclusion, it is necessary to briefly review the analysis of temporal characteristics of everyday activities.

The analytical approach examined each of the activities described by respondents as having taken place on a weekday and a weekend in terms of the periodicity, tempo, forms of synchronization, duration and sequence involved in the performance of activities. In terms of the dimension of periodicity, the analysis showed that the majority of activities had a high degree of regularity and frequency. This was particularly the case for activities that involved the co-presence of others, especially household members. The dimension of tempo was almost entirely evoked to describe contexts where the pace of activities was accelerated to meet a collectively timed event, often described in terms of 'getting back on track' to meet an impending fixed institutionally timed event (such as school pick-up time) or to keep to a pre-arranged activity coordinated with others (such as meeting for lunch). The dimension of synchronization was analysed in terms of the degree to which the performance of an activity involved coordination with other practitioners. In many cases, synchronization was closely related to periodicity as the frequent and regular performance of activities offered timings for which the practitioner (in this case interview respondents) could be confident of the availability and presence of others. Kathryn provided a nice example of how her extended family synchronized sociable activities focused on meeting for tea and coffee: '*it's just an unwritten rule, eleven o'clock every Sunday*'. By contrast, activities that involved the participation of others but had no discernible periodicity (e.g. occasional meeting with a friend for coffee) always required high degrees of arrangement within social networks that meant that, once agreed, those activity timings were 'fixed'. Activities that did not require coordination with others were described with a conspicuous lack of consideration regarding purposeful synchronization. Durations of activities were also closely associated with the co-participation of others. Overwhelmingly, activities performed by arrangement were of a longer duration than periodic activities, while those that required no co-participation of others tended to be of short durations. Finally, the sequencing of activities within the context of a day was almost entirely ordered around the temporal dimensions of periodicity and synchronization. This was because periodic or purposefully synchronized activities acted as 'anchor' points within the sequence of activities. Dinner parties, evening mealtimes, watching particular television programmes together and having 'movie nights' were all described as activities around which other activities in the day were sequenced, whether that was domestic tasks or stealing opportunities to read a book 'for half an hour' (Charlotte) or 'check the footie results' (Mark, aged 39).

When these deconstructed temporal dimensions of activities are reassembled in the context of each respondent's account of their entire day, the temporal relationships between activities are revealed in a new light. Take, for example, how the couple Bradley and Cindy described their previous weekday and weekend. After taking her daughter to school, Cindy, a home-worker, had gone to the gym (which she did twice a week) where she had arranged to meet friends. This activity was fixed, in that other practices were allocated around it, and Cindy spent between 10 am and 12 noon (duration and timing) at the gym before returning home for lunch and an afternoon of domestic labour. Bradley, an accountant, took his daughter for a short bike ride to *'get her out the house'* when he arrived home from work while Cindy finished preparation of their evening meal. They then watched television together. When Cindy went to sleep, Bradley read for *'half an hour'*, something he did in order to *'switch off'* before sleeping. The temporal ordering of the activities during Cindy and Bradley's weekday were the following: first, institutionally timed events of work and school; second, activities synchronized with others and/or with a high degree of periodicity; and, third, activities that were performed alone.

At the weekend, as with every Saturday morning, Bradley entertained his daughter, in this case with a '*leisurely*' trip to the park. During this time, Cindy '*dashed*' to the shops (tempo), as she wanted to buy something for their evening out, clothes shopping being a frequent but not regular activity for Cindy (periodicity). The afternoon consisted of domestic work while their daughter visited her grandparents. They described the need to complete housework in the afternoon so that they could '*properly relax*' (Cindy) when dining out with friends in the evening. This was a pre-arranged event (synchronization), '*the only weekend that we could all meet up*' and was an infrequent activity; they rarely ate out with friends. To compound the difficulties, they could only book a table for '*7.30 when really 8.30 would have been better so we can get Lucy settled properly*' (Cindy), although Bradley observed a relative upside to this arrangement because '*it does mean we're not in such a rush to get back for the baby-sitter as we leave that bit earlier*' (Bradley). The meal lasted all evening. Cindy and Bradley's description of their weekend followed the same temporal ordering of practices as their weekday, although with the absence of institutionally timed events such as paid work and school, but also revealed the sequencing necessary to facilitate activities synchronized with others. This patterning of the temporal ordering of activities was repeated across all respondents of the Bristol study.

The day is the context for the allocation of activities. Those activities come with different temporal requirements for their satisfactory performance. Activities that required the co-presence or participation of others tended to have a high degree of periodicity (as was the case for evening meals) that offered a basis for synchronization between participants or demanded that participants make prior arrangements (as was the case with Cindy and Bradley's dining out with friends). Consequently, such activities came to be fixed within the context of the day, requiring that other activities were sequenced to accommodate. Often, activities formed a sequential order so as to facilitate the performance of synchronized activities. Completing domestic tasks, some forms of childcare (doing the homework or bath-time) and some forms of leisure (shopping or going to the gym) were sequenced to fit within the ordering of other activities that had been coordinated to be performed with others. Finally, a third order of activities were those that required no coordination, synchronization or sequencing for their satisfactory performance. Activities such as reading, browsing the internet and hobbies (such as knitting) could be performed at any time of the day and were often described as activities that were useful for 'filling quiet moments' (and it is interesting to note that time spent reading has increased in the UK, Norway and France since the 1970s; Southerton et al. 2012b).

While the strength of the collective timings of everyday activities at a societal level might have weakened since 1937, this reanalysis of the Bristol study demonstrates that everyday temporal experiences are not simply matters of individualization. Rather, it shows that activities have temporal characteristics particularly related to the dimensions of periodicity, synchronization and sequence. These temporal characteristics contribute to the organization of the times when activities are performed and experienced. When viewed at an aggregate or societal level, such collective timings indicate the extent to which a society can be described as having strong or weak temporal rhythms of daily life. As illustrated by the collective timings of eating activities, Spain and France represent societies in which the patterning of times when meals happen in the context of a day represents relatively strong rhythms, especially when contrasted with the much weaker collective timings that feature in the UK. From the analysis of respondents' descriptions of the activities contained within their previous weekday and weekend, the critical characteristics that shaped the temporal organization of their daily activities related to whether an activity had a fixed temporal location within the day (i.e. an institutionally timed event), the degree to which it required coordination for the purpose of co-presence or participation of others, and the extent to which an activity was or could be positioned within a sequence of activities. Consequently, and as captured by the description of days in the life of Bradley and Cindy, the organization of a day and the temporal experiences that result represent a form of pragmatic shared (or coordinated) ordering of activity performances.

6.5   Conclusion

This chapter has addressed two questions. The first explored whether the forms of personal scheduling and coordination that featured so strongly in the temporal experiences of daily life reported by the respondents of the Bristol study (and expressed as experiences of hot and cold spots of activity) represent a contemporary social phenomenon. Analysis of day in the life diaries from 1937 revealed strong collective timings of daily activities that resulted from clearly defined institutionally timed events, particularly start and end times of work and mealtimes but also events such as Sunday lunch, Monday as wash day and market days. Diarists expressed limited senses of discretion in the allocation of activities within the context of the days that they described. While there was some language of haste and rush, there was little by way of narratives to describe the possibility of rearranging or allocating activities to different parts of the day or week. Perhaps because diarists described limited autonomy in the allocation of activities within the day, they also presented no consideration of seeking to arrange or coordinate their daily activities in order to create moments for 'quality time' in the ways that were so prominent in the narratives of respondents in the Bristol study. Overall, the main difference when comparing the diarists of 1937 with the narratives of respondents in the Bristol study, some 70 years later, was that the degree to which institutionally timed events represented binding, and therefore more clearly defined, collective timings of activities had been weakened. In 1937, the strength of collective timings meant there was much less need to coordinate personal schedules or to seek to arrange moments for quality time.

The second question returned to the Bristol study to consider whether the apparent weakening of collective timings implies greater individualization of temporal experiences as a consequence of more flexibility with respect to the timings of paid and unpaid work and a greater variety of options for leisure and consumption. Reanalysing the Bristol data by examining each activity performed in the context of a day in terms of five temporal dimensions demonstrated that practices which had a fixed temporal location within the day (institutionally timed events) remained significant in ordering the timings of activities but those timings were varied across respondents and therefore were less clearly defined as collective timings. This is corroborated by time diary data focused on the timing of UK eating events. Nevertheless, activities that featured a high degree of periodicity acted as fixed institutional events around which other activities are allocated in the context of a day. Secondly, activities that required coordination with other practitioners or synchronization with other activities also acted to order the allocation of practices within the day. Together, activities with fixed temporal locations and that required coordination with others determined the sequencing of all activities described by respondents, and it was this patterning of activity allocation from which the temporal ordering of the daily lives of respondents in the Bristol study was derived.

Comparison of the 1937 diaries and the Bristol study reveals a weakening of the collective timing of everyday, or synchronization with other, activities in contemporary lives. This does not mean that contemporary lives lack cohesive temporal rhythms but rather that those rhythms are less collectively binding with respect to the timings of activities. Greater choice and flexibility regarding economic, domestic and consumption activities might have undermined the collective timing of activities, but those activities retained a temporal ordering. The weakening of collectively timed activities does, however, make the task of coordinating daily lives, especially in the context of activities that require the participation of others for their satisfactory performance, more challenging. Put in simple terms, the collective timings underpinning the daily lives of the diarists in 1937 meant that there was little need to coordinate activities with other practitioners, whereas the respondents of the Bristol study were acutely aware of a need to coordinate and schedule their everyday activities and do so in a way that aligns with others in their households and social networks.

References

Bott, E. (1957). *Family and Social Network* (2nd ed., 1971). New York: Free Press.

Craig, L., Powell, A., & Smyth, C. (2014). Towards Intensive Parenting? Changes in the Composition and Determinants of Mothers and Fathers' Time with Children 1992–2006. *British Journal of Sociology, 65*(3), 555–579.

De Saint Pol, T., & Ricroch, L. (2012). Le Temps de l'alimentation en France [Time Spent on Eating in France]. Insee Premiere Report No. 1417. Retrieved from https://www.insee.fr/fr/statistiques/1281016.

Fine, G. (1996). *Kitchens: The Culture of Restaurant Work*. University of California Press.

Hall, D. (2015). *Worktown: The Astonishing Story of the Birth of Mass-Observation*. London: Weidenfeld & Nicolson.

OldandInteresting. (2019). History of Laundry—after 1800, Washing Clothes and Household Linen: 19th Century Laundry Methods and Equipment. Retrieved November 27, 2019, from http://www.oldandinteresting.com/history-of-washing-clothes.aspx

Sheridan, D. (2009). The Mass Observation Archive: A History. *Mass Observation Online* [Online], Marlborough, UK: Adam Matthew. November 26, 2019. Retrieved from http://www.massobservation.amdigital.co.uk/FurtherResources/Essays/TheMassObservationArchiveAHistory

Southerton, D. (2006). Analysing the Temporal Organisation of Daily Life: Social Constraints, Practices and Their Allocation. *Sociology, 40*(3), 435–454.

Southerton, D. (2009). Re-ordering Temporal Rhythms: Comparing Daily Lives of 1937 with Those of 2000 in the UK. In E. Shove, F. Trentmann, & R. Wilk (Eds.), *Time, Consumption and Everyday Life: Practice, Materiality and Culture* (pp. 49–63). Oxford: Berg.

Southerton, D., Diaz Mendez, C., & Warde, A. (2012a). Behavioural Change and the Temporal Ordering of Eating Practices: A UK–Spain Comparison. *International Journal of Sociology of Agriculture and Food, 19*(1), 19–36.

Southerton, D., Warde, A., Olsen, W., & Cheng, S. (2012b). Practices and Trajectories: A Comparative Analysis of Reading in France, Norway, Netherlands, UK and USA. *Journal of Consumer Culture, 12*(3), 237–262.

Warde, A., & Yates, L. (2017). Understanding Eating Events: Snacks and Meal Patterns in Great Britain. *Food, Culture, and Society, 20*(1), 15–36.

7

Socio-Temporal Rhythms, Social Practices and Everyday Life

7.1 Introduction

The empirical analyses of Chaps. 5 and 6 suggest that the time squeeze, whether presented as time scarcity or experiences of harriedness, is a consequence of the weakening of collectively timed everyday activities and the resulting challenges that individuals face in coordinating the performance of shared activities with others. In the 1937 diaries, strong collective timings of everyday activities shaped the timings (when), durations, periodicity, tempo and also the sequences of activity performances. These collective timings can be regarded as temporal rhythms, which represent and reflect the temporal patterning of daily lives. While respondents of the Bristol study also narrated rhythms of activity performance that reflected a temporal ordering based on the extent to which those activities related to an institutionally timed event required coordination with other people or synchronization with other practices, these rhythms were far more open to individualized discretion with respect to the timing, duration, periodicity, tempo and sequences in which they were performed. It is the weakening of collectively timed events that present the challenge of

© The Author(s) 2020
D. Southerton, *Time, Consumption and the Coordination of Everyday Life*,
Consumption and Public Life, https://doi.org/10.1057/978-1-349-60117-2_7

micro-coordination of activities in daily life and the associated feelings of harriedness and time scarcity described in Chap. 5.

In reaching this conclusion it is worthwhile stepping back from the analysis presented so far to reflect on the theoretical and conceptual steps taken. In seeking to examine and explain contemporary sense of everyday life as being time squeezed, critical social scientific theories of the relationship between time and society were explored. These theories, whether diagnosing processes that led to time scarcity or acceleration and time pressure, conceptualize time principally as the distribution of activities within the context of clock time. The Bristol study and analysis of Mass Observation diaries from 1937 therefore took the distribution of activities in time as its object of analysis and sought to examine the ways in which activities are organized, performed, coordinated and experienced within the context of a day or week. This has proved insightful with respect to highlighting the significance of the timings of everyday activities and how the degree to which they are collectively timed impacts on experiences of the time squeeze.

This analysis also suggests that the collective timing of activities also provides the basis for observations of temporal rhythms, in that the patterning of activity distributions within time represents the regularities of daily lives. While such rhythms can be observed through data that considers the timings of activities, such as that presented in Chap. 6, these observations offer little by way of explanation as to how such temporal rhythms of activity are formed or reproduced. To address such questions, this chapter argues for a need to 'start' conceptual enquiry from a different theoretical position: from a position that takes the organization and performance of 'practices' as the object of analysis and seeks to analyse the temporal features of those practices. In this analysis, everyday activities (the performance of a discrete act) are distinguished from practices (the doings and sayings of everyday life) in that a practice represents a configuration of activities that together form meaningful ways of doing and understanding everyday life. It is the ways in which activities are configured together into practices through which socio-temporal rhythms are formed, and it is through the performance of those practices that rhythms are reproduced.

Explaining what underpins the formation and reproduction of temporal rhythms is necessary to understand their significance in the organization of everyday lives, how they are experienced and, ultimately, to consider options for tackling 'time-related' social problems in ways that only consider how individuals distribute activities in the context of a day or week (which will be discussed in Chap. 8). A first step in explaining temporal rhythms is to consider and clarify how these terms can be conceptualized. The next section reviews theories of temporality and rhythm to argue that socio-temporal rhythms can be conceptualized as shared social phenomena related to (or of) time that form into circular (recurrent) and linear (sequential) rhythms of activity. Section 7.3 introduces theories of practice, especially 'social practice theory', as offering a conceptual framework for explaining how the organization and performance of practices shape the formation and reproduction of socio-temporal rhythms. Section 7.4 then applies insights from social practice theory to examine the temporal rhythms of laundry practices. In taking this approach, it is demonstrated that socio-temporal rhythms form out of the organization of social practices as entities and how those rhythms are reproduced by shaping the ways in which practice are performed.

7.2   Socio-Temporal Rhythms

The words temporal and temporalities (perceptions of social phenomena related to or of time) are widely used in the social sciences because temporal dimensions of duration, periodicity, tempo, sequence and synchronization can be associated with a broad range of phenomena. One consequence of this is that, conceptually, the application of the term temporalities is nebulous. When equally nebulous terms such as 'social' and 'rhythm' are added to form phrases such as 'socio-temporal rhythms', then those phrases come to represent broad descriptive terms in which the patterning of social activities in the context of time is intimated. This section seeks to offer some conceptual clarity to the commonly used phrase of 'socio-temporal rhythms'.

The influential work of Barbara Adam (1990, 1995), outlined in the opening chapter of this book, identified multiple forms of temporalities, including those related to the natural environment (such as the seasons, daytime and night-time), biological cycles (e.g. menstruation and ageing) and societal (e.g. events such as Easter or mealtimes). When it comes to societal temporalities, she distinguishes between the concepts of 'time', 'timing', 'rhythms' and 'tempo'. She describes time as the moments 'when' activities happen and the durations for which they last. This is different from conceptions of timings, such as right or wrong and good or bad timings, which are context-dependent interpretations of the relationship between everyday moments, durations (of time) and subjective activity experiences. The difference is important; time diaries are excellent at analysing 'when' and for 'how long' activities take place in 'clock time' but are limited in explaining the qualities and experiences of the timings of those activities. Rhythms represent a third variation and refer to recurrent activities that can take both linear (lunch tends to the next meal after breakfast) and cyclical (lunch tends to be eaten daily) forms, and together capture senses of rhythm that appear as forms of continuity and repetition (Sundays as days of rest). Finally, she describes tempo as experiences of fast and slow, of intensity of activities as in senses of rushing, emptiness (boredom) and stalling (to avoid an activity). Adam's purpose in making such a conceptual separation was twofold: first, to demonstrate that the social scientific focus on 'time' (when activities happen and their durations) has led to an overemphasis on clock time in explanations of societal temporalities and ,second, to encourage a focus on the temporal and especially on timings, temporal rhythms and tempos as a corrective to the dominance of (clock) 'time' in social theory.

Nowotny's (1992) classic account of time as a social construct—which draws inspiration from the theories of Durkheim (1915) on time as a social fact, Sorokin and Merton's (1937) notion of 'social time' as rhythms of collective life and Elias's (1992) account of events—further develops Adam's theoretical contention that the temporal is relativistic and irreducible to clock time. Nowotny argues that societal temporalities are produced through the interactions between social relations and institutionalized events. These are objectified through timekeeping devices such as clocks and calendars, which serve to reify time as a concept that organizes everyday social interactions and activities by providing symbolic and pragmatic means of societal coordination. Such coordination is represented in what Nowotny describes as social times: the instituted events of everyday life that provide for temporal regularities—such as mealtimes, work times and so on. The analyses of Chaps. 5 and 6 suggest that the capacity of 'social times' (or institutionalized events) to coordinate the collective timing of activities appears to have been weakened, such that temporal rhythms appear less cohesive and more individualized to the extent that they no longer act to comprehensively synchronize activities or coordinate social lives.

This is not to argue that social times have become insignificant. Van Tienoven et al. (2013) claim that three 'principles' underpin the formation and reproduction of social times in that they represent meaningful events, qualitatively different moments of time and intersubjective understandings of those times. Put another way, social times reflect shared and meaningful cultural conventions and expectations employed for making collective sense of the temporal flow of everyday activities. To examine the significance of such principles of social time in contemporary society, Van Tienoven et al. analysed the 'charging' patterns for electric key fobs of university staff. Key fobs required recharging within a 10-day cycle. The results revealed that the majority of those surveyed followed a weekly (seven-day) recharging pattern with Monday representing the day most commonly used for charging their key fobs. They conclude that the weekly charging pattern represents an instance of social time in which rhythm emerges from the relationship between the temporal ordering of days of the week, in which Monday signifies the start of the new week, and adhere to intersubjective cultural norms of weekly cycles for repetitive tasks with similar patterns evident for tasks such as household waste disposal, visits to the gym and food shopping. The cultural conventions that underpin social time and the flow of activities across a day, week, month or year act as the 'metronome' of daily life.

Zerubavel (1979, 1981, 1982), also introduced in Chap. 1, provides the most comprehensive account of how societal temporalities are ordered in everyday life to form into rhythms of activity. Building on the conceptual premise that societal temporalities are culturally derived and reproduced through social institutions, he identifies four major socio-temporal dimensions (duration, sequential structure, temporal location and rate of recurrence) that each structure the rhythm of activities and events in daily life. In doing so, and in contrast to popular lament, everyday activities can be understood as remarkably ordered such that they are predictable and familiar and act to reproduce the regularity of everyday life. Rush hours and peak electricity demand, both of which pose significant challenges to societal problems such as environmental sustainability, reflect the significance of these forms of socio-temporal rhythms in contemporary societies (see Shove 2009 for a discussion).

For Zerubavel, the seven-day weekly cycle, as implied in van Tienoven et al.'s analysis of the timings of key fob recharging, represents the most significant socio-temporal rhythms because 'through imposing a rhythmic beat on a vast array of major activities (including work, consumption and socializing), the week promotes the structuredness and orderliness of human life' (Zerubavel 1985: 2). As Walker (2014) observes, rhythms such as these play out at multiple scales in people's daily lives, whether related to the daily use of timing devices to control central heating so that homes are aligned to the rhythms of the comings and goings that occur within it, organizations that have their own rhythms of opening and closing times or energy infrastructures geared towards the 'load profiles' of peak times that occur when much of the population simultaneously uses energy (such as during early evening when many people return home from work). Critically, in terms of tackling the energy-related challenges that such rhythms pose, Walker points out that what is at stake is less the question as to whether socio-temporal rhythms exist and more the problem of coping with patterns of synchronicity when large numbers of people perform the same (resource-intensive) activities at the same time. Socio-temporal rhythms, he argues, reflect the synchronicity of social activities.

Lefebvre's account of rhythms and everyday life adds a further variation to the terms of societal temporalities and rhythms. For Lefebvre (2004: 15), everyday life is comprised of multiple rhythms: 'everywhere there is interaction between a place, a time, and an expenditure of energy, there is rhythm'. Such rhythms reflect 'repetitions and can be defined as movements and differences within repetition' (2004: 90), and represent phenomena that bring together performances, experiences and understandings of activities in moments of time and space. In setting out his broad conceptualization of temporal rhythms, Lefebvre distinguished between two analytical dimensions: cyclical rhythms, as events and activities that 'begin again' and are commonly found both in nature (seasons) and in social phenomena (holiday periods, the school year); and linear rhythms, as consecutive reproductions or pulses of activity. Returning to the example of travelling to work, cyclical rhythms such as the repetition of weekday commuting patterns are readily identifiable (especially to those who regularly commute), while linear rhythms can be identified in the journey itself with probably the familiar pattern of stopping and starting as one creeps through different sections of their journey. Finally, these rhythms are interconnected or nested, as is the case with the above example of the daily (cyclical) commute and the pulses and beats of each journey (linear). Such multiple rhythms operate at different interwoven spatial and temporal 'scales' such that social practices interact in rhythmically performed daily, monthly or yearly patterns and do so across different spatial scales. An example might be practices of travelling to work, which intersect with the spatial and temporal rhythms of the school day; rhythms of annual holiday periods; particularities of different industries and sectors; differences between rural, suburban and urban infrastructures; and so on. It is, according to Lefebvre, these intersecting circular and linear temporal rhythms from which everyday lives are produced, reproduced, experienced and understood (Blue 2019).

The above accounts of socio-temporal rhythms present them as being more than simply the patterning of activities across periods or units of time (e.g. of the day, week, month or year). In addition to the moments 'when' activities occur and the durations for which they last, temporalities also consist of timings, circular and linear rhythms and tempos of activity experiences. Such temporalities are shared across social groups and form to represent social times—marked by institutionally timed events—that represent meaningful, symbolic and pragmatic modes of coordinating the activities through which everyday lives consist (see also van Tienoven et al. 2017). The resulting societal temporalities come to regulate, order and organize activities into rhythms and do so at different scales—from the rhythms of an individual's daily life to the activities of organizations or at a societal level through the synchronicity of activities (see also Pantzer and Shove 2010). And, these multi-scalar socio-temporal rhythms underpin problematic societal phenomena as the examples of resource-intensive 'peak load' energy or 'rush hour' mobility practices illustrate.

In his argument that time and space are constituted through human activity, Schatzki (2010) recognizes the important contribution made by theories of socio-temporal rhythms to understandings of how the temporal features of social lives are embedded in meaningful and regular activities that can be analysed across multiple scales. However, he is also critical of their reliance on what he describes as the persistent category of objective time (and space) in explanations of societal phenomena. Objective time is not just the measurement (almost entirely through the use of clocks) of actions and motion, which was detailed in Chap. 2. For Schatzki, objective time also refers to the identification and description of social phenomena as being matters of the succession of activities:

> Almost all modern conceptions of objective time… concur that wherever events, objects, instants, phases, or anything else occur before and after one another, there is time… Similarly, rhythms and both linear and cyclical times are composed of successions. (Schatzki 2010: 6)

For Schatzki this is problematic because it objectifies time as something that is independent from, and therefore implies having the capacity to act upon or determine, human activity. While recognizing that many everyday activities have sequences and are recurrent, and also that analysing the sequences and periodicities of activities can offer insights into the temporal ordering of daily lives, Schatzki's key critique is that time is 'indeterminate' of human action. In other words, just because rhythms can be identified in which actions tend to precede or proceed others, or those actions tend to occur with regularities of timing, it does not necessarily follow that it is time which determines that patterning of activity. Rather, he argues, it is the ways in which social practices are arranged that reproduce temporal patterns in daily life. Temporal rhythms, for Schatzki, represent empirical observations of the organization of social practices but those rhythms do not explain the organization of practices.

7.3   Social Practice Theory

Following Schatzki's (2010) intervention, this section introduces social practice theory in order to consider its capacity for providing insights into the formation and reproduction of socio-temporal rhythms in everyday lives. Social practice theory belongs to a constellation of diverse positions that can broadly be described as theories of practice (Schatzki 2011). Emerging in the 1970s, they are identified with a heterogeneous set of authors that, according to Ortner (1984), include Bourdieu, Giddens, Sahlins, Foucault, Lyotard, Garfinkel, Charles Taylor and Judith Butler. What binds them is their insistence that practices represent the fundamental unit of social analysis (Reckwitz 2002; Rouse 2006) and therefore focus analytical attention on multiple and often context-dependent 'processes' that hold in tension the bases for societal change and reproduction (or stasis). This is in contrast with the dominant 'variance' theories (such as rational choice theory or the theory of planned behaviour) that seek to identify core variables so as to isolate cause and effects (Geels and Schot 2010) as the bases of change or stability.

Schatzki's social practice theory begins from the premise that a practice is a 'temporally unfolding and spatially dispersed nexus of doings and sayings' (1996: 89) and represents 'open-ended spatial-temporal manifolds of actions' (2005: 471). Practices are discrete spatiotemporal entities comprised of practical understandings (knowing how to identify, do and respond to any given practice), rules (explicit formulations, principles, precepts and instructions) and teleo-affective structures (normative or common ends and purposes). In setting out this definition, Schatzki makes the distinction between 'integrative' practices, which are 'the more complex practices found in and constitutive of particular domains of social life' (1996: 98), examples being cooking, farming or business practices, and dispersed practices. The latter refers to generic doings and sayings that apply across practices of activity and include 'describing… explaining, questioning, reporting, examining and imagining' (1996: 91). For Warde (2014), it is integrative practices that receive most attention from social scientists because they tend to be differentiated across social groups and because such practices are distinct and recognizable as discrete entities.

Integrated practices are, however, always interconnected to form what Schatzki describes as 'practice bundles'. Warde (2013, 2016) explores this interconnectivity further in his analysis of the practice of eating, which he defines as a 'compound practice' that rests at the intersection of several integrative practices. Four integrative practices related to eating stand out, each with its own specific formalization in terms of rules, procedures and standards. These are the supplying of food formalized in terms of understandings surrounding nutrition; cooking, formalized through codified instruction manuals (e.g. the recipe book); the organization of meal occasions, formalized through etiquette and manners; and aesthetic judgments of taste that are formalized through gastronomy. These four integrative practices have developed at different rates and according to different logics that have resulted in varying degrees of institutionalization and organization. The first two (supply and cooking) are more directly located within the sphere of production and have a greater degree of formal organization when contrasted with the latter two (meal occasions and aesthetic judgment) which belong to the sphere of consumption and are open to greater contestation.

A further critical conceptual distinction developed in social practice theory is between practices as 'entities' and as 'performances' (Shove et al. 2012). Practices are configured or shaped as entities (as recognizable, intelligible and describable) by the many elements that comprise their conditions of existence. While there is no single typology of the elements that configure practices, the most frequently cited (see Gram-Hanssen 2011; Shove et al. 2012) are cultural conventions and representations (meanings), material objects and infrastructures (materialities), and normative understandings of competent performance (skills and procedures). Arrangements of such 'elements' configure how practices are conducted and make them identifiable to practitioners and non-practitioners alike. Practices also exist as performances: it is through the 'doing' of practices that the pattern provided by the practice as entity becomes meaningful and the entity is reproduced or modified (Shove et al. 2012). It is this recursive interaction between 'practice as entity' and 'practice as performance' where the dynamics of reproduction and change are located (McMeekin and Southerton 2012).

Having outlined the core principles of social practice theory it is useful to consider how such an approach can be applied to explanations of time and temporality (see also Moran 2015 for an overview of time and social practice). The distinction between practices as entities and as performances represents a useful starting point for thinking through and disentangling the many ways in which social practices and socio-temporal rhythms can be understood and conceptualized. In his review of studies that examine time and practices, Blue (2019) distinguishes between approaches that consider 'time in practices' and 'practices in time'. The former refers to studies that explore how time and temporality feature in subjective experiences of practice performances. The Bristol study discussed in Chaps. 5 and 6 presents an example of this approach, analysing how practitioners allocated and coordinated practices within the temporal contexts of their day, week and month; how the performance of practices related to the temporal characteristics of different types of practice (e.g. need for co-presence for satisfactory performance) and how these allocations were experienced as practice performances within hot and cold spots of temporal activity. Other studies that explore time in practices include Spurling's (2015) analysis of how academic's manage their work practices; Jalas's (2006, 2009) studies of boat enthusiasts and the temporal experiences of caring for wooden boats; Perrons's (2003) study of homeworkers and their experiences of juggling work, leisure and childcare; Holmes's (2018) analysis of temporal experiences in hair salons; Paiva et al.'s (2017) account of neighbourhood 'time-styles'; Skinner's research on the temporal coordination of school drop-off and pick-up times; and the studies reported in Chap. 4 of communications practices and the changing temporalities of workplaces related to the use of mobile phones and emails. In these approaches, time is embedded in practice performances and the extent to which those performances reflect socio-temporal rhythms is dependent upon the degree to which they share similar timings and sequences and are synchronized (whether purposefully or not) with the performances of other practitioners across social groups.

Approaches that consider 'practices in time' (1) focus attention on how practices as entities are distributed within particular time periods, most usually the day or week, or (2) consider how those practices compete, colonize or cooperate in relation to their temporal locations within daily lives. Time diary studies, while not explicitly employing social practice theoretical approaches, represent a significant body of empirical work that reveals how practices (as entities) are distributed within (clock) time. Treating time as a finite, objective, resource and analysing how activities (which are usually combined into categories of activity, such as paid work, and in this way reflects practices) are distributed within a 24-hour day have produced some critical understandings of social change. These include: how changing forms of economic organization and occupational structures have altered the temporal distribution of working practices (e.g. Garhammer 1995; Gershuny 2005; Brannen 2005); how the rise of consumer culture has changed the temporal patterns of consumption practices (e.g. Schor 2010; Southerton 2011; Gershuny and Sullivan 2019); the ways in which changing patterns of domestic life effect the temporal patterns of personal and intimate practices (e.g. Hochschild 2003; Daly 1996; Lesnard 2008; Sullivan and Gershuny 2018); and how information and communications technologies create new temporal distributions of everyday practices (e.g. Hassan and Purser 2007; Wajcman 2015; Green and Haddon 2009). A logical extension of such approaches is that, because practices are distributed in time, public policies should seek to tackle substantive societal problems by intervening 'in time'. Recent examples include calls for shorter working weeks as a means to improve the productivity or well-being of the workforce, or to facilitate more discretionary time to enable practitioners to engage in 'meaningful' consumption and leisure practices focused on experiential services as opposed to the accumulation of material goods on the grounds of tackling environmental sustainability (e.g. see Gershuny's account of humane modernization, 2000; Bregman's account of the 15-hour workweek, 2017; and Schor's account of 'plenitude', 2010).

The second set of approaches—'Practices in time'—explicitly draw upon social practice theories to look beyond the broad allocation and distribution of practices within the context of a 24-hour day and place greater focus on the significance of tensions and connections between practices as entities (see Pantzar and Shove 2010 for an example). The analysis of the temporal ordering of daily activities in Chap. 6 provided an example where the degree to which activities required coordination with other people or synchronization with other activities in order to be performed satisfactorily shaped how 'practices' were ordered 'in time'.

In her analysis of temporalities and social practices, Shove (2009) explains how the core elements that comprise any practice are shared between, and competed over by other, practices. For example, a core premise of time diary studies is that activities compete for time, such that the more time practitioners spend watching television the less time available to devote to other practices. However, as Shove et al. (2012) explain, this is not merely competition over hours and minutes but about contestations as well as synergies between the elements from which practices such as television watching are comprised. Increases in television watching have been accompanied by normative concerns about proper or appropriate uses of time, with television often cited as threatening practices such as reading or family relationships. And yet, television watching as a practice also shares synergies with various material elements that connect it to other practices. The relationship between the material elements of electricity and broadcasting infrastructures are obvious examples. Spatial location and cultural conventions within domestic homes also connect television watching with a wide range of practices related to family life, personal relationships and socializing (e.g. watching a movie together or watching live television while exchanging social media messages about the event with geographically distant friends). And practices such as television watching involve skills and competencies related to the negotiation and coordination of when and how to perform the practice. Shove et al. give the example of 'prime time' television which at the level of practice as entity reflects the synchronization of millions of households watching television, and often the same television programmes, at the same time. Such synchronization is the outcome of collective negotiations within and across households, that include the skilful sequencing of a wide array of practices such as when to eat and clean the dishes or the 'right time' of the day to work and check emails. With digital innovations related to 'on-demand' television services it may no longer be the case that the television programme schedules of broadcaster's act to synchronize the majority of UK household evening schedules as reported by Silverstone (1993), but prime time television remains a strong feature of contemporary temporal patterns of leisure activities. (The Netflix effect in which download speeds on broadband networks decline during the evenings when millions of people are streaming programmes is, perhaps, a good contemporary parallel.)

The forms of connection and competition between practices and the elements through which they are comprised, according to the analysis of Shove et al. (2012), represent the basis upon which activities are held together (or, on the contrary, come apart) into meaningful practices. In their analysis, spatial and temporal contexts play an important role in binding activities and practices together. In spatial terms, activities are routinely performed and co-located in similar places. For example, kitchens represent places where the activities and practices of cooking, eating, cleaning, laundry, homework, listening to the radio and television watching are regularly performed (Southerton 2001). The kitchen provides a spatial context in which bundles of related activities and practices are co-located, connected and performed. Temporalities in the form of sequences, synchronizations and proximities operate in a similar way by providing temporal contexts for the bundling together of activities into recognizable practice entities. Shove et al. (2012) use Zerubavel's (1979) classic study of the temporalities of hospital life to illustrate. Zerubavel's analysis showed the multilayered and interconnected temporal rhythms that order the activities within hospitals, which include the rhythm of recurrent daily practices as performed by staff and patients. For staff this includes consultant, medicine and ward 'rounds', clinics and surgeries, while for patients this includes mealtimes and visitor periods. Such daily temporal rhythms 'intersect' with weekly rhythms that are most clearly visible in the distinction between weekdays and weekends, and also intersect with annual rhythms related to budgets, seasonal pressures (heat in the summer, cold in the winter) and holiday periods. For Shove et al. (2012), such intersecting temporal rhythms represent a socio-temporal order that reflects the range and form of connections between activities and practices and the degrees to which those connections act to bind activities into practices and bundle practices together. Socio-temporal rhythms provide the context in which practices are sequenced, the temporal proximity in which practices are performed and the degrees to which practice performances are synchronized across social groups.

Social practice theory is outlined in this section because it offers useful theoretical and conceptual tools for explaining how socio-temporal rhythms are formed. In doing so, it avoids Schatzki's critique of theories of temporalities by not reducing them either to the objective measurement of activities in (clock) time or to instances of succession as a determinant of activity performances. It does not, however, exclude the insights gained from studies that focus on objective time (as indicated by the summary of time diary studies that fall within 'practices in time' approaches), in that time diary studies and accounts of activity sequences remain valuable for identifying and describing the temporal patterning of social practices. A further conceptual advantage of social practice theories is its capacity to coherently explain social phenomena at multiple scales of analysis. This is best captured by the work of Nicolini (2009, 2012) in which he describes how social practice theory simultaneously 'zooms out' to analyse organizational forms (such as the conceptualization of practice as entities) and 'zooms in' to detail the experiences and accomplishments of activities (as captured by the concept of practices as performances). In other words, to explain the micro-detail of lived experiences and the broader social organization of those experiences does not require the switching between (and stitching together of) different theoretical lenses. In the framing presented above, social practice theory offers a theoretical lens that enables 'zooming in' to analyse how time is experienced in the performance of practices and 'zooming out' to analyse the socio-temporal organization of practices. Finally, by taking practices as the unit of analysis, the discussion of this section presents a theoretical position which suggests that socio-temporal rhythms reflect, or are the observable instances of, the organization of social practices but do not necessarily determine those practice arrangements.

7.4   Laundry Practices and Socio-Temporal Rhythms

The key theoretical insights from social practice theory presented in the previous section argue that to understand how socio-temporal rhythms are formed and reproduced requires an analysis of how practices as entities are organized (or arranged) and how those practices are performed (and experienced). This section examines this contention through an analysis of the practice of laundry. It does so by drawing on an empirical study consisting of 18 household interviews conducted in Manchester, England, that explored the ways in which respondents organized and performed laundry practices (see Mylan and Southerton [2018] for a full discussion of the methodological approach). This presents a departure from the empirical analysis presented in Chaps. 5 and 6, which examined how multiple activities were organized and experienced within temporal contexts of the day or week. Rather, the analysis of laundry takes the practice as the unit of analysis and explores the temporalities revealed by (first) 'zooming out' to examine the practice as entity and (second) 'zooming in' to explore the temporalities of its performance. In doing so, this section reconsiders the key contention from Chaps. 5 and 6 that the collective timings of everyday activities have weakened, undermining the capacity of temporal rhythms to coordinate the collective timings of everyday activities. Rather, contemporary experiences of the temporalities of activities reflect more individualized timings of activities and this represents a persistent challenge of the micro-coordination of daily lives.

The case of laundry is particularly interesting for exploring questions about the relationship between social practices and socio-temporal rhythms. This is because the times when laundry practices take place (its allocation in time) have changed significantly since its association with Monday (as wash day) in early twentieth-century Britain (see Chap. 6). Contemporary studies of laundry practices (e.g. Shove 2003; Pink 2012; Jack 2013; Watson 2014; Yates and Evans 2016; Anderson 2016) suggest it to no longer be a practice with distinct temporal rhythms. Rather, studies demonstrate that the widespread use of household washing and drying machines and subsequent decline of collective laundry services such as launderettes, together with redefined standards of cleanliness and an increased frequency at which people change their clothing, has resulted in laundry practices being spread across the week. It remains, however, an everyday practice that consumes relatively large amounts of time in everyday lives, especially for women. In 2016, American women spent 17 minutes and men 5 minutes per day on laundry activities, ranking laundry the third highest domestic activity in terms of time use (Bureau of Labor Statistics 2016). In 2017, survey data suggests UK households devoted 15 minutes per day to laundry, making it the second most time-consuming domestic chore (Garnett 2018), overwhelmingly performed by women (Scott and Clery 2013). A prominent explanation as to why laundry remains such a time-consuming activity with gendered divisions of labour is that it continues to be a meaningful and intersubjective practice expressive of care for others and the self (Kaufmann 1998; Pink 2012; Jack 2013).

Analysed as an entity, the temporalities of laundry practices can be conceptualized as circular and linear. Circularity is revealed most explicitly through the recurrence (or periodicity) of the practice. In the analysis of 1937 'day in the life' diaries circularity took the form of laundry performances having a weekly periodicity with Monday as wash day. Contemporary laundry temporalities present circularity with respect to the time of day in which activities take place. For example, referring to data on electricity consumption of domestic appliances, Yates and Evans (2016) show that most washing machines are operated between 7 am and 11 am and tumble dryers used primarily in the afternoon (see also Zimmermann et al. 2012). Anderson's (2016) analysis of time diary data additionally reveals a shift towards laundry being performed on the weekend, although the data does not differentiate between the activities through which the practice is constituted, and consequently, this analysis might well capture that the laundry activity of ironing takes place at weekends even if the activities of washing and drying occurs at different times of the week. In our qualitative study of laundry practice performances (see Mylan and Southerton 2018), interview respondents revealed circular temporal rhythms through either the designation of particular days for specific laundry activities (such as washing and drying on selected weekdays and ironing activities on weekends) or washing when the laundry basket was full (which itself created a cyclical rhythm for which the periodicity was dependent on the number of household members). Laundry practices reflect linear temporal rhythms through the typical sequencing of the activities from which the practice is comprised. In our study, the overwhelmingly typical sequence took the following form: designation of unclean items, storage (of unclean items), washing, drying, preparation of items for use (e.g. ironing) and storage of clean items (Mylan and Southerton 2018).

Analysed through the lens of laundry practice performances, and consistent with the theoretical accounts of Adam and Nowotny, these circular and linear rhythms act to contextualize laundry activities with respect to good (right) and bad (wrong) times for their performance. Good timings with respect to circular rhythms were captured by respondents through the designation of particular days of the week for particular activities, especially related to ironing and the periodic washing of bed linen. For example, Clare (30s, single, two children) stated that '*I tend to try and do it* [the ironing] *on a Monday evening which is a quieter night because I haven't got children's activities on*', while Liz (20s, couple, no children) explained a circular weekly rhythm: '*I'll do four loads, probably every other day, because I do a lot of exercise and so does my boyfriend so we have a constant cycle of clothes that need washing*'. Conversely, bad or wrong laundry times were described as moments when laundry activities were required outside of circular rhythms, most often when unexpected needs arose, such as Rachel's (50s, married, two children) description of '*the other morning, my son said "I've got no school shirts", I had to put one in, give it a rinse on this quick wash and then get it dried*', which resulted in '*chaos, panic and everyone being late when it wouldn't have been a problem if that had happened the day before or after when I put on a load anyway*'.

Linear rhythms, as experienced through practice performances, also contextualized good and bad moments for laundry. Good linear rhythms were expressed by respondents with respect to the anticipated tempo or flow through the sequence of laundry activities, which Marianne (50s, married, two children) described as '*when everything goes right it's like clockwork*' and Jude captured as being '*a well-oiled machine—load, dry, sort, put away*'. Unanticipated disruption to that flow was described by respondents as problematic because it pushed activities in the (anticipated) laundry sequence into the times of other practices. Examples given by respondents included forgetting to press start on the washing machine before leaving for work meaning that washing and drying activities were compressed into the post-work evening time or the '*piling up of ironing*' because the time allocated for the activity is missed due to unforeseen circumstances, such as an unexpected visit by friends in Darren's case. In other examples, unexpected additions to the volume of laundry could intensify the sequential flow of activities, as described by Rachel in the case of her teenage son's inability to align his laundry needs with the sequential flow of Rachel's laundry activities: '*he'll be "my washing basket's full, mum, it needs washing", so I'll think yeah but I need to get that lot dried and put away first*'. In such contexts, the capacity to anticipate potential moments of disruption to both circular and linear rhythms represented a critical skill for all laundry practitioners interviewed: '*I've got two wash baskets and basically see what's on top of them. Then I'll be thinking ahead… what's happening the next day, I'll be asking the kids "Have you had PE? Is there anything in your bag that needs washing?"*' (Jude, 40s, married, three children).

As these brief examples demonstrate, both as an entity and through their performance, laundry practices have circular and linear temporal rhythms consistent with the definition of temporalities outlined by theorists such as Adam, Nowotny, Zerubavel, Lefebvre and van Tienoven. Circular temporal rhythms of laundry practices as entities are revealed both by data on energy use of laundry appliances and by time use data on when laundry activities are performed during the week. These periodicities are consistent with those described by laundry practitioners in our Manchester study. Linear rhythms of the sequential flow of laundry activities interconnect with circular rhythms, washing being done on weekday mornings and drying later in the day; ironing being focused on weekends or the start of the working week. Together, this circularity and linearity underpinned the temporal rhythms of laundry practice performances. At the level of practice as entity, circular rhythms imply some degree of collective timing of practice performances as reflected in the aggregate patterning of the times when machines are used, and time diary respondents reported doing laundry activities. Given that, in theory, contemporary laundry practices could be performed at any time of the day or week at the discretion of practitioners, it is worth further considering if and how the organization of laundry practices as entities provide the basis for explaining how these observable socio-temporal rhythms of laundry practice performances are formed and reproduced.

To address this question, it is necessary to briefly consider how respondents of the Manchester study described and explained their laundry practice performances by analysing the three foundational elements (cultural meanings, skills and competence, and material arrangements) identified by Shove et al. (2012) to explain the organization of social practices. Cultural meanings were articulated through qualities of laundry outcomes, which were expressed through understandings of cleanliness, comfort and freshness. All respondents described laundry practices as a matter of removing germs, stains and smell from items of linen, with temperatures of wash adjusted accordingly for items that are most likely to be heavily soiled, such as sportswear, bedding and towels. Ruth (30s, married, one child) provided a typical example: *'if I'm doing sheets or anything like that, or towels, I try and do them on a high temperature… I just feel like it just gets the bacteria out better'*. Other prominent qualities of laundry meanings were comfort and freshness. Comfort was often expressed by the feel of items after wash with softness the desired outcome. Marianne was one of the 12 respondents who described the benefits of placing *'towels… in the tumble-dryer so that they're soft'*, while qualities of freshness were presented through drying clothes outside or, as in Jude's example, giving items a *'quick rinse… to freshen them up'* if they had been left in a *'stuffy drawer or wardrobe'* for too long.

Interpretations of competent or skilful performance (i.e. 'how to do' the laundry to a satisfactory standard) were articulated through the pragmatics of identifying dirty items, judging the flow of laundry items through sequences of activities and minimizing activity later in the sequence. Designating items as *'ready-to-wash'* involved the skilful sorting through a range of items as neatly articulated by Jude:

> It's see and smell I suppose, and remembering sometimes. Sometimes I'll just look at it and think they've had that on for a while. Often I'm pulling knickers out of leggings. Underwear is easy to tell, and socks. You kind of just know. You can see when they've been worn. And then lots of things have creases in and

sometimes that's enough to wash it. If it was a skirt or trousers that had too many wear creases in, and I can see that needs a wash to freshen it up and straighten it out again, so that's the key things. Mainly with tops I'd be going round sniffing them. It sounds so disgusting.

Identification of ready-to-wash items was achieved with the employment of 'rules of thumb', combining sensory indicators related to '*smell*', '*appearance*' and '*feel*' with recall of frequency and longevity of use. Judging the flow of laundry also required the skilful management of what most respondents described as '*making up a load*'. Rachel captured this process as '*I mean if somebody's only got a little bit* [in their washing basket] *I'll go and find something else to put in, rather than doing two or three things I'll look around and find something to go in with it*'. Finally, minimizing activity later in the laundry activity sequence was managed through competent performance at each stage, as captured by the skills of '*crease avoidance*' to avoid unnecessary ironing. Purchasing clothes made from non-crease fabrics, avoiding tumble dryers or using them with small loads, shaking out items before drying, lying items flat, hanging out and '*frequently turning*' items while drying on radiators were commonly described tactics.

As the above suggests, understanding and caring for linen and clothing represent an important part of the material element of laundry practices. To this can be added domestic appliances, the size and format of homes (particularly with respect to space for indoor and outdoor drying facilities), and the household domestic infrastructures of water and heating systems. All of these materialities played an important role in organizing the timings of both circular and linear laundry practice rhythms. In addition, weather conditions affected drying modes, which in turn were shaped by whether households had a tumble dryer or alternative options for indoor drying (e.g. the use of radiators). In some cases the domestic infrastructures of homes placed laundry practices in direct competition with other practice performances. In explaining why the activity of washing laundry always takes place in the morning, Liz revealed that:

we've got a combi-boiler so while the washing machine is on you can't have a shower because it just makes the water freezing and really low pressure. And because we both exercise most nights, we both come in and have a shower, so if the machine was on we wouldn't be able to have a shower or we'd have to have our showers and then put the machine on

Noisy washing machines disrupting evening conversations or television viewing and concern over placing too heavy a burden on water and electricity infrastructures by running several appliances at the same time were all mentioned as considerations with respect to the timing of laundry activities.

These three elements organized and conditioned the temporalities of laundry practice performances within the households studied. However, the performance of laundry practices also involved significant considerations regarding its coordination with the practices of other people (especially other household members) and synchronization with a range of other practices. As many of the examples provided above demonstrate, laundry is not an individualized practice, but one coordinated with the needs and rhythms of household members and synchronized with the rhythms of other practices. All respondents coordinated rhythms of laundry with the work and school-based practices of household members, but also with socializing and sporting activities (especially of teenagers) where particular items of clothing were required. Laundry practices were synchronized with a range of other domestic practices, notably loading the washing machine with the pre-work or preschool routines, drying activities (loading/unloading/folding) alongside the early evening routines of preparing dinner, and ironing alongside weekend routines of catching up with favourite television or radio shows. In Marianne's description, Saturday morning represents a choreography of practice synchronization as she '*finishes off the chores so the weekend can start*', which she explained in the following terms:

I'll sort of either be writing a shopping list or cleaning or organizing other things for the day... as I'm doing that round the house I'll put the loads in and out... The quick loads, the half an hour ones, I can just put them in and out between cleaning and sorting out homework and organizing anything else, so that it's all done and dusted for lunchtime on Saturday.

The case of laundry is particularly instructive for examining socio-temporal rhythms. It is a practice that illustrates rhythms at different scales—from the patterning of times when washing machines are used through to household rhythms and the experiences of individual practitioners. It reveals circular and linear rhythms, both of which contextualize appropriate times to perform the practice and frame expectations of acceptable timings, tempos, durations, periodicities and sequences of the activities from which the practice is comprised. Rhythms also reflect how practices such as laundry are synchronized with a range of other practices and coordinated across household members. While the socio-temporal rhythms of laundry practices might not reveal the apparently strong collective binding of everyday practices that 'Monday as wash day' represented in 1930s British, it is clear that laundry is a practice with discernible temporal rhythms that are widely shared and experienced across UK households today.

Returning to the question of how socio-temporal rhythms are formed and reproduced, this analysis of laundry through the lens of social practice theories reveals that its socio-temporal rhythms are formed through the organization of laundry practices as an entity and are reproduced through practice performances that shape temporal experiences. Analysed as an entity, the practice of laundry is organized through the cultural meanings related to expected qualities of laundry outcomes, the skills required for competent accomplishment and its material forms. As an entity, laundry practices interconnect with many other practices 'in time'. Such connections reflected competition, cooperation and synchronization with other practices in time and also coordination with others (most often household members) to ensure that the temporalities of laundry activities were aligned with their laundry needs and the temporalities of connected practices (as in the case of ensuring items of clothing were ready for the timings of work, school or leisure practices of others). These interconnections across practice entities organized the practice of laundry such that patterns of collective timings and of circular temporal rhythms can be observed (i.e. aggregate patterns of times when the different activities that comprise laundry practices are performed). At the level of practice as performance, respondents of the Manchester study described many variations in the ways that laundry activities were performed but did so within the context of shared experiences of the elements that organize the practice and, as a consequence, described shared experiences of circular and linear temporal rhythms ('practices in time') in the performance of the practice. The socio-temporal rhythms of laundry are formed through the organization of the practice and reproduced through the shared temporal experiences of their performance.

7.5   Conclusion

This chapter began with a summary of empirical analysis that suggests the time squeeze is a consequence of the weakening capacity of collectively timed activities to coordinate and synchronize everyday activities. It is the resulting need to micro-coordinate practices that creates senses of time pressure. Much social scientific enquiry into phenomena such as collective timings, synchronization and coordination tend to describe them generically as forms of socio-temporal rhythm. Defined as shared social phenomena related to or of time (socio-temporal), theories of rhythms were reviewed to argue that 'rhythms' take circular (recurrent) and linear (sequential) forms that can be observed in the aggregate patterning of the 'times when' (timing) everyday activities are performed across society. Such rhythms can be observed at multiple scales, from the micro-level rhythms experienced by individuals and households to the macro-level rhythms of peak hours in energy demand and rush hours. However, beyond representing empirical observations of shared temporal phenomena it remains less clear as to how such rhythms are formed and reproduced in ways that appear to render them more or less coherent in terms of the collective timing of activities.

Theories of practices, particularly social practice theory, represent a framework for examining and explaining how socio-temporal rhythms are formed and reproduced. Taking practices as the fundamental unit of analysis, they provide a conceptual framing that enables analysis across multiple scales through the application of the distinction between practices as entities and as performances. Practices as entities examine the ways in which practices are organized and enable the researcher to 'zoom out' to examine the critical elements that organize practices into distinct sets of activities. Practices as performances provide an analytical framework for 'zooming in' to examine how practices and their constituent activities are experienced and reproduced. Applied to consideration of temporalities, this theoretical and conceptual framework encourages analysis of both how practices are distributed 'in time' and how time is experienced in (the performance of) practices.

Applying social practice theory to an analysis of the temporalities of laundry practices revealed distinct circular (e.g. the timings of washing machine use and times when people report doing laundry activities) and linear (e.g. the sequential flow of laundry activities) rhythms. These temporal rhythms formed out of the organization of laundry practice as an entity—as demonstrated by the elements of cultural meanings, skills and competence and materialities that shaped the ways in which respondents from the Manchester study performed the practice—and produced the aggregate temporal patterns observed in circular and linear rhythms. The ways in which respondents synchronized doing the laundry with a range of other practices and coordinated the performance of laundry activities to align with the practices of other people acted to reproduce those rhythms in ways that demonstrated shared temporal experiences.

Socio-temporal rhythms form and reproduce through the organization and performance of social practices. The degrees to which those rhythms reflect strong collective timings of activities across social groups is, therefore, a reflection of the coherence of the practice as entity and the degree to which performance of the practice is constrained or shaped by the elements that organize it. As a consequence, it is less that the collective timings of activities have been eroded or become weakened (as would be one interpretation of the analysis presented in Chap. 6) and more the case that the organization of and interconnections between social practices (such as laundry) have shifted in form. In doing so the socio-temporal rhythms associated with the practice have changed. From this analysis, to understand time and temporality requires attention to the temporal organization of practices, and this fundamental theoretical statement raises a number of critical considerations when it comes to addressing 'problems of time'.

References

Adam, B. (1990). *Time and Social Theory*. Cambridge: Polity.

Adam, B. (1995). *Timewatch: The Social Analysis of Time*. London: Polity.

Anderson, B. (2016). Laundry, Energy and Time: Insights from 20 Years of Time-use Diary Data in the United Kingdom. *Energy Research & Social Science, 22*, 125–136.

Blue, S. (2019). Institutional Rhythms: Combining Practice Theory and Rhythmanalysis to Conceptualise Processes of Institutionalisation. *Time & Society, 28*, 922–950.

Brannen, J. (2005). Time and the Negotiation of Work-family Boundaries: Autonomy or Illusion. *Time & Society, 14*(1), 113–131.

Bregman, R. (2017). *Utopia for Realists: How We Can Build the Ideal World*. Little: Brown and Company/Hachette Book Group USA.

Bureau of Labor Statistics. (2016). American Time Use Survey: Household Activities. Retrieved from https://www.bls.gov/tus/charts/household.htm

Daly, K. (1996). *Families and Time: Keeping Pace in a Hurried Culture*. London: Sage.

Durkheim, E. (1915). *The Elementary Forms of Religious Life: A Study in Religious Sociology* (J. W. Swain, Trans.). London: Allen & Unwin.

Elias, N. (1992). *Time: An Essay*. Oxford: Blackwell.

Garhammer, M. (1995). Changes in Working Hours in Germany. *Time & Society, 4*(2), 167–203.

Garnett, K. (2018). The Average Brit Spends more than 2000 days Doing Chores in Their Lifetime. *Ideal Home Magazine*. Retrieved October 07, 2019, from https://www.idealhome.co.uk/news/time-spent-doing-chores-181435.

Geels, F. W., & Schot, J. (2010). Part 1: The Dynamics of Socio-technical Transitions: A Sociotechnical Perspective. In J. Grin, J. Rotmans, & J. Schot (Eds.), *Transitions to Sustainable Development: New Directions in the Study of Long Term Transformative Change* (pp. 11–104). London: Routledge.

Gershuny, J. (2000). *Changing Times: Work and Leisure in Post-industrial Society*. Oxford: Oxford University Press.

Gershuny, J. (2005). Busyness as the Badge of Honor for the New Superordinate Working Class. *Social Research, 72*(2), 287–314.

Gershuny, J., & Sullivan, O. (2019). *What We Really Do All Day: Insights from the Centre for Time Use Research*. Milton Keynes: Pelican Books.

Gram-Hanssen, K. (2011). Understanding Change and Continuity in Residential Energy Consumption. *Journal of Consumer Culture, 11*(1), 61–78.

Green, N., & Haddon, L. (2009). *Mobile Communications: An Introduction to the New Media*. Oxford: Berg.

Hassan, R., & Purser, R. E. (2007). *24/7: Time and Temporality in the Network Society*. Stanford, CA: Stanford Business Books.

Hochschild, A. (2003). *The Commercialization of Intimate Life*. Berkeley: University of California Press.

Holmes, H. (2018). Self-time: The Importance of Temporal Experience within Practice. *Time & Society, 27*(2), 176–194.

Jack, T. (2013). Laundry Routine and Resource Consumption in Australia. *International Journal of Consumer Studies, 37*(6), 666–674.

Jalas, M. (2006). Making Time: The Art of Loving Wooden Boats. *Time and Society, 15*, 343–363.

Jalas, M. (2009). Wooden Boats and Self-legitimizing Time. In E. Shove, F. Trentmann, & R. Wilk (Eds.), *Time, Consumption and Everyday Life: Practice, Materiality and Culture* (pp. 203–216). Oxford: Berg.

Kaufmann, J. C. (1998). *Dirty Linen: Couples and their Laundry*. London: Middlesex University Press.

Lefebvre, H. (2004 [1992]). *Rhythmanalysis: Space, Time and Everyday Life* (S. Elden and G. Moore, Trans.). London: Athlone.

Lesnard, L. (2008). Off-scheduling Within Dual-earner Couples: An Unequal and Negative Externality for Family Time. *American Journal of Sociology, 114*, 447–490.

McMeekin, A., & Southerton, D. (2012). Sustainability Transitions and Final Consumption: Practices and Socio-technical Systems. *Technology Analysis & Strategic Management, 24*(4), 345–361.

Moran, C. (2015). Time as a Social Practice. *Time & Society, 24*, 283–303.

Mylan, J., & Southerton, D. (2018). The Social Ordering of an Everyday Practice: The Case of Laundry. *Sociology, 25*(6), 1134–1151.

Nicolini, D. (2009). Zooming In and Out: Studying Practices by Switching Theoretical Lenses and Trailing Connections. *Organization Studies, 30*(12), 1391–1418.

Nicolini, D. (2012). *Practice Theory, Work, and Organization: An Introduction*. Oxford: Oxford University Press.

Nowotny, H. (1992). Time and Social Theory Towards a Social Theory of Time. *Time and Society, 1*, 421–454.

Ortner, S. (1984). Theory in Anthropology since the Sixties. *Comparative Studies in Society and History, 26*, 126–166.

Paiva, D., Cachinho, H., & Barata-Salgueiro, T. (2017). The Pace of Life and Temporal Resources in a Neighborhood of an Edge City. *Time and Society, 26*(1), 28–51.

Pantzar, M., & Shove, E. (2010). Temporal Rhythms as Outcomes of Social Practices: A Speculative Discussion. *Ethnologia Europaea, 40*, 19–29.

Perrons, D. (2003). The New Economy and the Work-Life Balance: Conceptual Explorations and a Case Study of New Media. *Gender, Work and Organization, 10*(1), 65–94.

Pink, S. (2012). *Situating Everyday Life*. London: Sage.

Reckwitz, A. (2002). Toward a Theory of Social Practices: A Development in Culturalist Theorizing. *European Journal of Social Theory, 5*(2), 243–263.

Rouse, J. (2006). Practice Theory. In S. Turner & M. Risjrod (Eds.), *Handbook of the Philosophy of Science, vol.15: Philosophy of Anthropology and Sociology* (pp. 500–540). Elsevier.

Schatzki, T. R. (1996). *Social Practices: A Wittgensteinian Approach to Human Activity and the Social*. Cambridge: Cambridge University Press.

Schatzki, T. R. (2005). Peripheral Vision: The Sites of Organizations. *Organizational Studies, 26*(3), 465–484.

Schatzki, T. R. (2010). *The Timespace of Human Activity: On Performance, Society, and History as Interminate Teleological Events*. Plymouth: Lexington Books.

Schatzki, T. R. (2011). Theories of Practice. In D. Southerton (Ed.), *Encyclopedia of Consumer Culture* (Vol. III, pp. 1447–1551). Thousand Oaks, CA: Sage.

Schor, J. (2010). *Plenitude: The New Economics of True Wealth*. New York: Penguin.

Scott, J., & Clery, E. (2013). Gender roles: An Incomplete Revolution? In A. Park, C. E. Bryson, J. Curtice, & M. Phillips (Eds.), *British Social Attitudes: The 30th Report*. London: NatCen Social Research.

Shove, E. (2003). *Comfort, Cleanliness and Convenience: The Social Organization of Normality*. Oxford: Berg.

Shove, E. (2009). Everyday Practice and the Production and Consumption of Time. In E. Shove, F. Trentmann, & R. Wilk (Eds.), *Time, Consumption and Everyday Life: Practice, Materiality and Culture* (pp. 17–34). Oxford: Berg.

Shove, E. (2010). Beyond ABC: Climate Change Policy and Theories of Social Change. *Environment and Planning A, 42*, 1273–1285.

Shove, E., Pantzar, M., & Watson, M. (2012). *The Dynamics of Social Practice: Everyday Life and how it Changes*. London: Sage.

Silverstone, R. (1993). Time, Information and Communication Technologies and the Household. *Time & Society, 2*(3), 283–311.

Sorokin, P. A., & Merton, R. K. (1937). Social Time: A Methodological and Functional Analysis. *American Journal of Sociology, 42*, 615–629.

Southerton, D. (2001). Consuming Kitchens: Taste, Context and Identity Formation. *Journal of Consumer Culture, 1*(2), 179–204.

Southerton, D. (2011). Introduction. In D. Southerton (Ed.), *Encyclopedia of Consumer Culture* (pp. xxiix–xxxiv). Thousand Oaks, CA: Sage.

Spurling, N. (2015). Differential Experiences of Time in Academic Work: How Qualities of Time are Made in Practice. *Time and Society, 24*, 367–389.

Sullivan, O., & Gershuny, J. (2018). Speed-Up Society? Evidence from the UK 2000 and 2015 Time Use Diary Surveys. *Sociology, 52*, 20–38.

van Tienoven, T. P., Glorieux, I., & Minnen, J. (2017). Exploring the Stable Practices of Everyday Life: A Multi-day Time-diary Approach. *The Sociological Review, 65*(4), 745–762.

van Tienoven, T. P., Glorieuz, I., Minnen, J., Daniels, S., & Weenas, D. (2013). If Only the French Republicans Had Known This: The Week as a Social Fact. *Societies, 3*, 399–413.

Wajcman, J. (2015). *Pressed for Time: The Acceleration of Life in Digital Capitalism.* Chicago: Chicago University Press.

Walker, G. (2014). The Dynamics of Energy Demand: Change, Rhythm and Synchronicity. *Energy Research and Social Science, 1*, 49–55.

Warde, A. (2013). What Sort of a Practice is Eating. In E. Shove & N. Spurling (Eds.), *Sustainable Practices: Social Theory and Climate Change* (pp. 17–30). London: Routledge.

Warde, A. (2014). After Taste: Culture, Consumption and Theories of Practice. *Journal of Consumer Culture, 14*(3), 279–303.

Warde, A. (2016). *The Practice of Eating.* Cambridge: Polity.

Watson, S. (2014). Mundane Objects in the City: Laundry Practices And The Making and Remaking of Public/Private Sociality and Space in London and New York. *Urban Studies, 52*(5), 876–890.

Yates, L., & Evans, D. M. (2016). Dirtying Linen: Understanding Household Laundry Habits. *Environmental Policy and Governance, 26*(2), 101–115.

Zerubavel, E. (1979). *Patterns of Time in Hospital Life: A Sociological Perspective.* Chicago, IL: University of Chicago Press.

Zerubavel, E. (1981). *Hidden Rhythms: Schedules and Calendars in Social Life.* Chicago: Chicago University Press.

Zerubavel, E. (1982). The Standardization of Time: A Sociohistorical Perspective. *American Journal of Sociology, 88*, 1–23.

Zerubavel, E. (1985). *The Seven Day Circle: The History and Meaning of the Week*. New York: Free Press.

Zimmermann, J.-P., Evans, M., Griggs, J., King, N., Harding, L., Roberts, P., & Evans, C. (2012). *Household Electricity Survey: A Study of Domestic Electrical Product Usage*. Intertek Report R66141. Retrieved from https://assets.publishing.service.gov.uk/government/uploads/system/uploads/attachment_data/file/208097/10043_R66141HouseholdElectricitySurveyFinalReportissue4.pdf.

8

Conclusion: Time, Consumption and Societal Problems

8.1   Introduction

This book set out to consider and explain the widely held perception that contemporary lives are an experience of a time squeeze. In doing so, it has explored a wide range of social scientific theories and empirical studies that, from different perspectives and applied to varying research questions, seek to explain the relationships between time and society. The diversity of themes and related studies have included the changing ways in which everyday activities are allocated within time (time use); time as a mechanism for coordinating social and economic activities; the significance of technologies in shaping the ways in which time is used and experienced; theories of social acceleration; the temporal organization of everyday activities; and the formation and reproduction of temporal rhythms through social practices. While the time squeeze has represented an 'entry' point for the phenomena discussed and explored, this book necessarily moved beyond this substantive concern to consider broader social scientific considerations for explaining the significance of time and temporality in contemporary social lives. In navigating and extending

© The Author(s) 2020   **177**
D. Southerton, *Time, Consumption and the Coordination of Everyday Life*,
Consumption and Public Life, https://doi.org/10.1057/978-1-349-60117-2_8

beyond the related theories and empirical studies, three critical contributions have been advanced.

First, and building on the notable work of Barbara Adam and Eviatar Zerubavel, was to present further evidence that understanding the relationships between time and society requires examination of the multiple temporalities experienced in daily lives—especially with respect to duration, periodicity, tempo, sequences and synchronization of activities—and not only a focus on the measurement and distribution of activities in finite periods of time (e.g. the day). This is not to argue that measurement and analysis of activity distributions is not important (as the chapters of this book demonstrate, time diary studies which take this approach represent a crucial body of empirical evidence), but to demonstrate that explanations for the temporal organization of everyday life go beyond analyses of clock time. As will be argued in Sect. 8.3 of this chapter, accounting for multiple temporal dimensions when seeking to address or intervene in social problems where time is identified as a critical contributory factor is important for opening up new avenues for policy-oriented solutions.

Second was to consider, at times indirectly, how changing patterns of consumption are embedded in temporalities. Whether related to the consumption of technologies (domestic, information, communication), leisure activities, the pleasures and anxieties associated with consumer culture, the relationship between work and consumption, or the forms of consumption that mediate various interpersonal relationships, the analysis presented in this book suggests that consumption and temporalities are indivisible. Consumption does not simply take time (although, of course, this is an important aspect of it), but is also embedded within conventions related to when consumption should happen, with whom, with what degree of frequency and at what appropriate pace. As the analyses of Chaps. 5, 6 and 7 revealed, the consumption of food, clothing or linen, leisure activities with children, partners and friends, communication and domestic technologies (and the energy embedded in their use) and so on are always temporal (phenomena of or related to time).

Third, just as Warde (2005) critically observed that consumption occurs for the purpose of engaging in meaningful social practices, this book has argued that time (or temporalities) is experienced and understood through the performance of social practices. Warde's statement is critical because it directly questions the methodological individualism that dominates studies of consumption, reducing the act of consumption to matters of individual discretion (choices) rather than recognizing that consumption happens because of the organization of practices (see Evans [2019] for a critical review of consumption studies). Similarly, and consistent with Schatzki's (2010) accounts of time-space action and social practice theory, the analysis of this book argues that time and temporalities cannot be reduced to individual decisions regarding the allocation of activities in time or individual discretion over the time that can be allocated to particular activities. Rather, time and temporalities are shaped by the organization of social practices—by the materialities, cultural meanings and forms of competency that shape the ways in which practices are performed. To understand time requires an analysis of social practices and the socio-temporal rhythms that they shape and reproduce.

These three contributions are further explored in this concluding chapter. It begins with an overview of the core arguments presented in the book. This overview covers three themes: the dominance of the clock, commodification and acceleration in accounts of societal change; coordination and synchronization of everyday activities and the declining strength of collectively timed events; and the formation and reproduction of socio-temporal rhythms through the organization of practices. The final section returns to some of the observations with which this book opened—that contemporary concern with time and the time squeeze are mobilized across a wide range of major societal problems, including environmental sustainability and concerns related to well-being. It considers the implications of this analysis, especially the social organization of practices and socio-temporal rhythms, for identifying effective policy or strategic responses that take account of temporalities. In this final analysis, the risks of treating time as an objective variable to be intervened in—by substituting, extending, displacing or resisting the allocation of activities in (clock) time—through policy is argued to be a weak, potentially counter-productive in some instances, response to the capacity of temporal thinking for providing solutions to social problems. Rather, focusing on the organization of practices and the socio-temporal rhythms that they shape offers alternative options for addressing major societal issues.

8.2   Commodification, Coordination, Synchronization and Rhythms

This book has been broadly divided into three parts. The first examined the many different theories and related empirical studies that frame understandings of time and society. These theories are dominated by conceptualizations of clock time. Throughout the nineteenth and early twentieth centuries, clock time played a critical role in the organization and management of industrial labour by increasing productivity and efficiency through the application of time and motion studies. Time quite literally came to be measured in units (minutes and hours) and assigned economic value with industrial workers exchanging their time for money. In addition, clock time increasingly regulated social and economic life, particularly economic activities related to the circulation of goods, human labour (times of work) and the times of consumption and leisure activities. Clock time came to discipline social lives, internalizing a valuing of not wasting time and of punctuality and seeking to extract more value from each unit of time. Through these processes clock time took on an abstract commodity form, depersonalized and detached from the contexts of the activities that it measures and regulates (a minute or hour is the same 'unit' regardless of the type of activity with which that time is associated). As with the money economy, this meant that time could be subject to accumulation in the form of the acceleration of activities performed per unit of time.

In the developing consumer culture particularly in the post-war period, the pursuit of time as an abstract commodity came to manifest itself through consumption. At first this was illustrated in the rise of mass production and consumption, which offered large volumes of consumer goods at ever-decreasing prices, thus increasing the accessibility of options for leisure and consumption. It was in this context that commentators such as Linder declared that leisure had become less leisurely because the accumulation of consumption goods and experiences meant that people sought to cram more activities into their non-work time. As mass production and consumption developed into post-Fordist production methods and a capacity for much greater variations of goods, forms of niche consumption through which status, identity and lifestyle could be expressed emerged. Best captured by Schor's analysis of work-spend cycles, the productivity gains of the mass and post-Fordist production regimes were taken to facilitate more consumption rather than less time in work. By the late twentieth century experiences of time were dominated by the pursuit of ever-more varied forms of consumption, expressed through consumer lifestyles and compressed within finite volumes of (clock) time.

Modernity can be characterized as the rise of clock time, but it was also a period of technological innovation that has changed how, and created new ways in which, everyday activities can be accomplished within the context of time periods such as the day or week. Innovations in transportation and communications technologies but also industrial and domestic labour have changed the ways in which time is used and experienced. Transportation and communications technologies have effectively reduced the temporal distance between people, while innovations in industrial and domestic technologies have enabled the fragmentation of activities across time (as illustrated by the freezer which fragments the sequential proximity of activities related to food provision and eating by separating the temporal proximity between food acquisition, preparation and eating). These processes are at the core of the sense that everyday lives have accelerated, with activities fragmented and decoupled from past temporal rigidities related to the periodicity and sequencing of activities, enabling new forms of synchronization as expressed in Hassan's (2003) concept of 'network time' and expectations related to immediacy and instantaneity (Urry 2009). Captured most comprehensively in the work of Hartmut Rosa, late modern experiences of time are represented as being dominated by the overwhelming acceleration bought about by technological innovation, rates of societal change and the intensification of the pace of everyday lives. Theories of acceleration suggest that the time squeeze is not simply a consequence of the forms of time scarcity that result from the pursuit of consumption but represents feelings of time pressure that result from the intensification of the sheer volume of discrete but fragmented activities that can be located in any unit of time accompanied by the rapid rates of societal and technological change of contemporary societies.

Together, these prominent social theories present a dominant account of contemporary perceptions and experiences of the time squeeze as being the consequence of two interconnected conditions: time scarcity (lack of available time in which to accomplish the activities that matter most to people) and time pressure (feelings of harriedness resulting from the intensity of activities contained with periods of time). The empirical evidence, especially that drawn from time diary data, casts some doubt on the veracity of these theories. As discussed in Chap. 3, the evidence that people work more to consume more is contentious. While data is difficult to compare over time and across countries (due to differences in the ways in which activities are categorized), much of the time diary evidence demonstrates that most people spend less time in paid and unpaid work today than people in the past. There are critically important variations. For example, women spend more time in paid and less in unpaid work than they did in the past and the educated professional and managerial classes have seen a more modest decline in working hours than those who are less educated working in manual occupations. It is also certainly the case that people consume a much greater volume and variety of consumer goods and leisure activities than they did in the past. However, whether time scarcity is at the source of perceptions and experiences of a time squeeze is not empirically corroborated by the data. When it comes to acceleration and intensity, time diary data shows little evidence of activity fragmentation or of an intensification of activities per unit of time. Qualitative studies of technologies or activities most frequently associated with the intensification of activities (e.g. office work, the use of mobile phones and email) provide some empirical evidence of experiences of acceleration but also of improvisations that include adjustments to manage the flow of activities and of deceleration. The empirical evidence suggests that rising levels of consumption and acceleration are, at best, only partial explanations of the phenomena that underpin time scarcity and time pressure.

By distinguishing between time scarcity and time pressure in empirical studies of how people negotiate time in the course of conducting their daily lives, the second part of this book has argued that experiences generically captured as the time squeeze are the consequence of the challenges faced in coordinating activities with others and synchronizing everyday activities. The dominant framing of clock time can be identified in the ways in which time scarcity was understood and described by people who felt it to be a contemporary phenomenon. Explanations for this condition were commonly framed in terms of working and consuming more in the pursuit of consumer lifestyles, the intensification and fragmentation of everyday activities, the search for quality time within personal relationships, and moral economies of maximizing (or not wasting) time. However, studies of the ways in which people experience the organization of everyday activities within the context of a day or week presented a far more ambivalent picture. Everyday lives were presented as containing moments in which the volume of activities scheduled into particular time periods represented experiences of intensity and feelings of harriedness (described as hot spots of activity in Chap. 5). These were countered by moments of time in which a low volume of activities was allocated so as to create temporal space within the day for the self or to spend with others described as 'quality time' (that can be characterized as 'cold spots'). It was these processes of allocating different types of activities to time frames within the day and week that produced generic feelings of time scarcity and moments of time pressure (harriedness) that were juxtaposed and scheduled with periods of quality time, and experienced as a challenge of temporal coordination with other people who also sought to schedule their daily activities in order to align temporal periods of hot and cold spots.

Contrasted with the temporal organization of past lives, as illustrated by the analysis of the Mass Observation 'day in the life' diaries from 1937 (Chap. 6), the challenge of coordinating personal schedules appears to be a contemporary phenomenon. The day in the life diaries certainly did not present everyday lives as one with a lower volume of activities; diarists reported a significant volume of paid and unpaid work activities as well as leisure and consumption. The striking contrast was, however, related to the collective timing of those activities. In 1937, the allocation and coordination of activities was strongly associated with times of the day (such as meal and work times) and week (Monday as wash day, market day, Sunday as a day of rest). These strong collective timings represented institutionally timed events that acted to coordinate and organize the temporal rhythm of everyday activities. In this context, the need for individuals to (micro-)coordinate and schedule their activities to align with those of others was far less evident.

This does not necessarily mean that the temporalities of contemporary everyday lives are more individualized offering greater freedoms in the allocation of activities within the context of the day or week. Rather, analysis of the temporal dimensions (duration, periodicity, tempo, sequence and synchronization) of activities suggests a temporal ordering of those activities based on the degrees of co-participation required for its satisfactory performance. Institutionalized events (particularly times of school and work) with a high degree of periodicity still act to fix moments within the day around which other types of activities are scheduled, but there are fewer such institutionalized events and their collective timings are less binding (or more flexible) when compared with diarists' accounts of life in 1937. At a secondary level, activities that required coordination with other practitioners or synchronization with other activities also acted to order the allocation of activities within the day. Around these types of activities were those that did not require the co-participation of others (such as reading), and which could be sequenced to fit around other activities. Contemporary lives might not reflect the strong collective timings of activities that featured in past lives, but the organization of those activities still reflect a form of temporal ordering.

The final part of this book explored the significance of collective timings of activities and whether the apparent weakening of collective timings undermines socio-temporal rhythms. In a departure from the analytical approach adopted in early chapters, in which the theoretical framing of the time squeeze led to a focus on how activities are allocated and distributed in the context of a day or week, Chap. 7 took social practices as the object of analysis to explore how socio-temporal rhythms are formed and reproduced. Socio-temporal rhythms were defined as shared (socio) phenomena related to or of time (temporal) that take a circular or linear form (rhythm), with circular referring to recurrent activities and linear relating to sequential performances of activities.

An empirical analysis of laundry practices (Mylan and Southerton 2018) presented an instructive case through which to consider the relationship between the organization of a social practice and the socio-temporal rhythms formed through performance of that practice. The timing of practices of laundry has shifted quite significantly from the designation of Monday as wash day that was illustrated in the analysis of diaries from 1937. Contemporary laundry practices, dominated by the self-servicing of laundry needs through the household washing machine, can now be performed on any day of the week and at different times of the day. Data that captures the times at which washing and drying appliances are used and time diary records of the times when people report performing laundry activities, however, does provide evidence of some degree of collective timings. That data suggests that activities of washing are largely allocated to weekday mornings, drying to weekday afternoons and ironing to weekends. Of course, there is much variation such that much washing and drying of laundry items happen on weekends and ironing takes place during weekdays. Laundry is a practice in which the strong collective timings of the activity that could be associated with past performances of the practice are no longer evident, although some patterning of the times when the activities that comprise the practice are performed does imply a persistence of socio-temporal rhythms.

Analysis of interviews conducted with households based in Manchester, England, revealed that the performance of laundry practices could be described in terms of circular and linear temporal rhythms. Circular rhythms referred to recurrence of laundry activities while linear rhythms described the sequential flow of activities from the designation of unclean items, storage (of unclean items), washing, drying and preparation of items for use (e.g. ironing) through to the storage of clean items. Data that captures the patterning of laundry practices at a societal level represents the aggregate manifestation of circular and linear rhythms. The accounts of laundry practice performances provided by respondents from the Manchester study provided insights into how those socio-temporal rhythms are formed through the organization of the practice as an entity. Cultural meanings (qualities of laundry outcomes), the skills and competencies necessary to perform the practice to an appropriate standard and the materialities (machines, domestic infrastructure and organization of domestic space) that afford and shape ways of conducting laundry activities all represented the key elements through which the entity of laundry practices was understood and organized. It was the organization of these elements through which the practice of laundry came to represent shared temporal patterns of activity. In the performance of laundry practices, respondents also narrated a range of temporal experiences related to the coordination of different laundry activities to meet the needs of other people (most often within the household) and to be synchronized with other practices. The latter included synchronization with institutionally timed events (particularly school and work times) as well as other domestic practices whether for the purpose of containing domestic activities within a particular time frame (doing laundry while also cleaning the house) or to render the practice performance more enjoyable (ironing while listening to the radio).

The example of laundry practices demonstrates that socio-temporal rhythms are formed and reproduced through the organization and performance of social practices. In this analysis, social practices represent meaningful configurations of activities that are commonly identified as recognizable and widely shared practices. Shared practices are 'held together' by elements that shape the range of possible and acceptable ways of performing those activities. It is these elements—materialities, cultural meanings and forms of competency—that organize the ways in which practices are performed and in so doing generate circular and linear rhythms. In this way, the analysis of transportation and information and communications technologies discussed in Chap. 4 represents examples around which the material elements of social practices change and reconfigure the ways in which practices are performed. However, this does not equate to a direct causal relationship between technologies and time in the ways suggested by theories of acceleration because, as demonstrated by the work of Wajcman (2015), the cultural meanings and modes of competency associated with the practices in which such technologies are enrolled mean that multiple temporalities can be identified, and hence her conclusions that empirical studies show both acceleration and deceleration of experiences of office-based and domestic practices (see

Chap. 4). This theoretical reasoning also offers an explanation for the apparent paradox that people feel that time is increasingly scarce when time diary data broadly reveals the availability of more minutes free from paid and unpaid labour today than people enjoyed in the past. This is because regardless of the amount of 'time' that one has available for the allocation of activities, if the 'times' available for the competent performance of social practices are congested by competing practices, the experiences of time scarcity will result.

Viewed through this theoretical lens, narratives of the time squeeze reflect observations of the changing organization of practices and experiences of shifting socio-temporal rhythms that are reproduced through practice performances. It is less the case that socio-temporal rhythms have been undermined and more that the elements (cultural meanings, skills and materialities) through which practice entities are organized no longer constrain the timings of those practices to the extent that could be observed in the strong collective timings of practices in past everyday lives. However, practice performances still demand coordination with other people and synchronization with other practices. And it was the difficulties of coordination and synchronization that dominated experiences of both time scarcity and time pressure in the narratives of respondents from the Bristol study. Explained in these terms, to address societal issues related to time requires an analytical focus on the organization of social practices and how the related performances of those practices form and reproduce the socio-temporal rhythms through which everyday lives (and senses of time squeeze) are experienced.

8.3   Implications

In the opening chapter of this book a range of societal problems commonly associated with the time squeeze were described. While a language of urgency to tackle societal problems is often evoked, as is particularly the case with climate change and environmental crises, when it comes to addressing these problems the issue of time scarcity is often identified as a 'barrier' to change (Cross 2005). Environmental sustainability is a good example, in which surveys repeatedly reveal that the significant majority of the public believe that lifestyle changes are necessary to avert the dangers of environmental change, but when it comes to changing their own lifestyle fail to act beyond minor adjustments. The time squeeze is often identified as one of the reasons why this is the case (see Southerton 2013 for a further discussion)—people simply do not have the time to make the necessary changes to their lifestyles not least because many of those changes require the investment of more time or incur significant inconvenience. A similar narrative can be found in other societal problems, such as family breakdown, social justice, ecological deterioration (such as plastics in the oceans or declining biodiversity), lifestyle diseases (such as obesity or type 2 diabetes), the declining quality of civil society engagement and concerns related to well-being and mental health. In all of these societal problems lack of time for individuals to take action in their own lives is diagnosed as a key contributing factor to the cause of the problem and a critical barrier to solutions.

Time, as discursively presented in these societal problems, is framed as clock time and based on a logic of zero-sum calculations in which the number of activities per unit of time is added, subtracted or substituted. Hence, the language of saving or making time for people to act accordingly in order to address societal problems comes to represent the main target of time-related policies or strategic interventions. Derived from the perspective of methodological individualism (that social phenomena are reducible to the motivations and actions of individuals), such a framing also locates the capacity to act as principally a matter of individual agents selecting to allocate activities within time in different ways. Both time and individual action become units of discretionary allocation within the context of everyday lives.

Translated into policy or strategic interventions, this framing of time presents it as being an abstract resource to be 'saved', 'sped-up' or 'freed-up'. While not an exhaustive list, four forms of time-related strategic interventions are readily identifiable: first, policies or interventions that seek to facilitate the 'substitution of time' frames for particular activities. A clear example is flexible work time schedules that allow employees to begin or finish work at times that differ from the core working hours of the organization (e.g. with core hours of 10 am–4 pm, enabling employees to start at 8 am and finish at 4 pm or start at 10 am and finish at

6 pm). Such policies offer employees greater discretion over the allocation of working time, particularly useful for dual income couples who are seeking to share domestic responsibilities such as pre- and post-school care of children (see Chap. 3 for a further discussion of flexible working time). In this way, times of the day can be substituted to cater for work and non-work activities.

A second set of approaches can be described as seeking to 'extend time'. The relaxation of regulations related to the times when consumption can take place has been a notable feature of the past 30 years. Licensing laws for public houses and nightclubs, shop opening times and Sunday trading are often cited as policy changes that have led to a 24/7 society (Anttila and Oinas 2018). Together with a global economy in which hours of work have extended across the 24-hour period and over weekends, while other leisure time regulations such as television programme schedules with a start and end time for broadcasting are rendered obsolete in an age of media streaming and on-demand viewing, the times in which activities can take place have been extended. Extending the times in which activities related to work and consumption typically occur opens up greater opportunities for individuals to allocate those activities within the context of a day or week.

The third is market-based solution directed at alleviating the challenges created by perceptions of time scarcity by seeking to 'displace time'. Digital technologies related to online shopping, smart devices in the home and personal digital assistants represent solutions that seek to remove activities from their conventional timings in the promise of freeing that time for individuals to pursue other activities. In the case of online grocery shopping, for instance, selecting items from a web-based browsing site removes the physical act of visiting a supermarket and means that the selection of goods and services can take place at any time, while home delivery removes the need to return home immediately after shopping in order to ensure that frozen or chilled items are kept at an optimal temperature. Whether online shopping reduces the overall amount of time required for shopping activities—especially given that it usually requires scheduling times to be at home for delivery, auditing delivered items and returning unsuitable items—matters less than the capacity for such digitally mediated services to displace the time required for the activity to be performed. In the case of smart home technologies, such as the refrigerator or home heating, the promise is that much of the time-related activities associated with the stocking of key food items or the turning on and off of the heating can be automated or controlled while away from the home. In these examples, the time required for everyday household management activities is displaced through the use of digitally mediated goods and services.

The final approach to addressing time-related problems can be found in popular movements (including the Slow Food Movement, Slow Cities, Society for the Deceleration of Time, the Simple Living Network and Manifesto for Slow Science) that seek to resist the apparent dominant trends underpinning the time squeeze. This is best captured in the Slow Living Movement, which seeks to resist the overloading of everyday life with increased volumes of activities (often described as downshifting or voluntary simplicity) by deliberately seeking out 'slow' activities. Slowness is presented as the antithesis of the orthodoxy of consumer culture in which people are locked into work-spend cycles, overconsumption and a dislocation of pleasure from sociability as the egoist pursuit of immediacy undermines the pleasures derived from cultural experiences of sociability. Its core ideology is that:

> 'Having time' for something means investing it with significance through attention and deliberation. To live slowly in this sense, then, means engaging with 'mindful' rather than 'mindless' practices which make us consider the pleasure or at least the purpose of each task to which we give our time. (Parkins and Craig 2006: 3)

Slow living, in its many forms, is a movement focused on the mindful pursuit of slowness, of savouring the moment, of consciously resisting the relentless drive for acceleration of activities in daily life and the accumulation of ever-more material goods. In this respect, the movement is not simply focused on time but a cultural critique of consumerism. However, time remains framed in zero-sum terms and as a matter of individual time-orientation (sometimes presented as 'time personalities', e.g. Kaufman-Scarborough and Lindquist 2003), for which the movement advocates adoption of the principles of slowness in one's allocation of activities within time.

These four approaches, whether related to public policy, organizational strategies (as with flexible working hours), market-based solutions or social movements, represent honourable attempts to assist individuals with the micro-coordination and synchronization of activities. However, because all conceptualize the problem of time through a zero-sum framing of the allocation of activities within (clock) time and therefore present the problem of time as a matter for individuals to resolve, they largely act to reproduce the temporal challenges created by the need for micro-coordination and synchronization of activities. Flexible time, for example, is certainly beneficial for managing the times of work but, as we have seen in Chap. 3, they do little to alleviate senses of time scarcity. Extending and displacing the times in which activities can take place certainly offers more minutes within the day to accomplish activities but in doing so opens up more (clock) time in which a diverse range of activities can and need to be coordinated with others and synchronized with other activities. And to be effective, strategies of slow living are entirely dependent on others both adopting slow living and aligning their schedules accordingly (and as the fascinating study of slow food by Hsu [2015] reveals, many of its core principles involve significant degrees of coordination and activity synchronization that exacerbate senses of feeling harried). Whether such approaches actually alleviate senses of the time squeeze is, however, not the primary concern here. Rather, the critical question is whether a singular focus on time as a matter of activity allocation in the context of a day or week limits capacity for considering how other perspectives and understandings of time might be applied in the context of seeking solutions to time-related societal problems.

The analysis presented in this book suggests that attention to the organization of social practices and the socio-temporal rhythms that they form offers an alternative and potentially instructive approach to tackling time-related societal issues. Such an approach draws attention to two related, but different, sets of processes. First is to focus attention on the ways in which social practices are organized, with particular reference to the elements of materialities, cultural meanings and standards of competent accomplishment. Strategic interventions across all three elements provide the basis for changes in the ways in which practices are performed (see Shove et al. 2012 and Spurling et al. 2013 for a comprehensive discussion) and socio-temporal rhythms are formed. The second is to consider the circular and linear temporal rhythms that are reproduced through the performance of interconnected practices. Circular rhythms are most readily identifiable in the periodicities (or regularities) and timings of practices. In the case of laundry practices such rhythms were found in the weekly cycles and timings of different laundry activities, such as washing clothes on weekday mornings. Linear rhythms are identifiable in the sequencing and synchronization of practices. In the case of laundry such rhythms include the sequential flow of laundry activities and the synchronization of particular activities with other practices. Both are experienced as nested socio-temporal rhythms (i.e. people rarely distinguish between circular and linear rhythms when discussing the patterning of their daily life), but the analytical distinction is useful for considering how interventions in the organization of practices might be utilized to shift socio-temporal rhythms. To provide a very brief example, the promotion of collective laundry provision (e.g. out-of-home laundry services) would require a change in the materialities of the laundry system, shifts in cultural meanings away from laundry as an expression of personal care within the household and new standards of competence and skills in appropriate laundry standards. Such an intervention would lead to quite different circular and linear rhythms of laundry practices, with the potential to reduce the volume of individual washing machines (together with their energy and water consumption) being used on weekday mornings and radically change the labour involved in delivering clean linen.

The practice of eating provides a different case through which to illustrate the implications of such an approach with respect to societal problems associated with food consumption. What we eat matters hugely, and concerns about the nutritional content of our diets, obesity, carbon emissions and food security are prominent in public debates. Policy responses tend towards an emphasis on informing consumers of the risks of different food product choices using various types of labelling (Nabec 2017), through attempts to nudge behaviour through choice editing (Spaargaren et al. 2013) or, when the public case is strong enough, through taxation (e.g. the sugar tax). Reference to convenience foods, fast foods and the dangers of snacking are also frequently targeted through social marketing campaigns with various celebrity chefs endorsing cookery books offering quick-to-prepare meals for the time-pressed consumer (Rousseau 2015; Piper 2015). The socio-temporal rhythms that form out of the organization of eating practices, however, receive very limited attention.

Yet, the social organization of eating practices and their socio-temporal rhythms are particularly important in shaping diets, and it would appear that particular forms of temporal rhythm are beneficial. As illustrated by a comparison of the UK and Spain (discussed in Chap. 6), the collective timing of eating activities varies significantly across societies. France, like Spain, has retained a temporal structure focused around three meals per day, each with strong collective timings, with lunch remaining an important event within the day. Laporte and Poulain (2014) explain that it is the continued cultural significance of lunch as a regular and structured event that helps explain why the French are less obese than the British. In France, lunches are prepared in workplace canteens by professional chefs in line with a template of main meals structured with nutritional balance in mind and which compare favourably to the dominance of the (quick) sandwich eaten by the majority of British workers at some point around the middle of the day. In both countries the organization of eating practices results in circular rhythms: most people eat lunch most days in both countries. However, in France linear rhythms sequence work practices around the lunch hour and follow a sequence of eating during that hour (e.g. two courses) whereas the UK lunchtime sandwiches are sequenced to fit within the linear rhythms of work-related practices.

In a different example, a study of Norwegian oil-rig workers sought to explain why they tended to gain weight during periods 'onshore' when compared with working 'offshore'. The organization of oil-rig working involved periods of between 7 and 10 days 'offshore' followed by long periods of non-work time while 'onshore'. When working offshore, oil-rig workers had access to free, prepared, unlimited and 'luxurious' foods with high meat and fat contents, available at any time of the day or night and with an abundant variety. Furthermore, beyond their work shifts offshore workers had few alternatives for leisure outside of the catering facilities. The assumption would be that when humans are offered free and ample foods with plenty of time in which to consume it, they would eat more. Østgård (1990) concludes that the rigid schedules of collectively timed events when offshore presented rigid socio-temporal rhythms that tempered dietary intake (Østgård 1990). Finally, a Danish study demonstrated that taking lunch with others (most usually work colleagues), which required a degree of coordination, regulated appetite and revealed lower instances of body-weight issues when compared with those who ate lunch independently from others. Those who ate independently either had unregulated episodes of eating (i.e. snacking) throughout the day or postponed lunch altogether, leading to particularly large evening meals (Kristensen and Holm 2006). As these examples show, the organization of eating practices produces socio-temporal rhythms with implications for diet and obesity.

The temporal rhythms of eating practices provide a glimpse into its potential to look beyond the individual consumer and the food consumption choices that they make to explore new avenues for societal responses to issues such as obesity. Presented in this light, reinstituting the UK lunch hour—which would necessitate a material provisioning system to cater for workplace meals (as is the case in France), reinforcing cultural meanings about commensal eating, and supporting the skills and competency to adjust work-based practices to be sequenced around that lunch hour—could represent a systemic policy for improving the diet of the nation.

Recognizing that socio-temporal rhythms are formed from the organization of social practices and that those rhythms shape patterns of consumption opens up new lines of enquiry for a broader range of issues, particularly with respect to sustainable consumption. The most significant of which is that such an approach locates individual action (or behaviour) as being, at most, a partial consideration in seeking to foster systemic change in the domain of consumption. As has been argued elsewhere, responses to questions regarding sustainable consumption have been dominated by methodological individualism. From this perspective, solutions are presented either as technological fixes that will enable the continuation of current lifestyles but in more resource-efficient ways or through appeals to individual behaviour change (Welch and Southerton 2019). These approaches are located within what Whitford (2002: 325) refers to as 'the portfolio model of the actor', a model in which 'individuals carry a relatively stable and pre-existing set of beliefs and desires from context to context. Given the situation, they select from this portfolio "those elements that seem relevant and [use] them to decide on a course of action".' When applied to consumption the individual is presented as a sovereign consumer, where consumption is largely a matter of personal decision-making within commercial markets that, in turn, respond to (aggregate) consumer demands and provide the sovereign consumer with a range of product choices from which to shape their lifestyle (Southerton et al. 2004). Within the portfolio model of action, consumer choices are the outcome of an individual's values and attitudes. The implications of such causal models are simple enough, to change behaviour (e.g. towards more sustainable ways of life) requires changes in the attitudes that shape, and values that frame, consumer choices (Shove 2010). When consumers' fail to respond accordingly, their 'deficit of action' is explained in terms of their lack of adequate knowledge or wilfully ignoring advice (Evans 2011; Jackson 2015).

Social practice theories present an alternative conceptualization of consumption (and human action more generally) as embedded in the organization of practices and reproduced through the performance of those practices (see Welch and Warde [2015] or Warde et al. [2017] for overviews). Patterns of consumption change as a consequence of shifts in the organization of practices. The analysis presented in this book argues that a critical outcome of the organization of practices is socio-temporal rhythms, which at an aggregate level reflect the temporal patterns of daily life and at the level of individuals, households or organizations can be analysed as the circular (periodicities and timings) and linear (sequential and synchronized) rhythms of daily activities. It follows that to seek to change or shift the forms of consumption reproduced through those rhythms the target for intervention needs to be the organization of social practices. And, because socio-temporal rhythms are embedded in periodicities, timings, sequences and the synchronization of activities, changes in the organization of practices are likely to have greater chance of sustained success in a way that behaviour change initiatives often fail to achieve (see Thøgersen and Berit Møller 2008 and Evans et al. 2012 for discussions of the temporary impacts of behaviour change initiatives).

At the core of this suggestion is that when developing policy, strategies or interventions that seek to change human actions and the consumption that they entail, attention needs to be given to the socio-temporal rhythms that form through the organization of social practices (see Southerton and Evans [2017] for a review of policy approaches to consumption). This could include a focus on seeking to institute collectively timed events, such as lunch hours featuring commensal dining in workplaces and promotion of fixed start and end times to the working day. Such examples focus directly on the timings of activities. However, the analysis of this book suggests looking beyond time per se to focus as much on the organization of practices and consider opportunities for forging new or different socio-temporal rhythms that could shift everyday lives in positive societal directions.

Much emphasis in recent policy debate has focused on notions of sharing (Schor 2016; Frenken and Schor 2017) or collaborative consumption (Yates 2018), which in a large part is down to their capacities for collectivizing the consumption of goods and services and thus reduce the resource intensity of patterns of consumption. Policies, interventions and innovations that seek to facilitate the alignment of personal schedules (and therefore synchronize the collective timings of daily activities) offer the scope to foster socio-temporal rhythms that make collective forms of consumption more accessible. The examples of reinstituting workplace lunch hours and developing out-of-home laundry service infrastructures are based on these principles. This does, however, require recognition that fostering collective timings of activities has implications for other resource-intensive rhythms of everyday lives. Peak loads of energy demand are a good example. While removing laundry from the home would offer the potential for laundry services to wash and dry clothes during times of off-peak energy demand (thus reducing peaks), reinstituting collective timings of eating occasions would have the opposite effect. The idea of seeking to flatten peak loads by reducing the collective timing of events would, according to the analysis presented in this book, have detrimental consequences for the organization of daily life because it would only further increase the challenge of coordination of people and synchronization of activities. As such, policies that seek to shift the socio-temporal rhythms of everyday patterns of consumption should work with, and seek to utilize, collective timings to even out energy demand as opposed to seeking to undermine those timings. The range of digital technologies, platforms and delivery systems now available (and developed for online shopping) could offer innovative opportunities to align such systems of provision for domestic consumption (with platforms coordinating multiple services to produce collectively timed delivery events within local neighbourhoods) and creating new socio-temporal rhythms of everyday lives (see also Moran [2015] for a discussion of how new technologies offer scope to reorganize social practices and their temporalities).

While speculative, these suggestions draw together two critical arguments derived from social practice theories. The first is that to change consumption requires attention to the ways in which practices are organized (Warde 2005, 2017), their dynamics (Shove et al. 2012), and the potential to reconfigure practices in ways that foster socially beneficial outcomes (Geels et al. 2015; Welch and Southerton 2019). The second is that socio-temporal rhythms are the consequence of the social organization of shared practices which underpin rhythms of human activity. As such, time scarcity and time pressure are reflections of the ways in which practices are organized and that, in the search for greater individual discretion in the allocation of activities within time, the contemporary organization of social practices has weakened collectively timed activities and generated the need for their micro-coordination. Attention to the socio-temporal rhythms that are formed from the organization of practices, with an emphasis on seeking to align practices and reinstitute collectively timed events, offers scope not just to alleviate the cognitive load of micro-coordinating activities in daily life but also for seeking to foster new forms of collective consumption.

References

Anttila, T., & Oinas, T. (2018). 24/7 Society: The New Timing of Work? In M. Tammelin (Ed.), *Family, Work and Well-Being* (pp. 63–76). Cham: Springer.

Cross, G. (2005). A Right to Be Lazy?: Busyness in Retrospective. *Social Research: An International Quarterly, 72*(2), 263–286.

Evans, D. M. (2011). Blaming the Consumer—Once Again: The Social and Material Contexts of Everyday Food Waste Practices in Some English Households. *Critical Public Health, 21*(4), 429–440.

Evans, D. M. (2019). What is Consumption, Where Has it Been Going, and Does it Still Matter? *The Sociological Review, 67*(3), 499–517.

Evans, D. M., McMeekin, A., & Southerton, D. (2012). Sustainable Consumption, Behaviour Change Policies, and Theories of Practice. In A. Warde & D. Southerton (Eds.), *The Habits of Consumption* (pp. 113–129). Helsinki: Open Access Book Series of the Helsinki Collegium of Advanced Studies.

Frenken, K., & Schor, J. (2017). Putting the Sharing Economy into Perspective. *Environmental Innovation and Societal Transitions, 23*, 3–10.

Geels, F., McMeekin, A., Mylan, J., & Southerton, D. (2015). A Critical Appraisal of Sustainable Consumption and Production Research: The Reformist, Revolutionary and Reconfiguration Agendas. *Global Environmental Change, 34*, 1–12.

Hassan, R. (2003). Network Time and the New Knowledge Epoch. *Time & Society, 12*(2/3), 225–241.

Hsu, E. L. (2015). The Slow Food Movement and Time Shortage: Beyond the Dichotomy of Fast or Slow. *Journal of Sociology, 51*(3), 628–642.

Jackson, P. (2015). *Anxious Appetites: Food and Consumer Culture*. London: Bloomsbury.

Kaufman-Scarborough, C., & Lindquist, J. D. (2003). Understanding the Experience of Time Scarcity: Linking Consumer Time-personality and Marketplace Behaviour. *Time & Society, 12*(2–3), 349–370.

Kristensen, S., & Holm, L. (2006). Modern Meal Patterns: Tensions Between Bodily Needs and the Organization of Time and Space. *Food and Foodways, 14*(3), 151–173.

Laporte, C., & Poulain, J.-P. (2014). Restauration d'entreprise en France et au Royaume-Uni: Synchronisation sociale alimentaire et obesite. *Ethnologie Francaise XLIV, 1*, 861–872.

Moran, C. (2015). Time as a Social Practice. *Time & Society, 24*, 283–303.

Mylan, J., & Southerton, D. (2018). The Social Ordering of an Everyday Practice: The Case of Laundry. *Sociology, 25*(6), 1134–1151.

Nabec, L. (2017). Improving Dietary Behaviour with Nutrition Labelling: Towards a Research Agenda that Serves Consumer Well-being. *Recherche et Applications en Marketing (English Edition), 32*(2), 71–97.

Østgård, L. I. (1990). Food Habits among Norwegian Offshore Oilworkers: Adaptation to Spectrum and Abundance of Food Choice. In J. C. Somogyi & E. H. Koskinen (Eds.), *Nutritional Adaptation to New Life-Styles* (pp. 165–175). Helsinki: Karger.

Parkins, W., & Craig, G. (2006). *Slow Living*. Oxford: Berg.

Piper, N. (2015). Jamie Oliver and Cultural Intermediation. *Food, Culture & Society, 18*(2), 245–264.

Rousseau, S. (2015). The Celebrity Quick-Fix. *Food, Culture & Society, 18*(2), 265–287.

Schatzki, T. R. (2010). *The Timespace of Human Activity: On Performance, Society, and History as Interminate Teleological Events*. Plymouth: Lexington Books.

Schor, J. (2016). Debating the Sharing Economy. *Journal of Self-Governance and Management Economics, 4*(3), 7–22.

Shove, E. (2010). Beyond ABC: Climate Change Policy and Theories of Social Change. *Environment and Planning A, 42*, 1273–1285.

Shove, E., Pantzar, M., & Watson, M. (2012). *The Dynamics of Social Practice: Everyday Life and how it Changes*. London: Sage.

Southerton, D. (2013). Temporal Rhythms, Habits and Routines: From Consumer Behaviour to the Temporal Ordering of Practices. *Time and Society, 22*(3), 335–355.

Southerton, D., & Evans, D. M. (2017). Consumption Policies with Different Theoretical Frameworks. In *Routledge Handbook on Consumption* (pp. 213–214). Routledge.

Southerton, D., Warde, A., & Hand, M. (2004). The Limited Autonomy of the Consumer: Implications for Sustainable Consumption. In D. Southerton, H. Chappells, & B. Van Vliet (Eds.), *Sustainable Consumption: The Implications of Changing Infrastructures of Provision* (pp. 32–48). London: Edward Elgar.

Spurling, N., McMeekin, A., Shove, E., Southerton, D., & Welch, D. (2013). *Interventions in Practice: Re-framing Policy Approaches to Consumer Behaviour*. Sustainable Practices Research Group Report, Sept.

Thøgersen, J., & Berit Møller, B. (2008). Breaking Car Use Habits: The Effectiveness of a Free One-Month Travelcard. *Transportation, 35*(3), 329–345.

Urry, J. (2009). Speeding Up and Slowing Down. In H. Rosa & W. Scheuerman (Eds.), *High Speed Society. Social Acceleration, Power and Modernity* (pp. 179–198). University Park: Pennsylvania State University Press.

van Spaargaren, G., Koppen, C., Janssen, A. M., Hendriksen, A., & Kolfschoten, C. J. (2013). Consumer Responses to the Carbon Labelling of Food. *Sociol Ruralis, 53*, 432–453.

Wajcman, J. (2015). *Pressed for Time: The Acceleration of Life in Digital Capitalism*. Chicago: Chicago University Press.

Warde, A. (2005). Consumption and Theories of Practice. *Journal of Consumer Culture, 5*(2), 131–154.

Warde, A. (2017). *Consumption: A Sociological Analysis.* London: Palgrave Macmillan.

Warde, A., Welch, D., & Paddock, J. (2017). Studying Consumption Through the Lens of Practice: Routledge Handbook on Consumption. In M. Keller, B. Halkier, T. A Wilska, & M. Truninger (eds.), *Handbook on Consumption* [1.3]. London: Routledge.

Welch, D., & Southerton, D. (2019). After Paris: Transitions for Sustainable Consumption. *Sustainability: Science, Practice and Policy, 15*(1), 31–44.

Welch, D., & Warde, A. (2015). Theories of Practice and Sustainable Consumption. In L. Reisch & J. Thøgersen (Eds.), *Handbook of Research on Sustainable Consumption* (pp. 84–100). Cheltenham UK: Edward Elgar Publishing Ltd.

Whitford, J. (2002). Pragmatism and the Untenable Dualism of Means and Ends: Why Rational Choice Theory Does not Deserve paradigmatic Privilege. *Theory & Society, 31*, 325–363.

Yates, L. (2018). Sharing, Households and Sustainable Consumption. *Journal of Consumer Culture, 18*(3), 433–452.

References

1900s.org.uk. (2019). Monday Washdays: The Laundry in Bygone Years. Retrieved November 27, 2019, from https://www.1900s.org.uk/1900s-washdays.htm

Adam, B. (1989). Feminist Social Theory Needs Time. Reflections on the Relation between Feminist Thought, Social Theory and Time as an Important Parameter in Social Analysis. *Sociological Review, 37*, 458–473.

Adam, B. (1990). *Time and Social Theory*. Cambridge: Polity.

Adam, B. (1995). *Timewatch: The Social Analysis of Time*. London: Polity.

Adam, B. (1998). *Timescapes of Modernity: The Environment and Invisible Hazards*. London: Routledge.

Adam, B. (2004). *Time*. Cambridge: Polity.

Adkins, C., & Premeaux, S. (2014). The Use of Communication Technology to Manage Work-Home Boundaries. *Journal of Behavioral & Applied Management, 15*(2), 82–100.

Agar, J. (2003). *Constant Touch: A Global History of the Mobile Phone*. Cambridge: Icon Books.

Agger, B. (1989). *Fast Capitalism*. Urbana: University of Illinois Press.

Agger, B. (2007). Time Robbers, Time Rebels: Limits to Fast Capital. In R. Hassan & R. E. Purser (Eds.), *24/7: Time and Temporality in the Network Society* (pp. 219–234). Stanford, CA: Stanford Business Books.

© The Author(s) 2020   **201**
D. Southerton, *Time, Consumption and the Coordination of Everyday Life*,
Consumption and Public Life, https://doi.org/10.1057/978-1-349-60117-2

Agger, B. (2011). iTime: Labor and Life in a Smartphone Era. *Time & Society,* *20*(1), 119–136.

Aguiar, M., & Hurst, E. (2007). Measuring Trends in Leisure: The Allocation of Time Over Five Decades. *Quarterly Journal of Economics, 122*, 969–1006.

Aguiar, M., & Hurst, E. (2009). Summary of Trends in American Time Allocation: 1965–2005. *Social Indicators Research, 93*, 57–64.

Anderson, B. (2016). Laundry, Energy and Time: Insights from 20 Years of Time-use Diary Data in the United Kingdom. *Energy Research & Social Science, 22*, 125–136.

Anttila, T., & Oinas, T. (2018). 24/7 Society: The New Timing of Work? In M. Tammelin (Ed.), *Family, Work and Well-Being* (pp. 63–76). Cham: Springer.

Baker, A., Roach, G., Ferguson, S., & Dawson, D. (2003). The Impact of Different Rosters on Employee Work and Non-Work. *Time & Society, 12*(2–3), 315–332.

Barley, S., Meyerson, D., & Gordal, S. (2011). Email as a Source and Symbol of Stress. *Organizational Studies, 22*(4), 887–906.

Bartlett, R. (2004). *The Hanged Man: A Story of Miracle, Memory, and Colonialism in the Middle Ages.* New Jersey: Princeton University Press.

Bauman, Z. (1990). *Thinking Sociologically.* Oxford: Blackwell.

Bauman, Z. (1991). *Modernity and Ambivalence.* Cambridge: Polity Press.

Bauman, Z. (1992). *Intimations of Postmodernity.* London: Routledge.

Beck, U. (1992). *Risk Society: Towards a New Modernity.* London: Sage.

Beck, U., & Beck-Gernsheim, E. (1996). Individualization and 'Precarious Freedoms': Perspectives and Controversies of a Subject-orientated Sociology. In S. Lash, P. Heelas, & P. Morris (Eds.), *Detraditionalisation.* London: Blackwell.

Beck, U., & Beck-Gernsheim, E. (2001). *Individualization: Institutionalized Individualism and its Social and Political Conseqeuences.* London: Sage.

Bell, D. (1976). *The Cultural Contradictions of Capitalism.* New York: Basic Books.

Bennett, T., Savage, M., Silva, E., Warde, A., Gayo-Cal, M., & Wright, D. (2009). *Culture, Class, Distinction.* London: Routledge.

Bergmann, W. (1992). The Problem of Time in Sociology: An Overview of the Literature on the State of Theory and Research on the Sociology of Time, 1900–82. *Time & Society, 1*, 81–134.

Bittman, M., Brown, J., & Wajcman, J. (2009). The Mobile Phone, Perpetual Contact and Time Pressure. *Work, Employment & Society, 23*, 673–679.

Bittman, M., & Wajcman, J. (2000). The Rush Hour; the Character of Leisure Time and Gender Equity. *Social Forces, 79*(1), 165–189.

Blue, S. (2019). Institutional Rhythms: Combining Practice Theory and Rhythmanalysis to Conceptualise Processes of Institutionalisation. *Time & Society, 28*, 922–950.

Bocock, R. (1993). *Consumption*. London: Routledge.

Bott, E. (1957). *Family and Social Network* (2nd ed., 1971). New York: Free Press.

Bourdieu, P. (1979). *Algeria 1960*. Cambridge: Cambridge University Press.

Bourdieu, P. (1984). *Distinction: A Social Critique of the Judgment of Taste*. London: Routledge & Kegan Paul.

Brannen, J. (2005). Time and the Negotiation of Work-family Boundaries: Autonomy or Illusion. *Time & Society, 14*(1), 113–131.

Brannen, J., O'connell, R., & Mooney, A. (2013). Families, Meals and Synchronicity: Eating Together in BRITISH Dual Earner Families. *Community, Work & Family, 16*, 417–434.

Breedveld, K. (1998). The Double Myth of Flexibilization: Trends in Scattered Work Hours, and Differences in Time Sovereignty. *Time & Society, 7*(1), 129–143.

Bregman, R. (2017). *Utopia for Realists: How We Can Build the Ideal World*. Little: Brown and Company/Hachette Book Group USA.

Bryan, M. (2017). Flexible Working in the UK and its Impact on Couples' Time Coordination. *Review of Economics of the Household, 15*(4), 1415–1437.

Bureau of Labor Statistics. (2016). American Time Use Survey: Household Activities. Retrieved from https://www.bls.gov/tus/charts/household.htm

Castells, M. (1996). *The Information Age: Economy, Society and Culture, Vol.1: The Rise of the Network Society*. Oxford: Blackwell.

Castells, M. (1998). *The Information Age: Economy, Society and Culture, Vol.3: End of Millennium*. Oxford: Blackwell.

Center for the Digital Future. (2013). *The Digital Future Project 2013— Surveying the Digital Future Year Eleven*. Los Angeles: University of Southern California.

Chesley, N. (2005). Blurring Boundaries? Linking Technology Use, Spillover, Individual Distress, and Family Satisfaction. *Journal of Marriage and the Family, 67*, 1237–1248.

Chung, H. (2018). *Gender, Flexibility Stigma, and the Perceived Negative Consequences of Flexible Working in the UK*. Social Indicators Research, Online First.

Colville, R. (2016). *The Great Acceleration: How the World is Getting Faster*. London: Bloomsbury.

Cook, D. (2000). The Rise of 'the Toddler' as Subject and as Merchandising Category in the 1930s. In M. Gottdiener (Ed.), *The New Means of Consumption* (pp. 111–130). Lanham, MD: Rowman & Littlefield.

Cook, D. (2004). *The Commodification of Childhood: The Children's Clothing Industry and the Rise of the Child Consumer.* Duke University Press.

Couldrey, N. (2012). *Media, Society, World: Social Theory and Digital Media Practice.* Cambridge: Polity Press.

Craig, L., & Mullan, K. (2011). How Mothers and Fathers Share Childcare: A Cross-national Time-use Comparison. *American Sociological Review, 76*(6), 834–861.

Craig, L., Powell, A., & Smyth, C. (2014). Towards Intensive Parenting? Changes in the Composition and Determinants of Mothers and Fathers' Time with Children 1992–2006. *British Journal of Sociology, 65*(3), 555–579.

Credit Loan. (2019). Who Does the Household Chores? Retrieved from https://www.creditloan.com/blog/love-and-household-labor/

Cross, G. (2005). A Right to Be Lazy?: Busyness in Retrospective. *Social Research: An International Quarterly, 72*(2), 263–286.

Daly, K. (1996). *Families and Time: Keeping Pace in a Hurried Culture.* London: Sage.

Darier, E. (1998). Time to be Lazy. Work, the Environment and Subjectivities. *Time & Society, 7*(2), 193–208.

De Saint Pol, T., & Ricroch, L. (2012). Le Temps de l'alimentation en France [Time Spent on Eating in France]. Insee Premiere Report No. 1417. Retrieved from https://www.insee.fr/fr/statistiques/1281016.

DEMOS. (1995). *The Time Squeeze.* London: Demos.

Dodd, N., & Wajcman, J. (2017). Simmel and Benjamin: Early Theorists of the Acceleration Society. In J. Wajcman & N. Dodd (Eds.), *The Sociology of Speed: Digital, Organizational, and Social Temporalities* (pp. 13–24). Oxford: Oxford University Press.

Dumazedier, J. (1967). *Toward a Leisure of Society.* New York: Free Press.

Durkheim, E. (1915). *The Elementary Forms of Religious Life: A Study in Religious Sociology* (J. W. Swain, Trans.). London: Allen & Unwin.

Ehrenreich, B., & English, D. (1979). *For Her Own Good: 150 Years of the Experts' Advice to Women.* London: Pluto Press.

Ehrenreich, B., & Hochschild, A. (Eds.). (2003). *Global Women: Nannies, Maids, and Sex Workers in the New Economy.* New York: Metropolitan Boons.

Elias, N. (1992). *Time: An Essay.* Oxford: Blackwell.

Energy Saving Trust. (2013). *At Home With Water*, Energy Saving Trust Report. Retrieved from https://www.energysavingtrust.org.uk/policy-research/home-water

Evans, D. M. (2011). Blaming the Consumer—Once Again: The Social and Material Contexts of Everyday Food Waste Practices in Some English Households. *Critical Public Health, 21*(4), 429–440.

Evans, D. M. (2019). What is Consumption, Where Has it Been Going, and Does it Still Matter? *The Sociological Review, 67*(3), 499–517.

Evans, D. M., McMeekin, A., & Southerton, D. (2012). Sustainable Consumption, Behaviour Change Policies, and Theories of Practice. In A. Warde & D. Southerton (Eds.), *The Habits of Consumption* (pp. 113–129). Helsinki: Open Access Book Series of the Helsinki Collegium of Advanced Studies.

Evans-Pritchard, E. (1969). *The Neur*. New York: Oxford University Press.

Fagan, C. (2001). Time, Money and the Gender Order. Work Orientations and Working-Time Preferences, Gender. *Work and Organizations, 8*(3), 239–267.

Featherstone, M. (1987). Lifestyle and Consumer Culture, *Theory. Culture & Society, 4*(1), 55–60.

Featherstone, M. (1991). *Consumer Culture and Postmodernism*. London: Sage.

Featherstone, M. (1997). Lifestyle and Consumer Culture. *Theory, Culture & Society, 4*(1), 55–70.

Fine, G. (1996). *Kitchens: The Culture of Restaurant Work*. University of California Press.

Fisher, K., Egerton, M., Gershuny, J., & Robinson, J. P. (2006). Gender Convergence in the American Heritage Time Use Study (AHTUS). *Social Indicators Research, 82*, 1–33.

Frenken, K., & Schor, J. (2017). Putting the Sharing Economy into Perspective. *Environmental Innovation and Societal Transitions, 23*, 3–10.

Frisby, D., & Featherstone, M. (Eds.). (1997). *Simmel on Culture: Selected Writings*. London: Sage.

Garhammer, M. (1995). Changes in Working Hours in Germany. *Time & Society, 4*(2), 167–203.

Garnett, K. (2018). The Average Brit Spends more than 2000 days Doing Chores in Their Lifetime. *Ideal Home Magazine*. Retrieved October 07, 2019, from https://www.idealhome.co.uk/news/time-spent-doing-chores-181435.

Geels, F., McMeekin, A., Mylan, J., & Southerton, D. (2015). A Critical Appraisal of Sustainable Consumption and Production Research: The

Reformist, Revolutionary and Reconfiguration Agendas. *Global Environmental Change, 34*, 1–12.

Geels, F. W., & Schot, J. (2010). Part 1: The Dynamics of Socio-technical Transitions: A Sociotechnical Perspective. In J. Grin, J. Rotmans, & J. Schot (Eds.), *Transitions to Sustainable Development: New Directions in the Study of Long Term Transformative Change* (pp. 11–104). London: Routledge.

Gershuny, J. (1978). *After Industrial Society? The Emerging Self-service Economy.* London: Macmillan.

Gershuny, J. (2000). *Changing Times: Work and Leisure in Post-industrial Society.* Oxford: Oxford University Press.

Gershuny, J. (2005). Busyness as the Badge of Honor for the New Superordinate Working Class. *Social Research, 72*(2), 287–314.

Gershuny, J. (2009). Veblen in Reverse: Evidence from the Multinational Time-use Archive. *Social Indicators Research, 93*, 37–45.

Gershuny, J. (2011). Increasing Paid Work Time? A New Puzzle for Multinational Time-diary Research. *Social Indicators Research, 101*, 207–213.

Gershuny, J. (2018). *Gender Symmetry, Gender Convergence and Historical Work-time Invariance in 24 Countries.* Centre for Time Use Research, Working Paper 2: 1–16.

Gershuny, J., Godwin, M., & Jones, S. (1994). The Domestic Division of Labor: A Process of Lagged Adaptation? In M. Anderson, F. Bechhofer, & J. Gershuny (Eds.), *The Social and Political Economy of the Household.* Oxford: Oxford University Press.

Gershuny, J., & Harms, T. (2016). Housework Now Takes Much Less Time: 85 Years of US Rural Women's Time Use. *Social Forces, 95*(2), 503–524.

Gershuny, J., & Sullivan, O. (2019). *What We Really Do All Day: Insights from the Centre for Time Use Research.* Milton Keynes: Pelican Books.

Giddens, A. (1990). *The Consequences of Modernity.* Cambridge: Polity.

Giddens, A. (1991). *Modernity and Self-Identity.* Cambridge: Polity.

Gillis, J. R. (1996). *A World of Their Own Making: Myth, Ritual and the Quest for Family Values.* New York: Basic.

Gimenez-Nadal, J. I., & Sevilla-Sanz, A. (2012). Trends in Time Allocation: A Cross-country Analysis. *European Economic Review, 56*(6), 1338–1359.

Gleick, J. (1999). *Faster: The Acceleration of Just About Everything.* New York: Abacus.

Glennie, P., & Thrift, N. (1996). Reworking E.P. Thompson's "Time, Work-Discipline and Industrial Capitalism". *Time & Society, 5*(3), 275–299.

Glennie, P., & Thrift, N. (2009). *Shaping the Day: A History of Timekeeping in England and Wales 1300–1800*. Oxford: Oxford University Press.

Goggin, G. (2012). *New Technologies and the Media*. New York: Palgrave Macmillan.

Gram-Hanssen, K. (2011). Understanding Change and Continuity in Residential Energy Consumption. *Journal of Consumer Culture, 11*(1), 61–78.

Green, F. (2006). *Demanding Work: The Paradox of Job Quality in the Affluent Economy*. Princeton: Princeton University Press.

Green, N., & Haddon, L. (2009). *Mobile Communications: An Introduction to the New Media*. Oxford: Berg.

Gronow, J. (1997). *Sociology of Taste*. London: Routledge.

Gronow, J., & Warde, A. (2001). *Ordinary Consumption*. London: Routledge.

Hall, D. (2015). *Worktown: The Astonishing Story of the Birth of Mass-Observation*. London: Weidenfeld & Nicolson.

Harrington, R. (2003). Trains, Technology and Time-travellers: How the Victorians Re-invented Time. Retrieved December 16, 2019, from https://web.archive.org/web/20080828054933/http://www.greycat.org/papers/timetrav.html

Harvey, D. (1989). *The Condition of Postmodernity*. Oxford, UK: Blackwell.

Harvey, M. (1999). Economies of Time: A Framework for Analysing the Restructuring of Employment Relations. In A. Felstead & N. Jewson (Eds.), *Global Trends in Flexible Labour*. London: Macmillan.

Hassan, R. (2003). Network Time and the New Knowledge Epoch. *Time & Society, 12*(2/3), 225–241.

Hassan, R. (2005). Timescapes of the Network Society. *Fast Capitalism* 1(1). Retrieved from http://www.uta.edu/huma/agger/fastcapitalism/1_1/hassan.html.

Hassan, R., & Purser, R. E. (2007). *24/7: Time and Temporality in the Network Society*. Stanford, CA: Stanford Business Books.

Hebdige, D. (1979). *Subcultures: The Meaning of Style*. London: Routledge.

Heidegger, M. (1927). *Being and Time* (J. Stambaugh, Trans.). New York: Harper and Row.

Hewitt, P. (1993). *About Time: The Revolution in Work and Family Life*. Rivers Oram Press.

Hochschild, A. R. (1997). *The Time Bind: When Home Becomes Work and Work Becomes Home*. CA Henry Holt.

Hochschild, A. (2003). *The Commercialization of Intimate Life*. Berkeley: University of California Press.

Hockey, J., & James, A. (2003). *Social Identities Across the Life Course*. London: Palgrave Macmillan.

Holmes, H. (2018). Self-time: The Importance of Temporal Experience within Practice. *Time & Society, 27*(2), 176–194.

Hsu, E. L. (2015). The Slow Food Movement and Time Shortage: Beyond the Dichotomy of Fast or Slow. *Journal of Sociology, 51*(3), 628–642.

Jack, T. (2013). Laundry Routine and Resource Consumption in Australia. *International Journal of Consumer Studies, 37*(6), 666–674.

Jackson, P. (2015). *Anxious Appetites: Food and Consumer Culture*. London: Bloomsbury.

Jalas, M. (2006). Making Time: The Art of Loving Wooden Boats. *Time and Society, 15*, 343–363.

Jalas, M. (2009). Wooden Boats and Self-legitimizing Time. In E. Shove, F. Trentmann, & R. Wilk (Eds.), *Time, Consumption and Everyday Life: Practice, Materiality and Culture* (pp. 203–216). Oxford: Berg.

Johnson, N., & Keane, H. (2017). Internet Addiction? Temporality and life Online in the Networked Society. *Time & Society, 26*(3), 267–285.

Kaufmann, J. C. (1998). *Dirty Linen: Couples and their Laundry*. London: Middlesex University Press.

Kaufman-Scarborough, C., & Lindquist, J. D. (2003). Understanding the Experience of Time Scarcity: Linking Consumer Time-personality and Marketplace Behaviour. *Time & Society, 12*(2–3), 349–370.

Kern, S. (1983). *The Culture of Time and Space 1880–1918*. Cambridge, MA: Harvard University Press.

Keynes, J. M. (1936). Economic Prospects for our Grandchildren. In D. E. Moggridge (Ed.), *Essays in Persuasion: The Collected Writings of John Maynard Keynes* (Vol. 9, pp. 321–332). London: Macmillan Press.

Kremer-Sadlik, T., & Paugh, A. L. (2007). Everyday Moments: Finding 'Quality time' in American Working Families. *Time & Society, 16*(2–3), 287–308.

Kristensen, S., & Holm, L. (2006). Modern Meal Patterns: Tensions Between Bodily Needs and the Organization of Time and Space. *Food and Foodways, 14*(3), 151–173.

Kunda, G. (2001). *Scenes from a Marriage: Work, Family and Time in Corporate Drama*. Paper Presented to the International Conference on Spacing and Timing, November, Palermo, Italy.

Lamont, M. (1992). *Money, Morals & Manners: The Culture of the French and American Upper-Middle Class*. London: Chicago Press.

Landes, D. (1983). *Revolution in Time: Clocks and the Making of the Modern World*. Cambridge, MA: Harvard University Press.

Laporte, C., & Poulain, J.-P. (2014). Restauration d'entreprise en France et au Royaume-Uni: Synchronisation sociale alimentaire et obesite. *Ethnologie Francaise XLIV, 1*, 861–872.

Larsson, J., & Sanne, C. (2005). Self-help Books on Avoiding Time Shortage. *Time & Society, 14*(2/3), 213–230.

Leccardi, C. (2007). New Temporal Perspectives in the "High-Speed Society". In R. Hassan & R. E. Purser (Eds.), *24/7: Time and Temporality in the Network Society* (pp. 25–36). Stanford, CA: Stanford Business Books.

Leete, L., & Schor, J. (1994). Assessing the Time-Squeeze Hypothesis: Hours Worked in the United States, 1969–89. *Industrial Relations, 33*(1), 25–43.

Lefebvre, H. (2004 [1992]). *Rhythmanalysis: Space, Time and Everyday Life* (S. Elden and G. Moore, Trans.). London: Athlone.

Lesnard, L. (2008). Off-scheduling Within Dual-earner Couples: An Unequal and Negative Externality for Family Time. *American Journal of Sociology, 114*, 447–490.

Linder, S. B. (1970). *The Harried Leisure Class*. New York: Columbia University Press.

Lott, Y., & Chung, H. (2016). Gender Discrepancies in the Outcomes of Schedule Control on Overtime Hours and Income in Germany. *European Sociological Review, 32*(6), 752–765.

Luhmann, N. (1976). The Future Cannot Begin: Temporal Structures in Modern Society. *Social Research, 43*, 130–152.

MacKenzie, D. (2017). Capital's Geodesic: Chicago, New Jersey, and the Material Sociology of Speed. In J. Wajcman & N. Dodd (Eds.), *The Sociology of Speed: Digital, Organizational, and Social Temporalities* (pp. 55–71). Oxford: Oxford University Press.

Majamäki, M., & Hellman, M. (2016). "When Sense of Time Disappears"—Or does it? Online Video Gamers' Time Management and Time Apprehension. *Time & Society, 25*(2), 355–373.

Mannheim, K. (1952). The Problem of Generations. In K. Mannheim (Ed.), *Essays on the Sociology of Knowledge*. London: Routledge Kegan & Paul.

Marx, K. (1976[1867]). *Capital, Vol. I*. Penguin: London.

Marx, K. (1996[1848]). *The Communist Manifesto*. London: Pluto Press.

Mass Observation Archive. (2009). *Meet Yourself on Sunday*. London: Bloomsbury House.

Massey, D. (1994). A Global Sense of Place. In D. Massey (Ed.), *Space, Place and Gender* (pp. 146–156). Cambridge, UK: Polity Press.

May, J., & Thrift, N. (2001). *TimeSpace: Geographies of Temporality*. New York, NY: Routledge.

McMeekin, A., & Southerton, D. (2012). Sustainability Transitions and Final Consumption: Practices and Socio-technical Systems. *Technology Analysis & Strategic Management, 24*(4), 345–361.

McMenamin, T. (2007). A Time to Work: Recent Trends in Shift Work and Flexible Schedules. *Monthly Labour Review, 130*, 3–15.

Minnen, J., Glorieux, I., & Pieter van Tienoven, T. (2016). Who Works When? Towards a Typology of Weekly Work Patterns in Belgium. *Time & Society, 25*(3), 652–675.

Moran, C. (2015). Time as a Social Practice. *Time & Society, 24*, 283–303.

Mylan, J., & Southerton, D. (2018). The Social Ordering of an Everyday Practice: The Case of Laundry. *Sociology, 25*(6), 1134–1151.

Nabec, L. (2017). Improving Dietary Behaviour with Nutrition Labelling: Towards a Research Agenda that Serves Consumer Well-being. *Recherche et Applications en Marketing (English Edition), 32*(2), 71–97.

Nicolini, D. (2009). Zooming In and Out: Studying Practices by Switching Theoretical Lenses and Trailing Connections. *Organization Studies, 30*(12), 1391–1418.

Nicolini, D. (2012). *Practice Theory, Work, and Organization: An Introduction*. Oxford: Oxford University Press.

Nowotny, H. (1992). Time and Social Theory Towards a Social Theory of Time. *Time and Society, 1*, 421–454.

O'Malley, M. (1992). Time, Work and Task Orientation: A Critique of American Historiography. *Time and Society, 1*(3), 341–358.

OldandInteresting. (2019). History of Laundry—after 1800, Washing Clothes and Household Linen: 19th Century Laundry Methods and Equipment. Retrieved November 27, 2019, from http://www.oldandinteresting.com/history-of-washing-clothes.aspx

Organisation for Economic Co-operation and Development. (2018). 'Time Use Portal', https://stats.oecd.org/Index.aspx?DataSetCode=TIME_USE

Ortner, S. (1984). Theory in Anthropology since the Sixties. *Comparative Studies in Society and History, 26*, 126–166.

Østgård, L. I. (1990). Food Habits among Norwegian Offshore Oilworkers: Adaptation to Spectrum and Abundance of Food Choice. In J. C. Somogyi

& E. H. Koskinen (Eds.), *Nutritional Adaptation to New Life-Styles* (pp. 165–175). Helsinki: Karger.

Paiva, D., Cachinho, H., & Barata-Salgueiro, T. (2017). The Pace of Life and Temporal Resources in a Neighborhood of an Edge City. *Time and Society, 26*(1), 28–51.

Pantzar, M., & Shove, E. (2010). Temporal Rhythms as Outcomes of Social Practices: A Speculative Discussion. *Ethnologia Europaea, 40,* 19–29.

Parkins, W., & Craig, G. (2006). *Slow Living.* Oxford: Berg.

Pedersen, V., & Lewis, S. (2012). Flexible Friends? FLEXIBLE Working Time Arrangements, Blurred Work-life Boundaries and Friendship. *Work, Employment and Society, 26*(3), 464–480.

Perrons, D. (2003). The New Economy and the Work-Life Balance: Conceptual Explorations and a Case Study of New Media. *Gender, Work and Organization, 10*(1), 65–94.

Perrons, D., Fagan, C., McDowell, L., Ray, K., & Ward, K. (2005). Work, Life and Time in the New Economy: An Introduction. *Time & Society, 14*(1), 51–64.

Pink, S. (2012). *Situating Everyday Life.* London: Sage.

Piper, N. (2015). Jamie Oliver and Cultural Intermediation. *Food, Culture & Society, 18*(2), 245–264.

Pisarski, A., Lawrence, S. A., Bohle, P., & Brook, C. (2008). Organizational Influences on the Work Life Conflict and Health of Shiftworkers. *Applied Ergonomics, 39*(5), 580–588.

Power Inquiry. (2006). The Report of Power: An Independent Inquiry into Britain's Democracy. Joseph Rowntree Charitable Trust. Retrieved from http://www.jrrt.org.uk/sites/jrrt.org.uk/files/documents/PowertothePeople_001.pdf

Putnam, R. (2000). *Bowling Alone: The Collapse and Revival of American Community.* New York: Simon & Schuster.

Rainie, L., & Wellman, B. (2012). *Networked: The New Social Operating System.* Cambridge, MA: MIT Press.

Reckwitz, A. (2002). Toward a Theory of Social Practices: A Development in Culturalist Theorizing. *European Journal of Social Theory, 5*(2), 243–263.

Reisch, L. (2001). Time and Wealth: The Role of Time and Temporalities for Sustainable Patterns of Consumption. *Time and Society, 10*(2/3), 387–405.

Rifkin, J. (1987). *Time Wars: The Primary Conflict in Human History.* New York: Simon & Schuster.

Roberts, K. (1976). The Time Famine. In S. Parker (Ed.), *The Sociology of Leisure*. Allen & Unwin.

Robinson, J., & Godbey, G. (1997). *Time for Life: The Surprising Ways That Americans Use Their Time*. Pennsylvania State Press.

Rosa, H. (2003). Social Acceleration: Ethical and Political Consequences of a Desynchronized High-speed Society. *Constellations, 10*(1), 3–33.

Rosa, H. (2013 [2005]). *Social Acceleration: A New Theory of Modernity*. New York, NY: Columbia University Press.

Rosa, H. (2017). De-Synchronization, Dynamic Stabilization, Dispositional Squeeze: The Problem of Temporal Mismatch. In J. Wajcman & N. Dodd (Eds.), *The Sociology of Speed: Digital, Organizational, and Social Temporalities* (pp. 25–41). Oxford: Oxford University Press.

Rosa, H. (2019 [2016]). *Resonance. A Sociology of Our Relationship to the World* (J. Wagner, Trans.). Cambridge: Polity.

Rosa, H., & Scheuerman, W. E. (Eds.). (2009). *High-speed Society: Social Acceleration, Power, and Modernity*. University Park: Pennsylvania State University Press.

Rouse, J. (2006). Practice Theory. In S. Turner & M. Risjrod (Eds.), *Handbook of the Philosophy of Science, vol.15: Philosophy of Anthropology and Sociology* (pp. 500–540). Elsevier.

Rousseau, S. (2015). The Celebrity Quick-Fix. *Food, Culture & Society, 18*(2), 265–287.

Rutherford, S. (2001). Are You Going Home Already?: The Long Hours Culture, Women Managers and Patriarchal Closure. *Time and Society, 10*(2/3), 259–276.

Rutter, J., & Southerton, D. (2000). E-commerce: Delivering the Goods? *Consumer Policy Review, 10*(3), 139–144.

Sabelis, I. (2001). Time Management. *Time & Society, 10*(2–3), 387–400.

Schatzki, T. R. (1996). *Social Practices: A Wittgensteinian Approach to Human Activity and the Social*. Cambridge: Cambridge University Press.

Schatzki, T. R. (2005). Peripheral Vision: The Sites of Organizations. *Organizational Studies, 26*(3), 465–484.

Schatzki, T. R. (2010). *The Timespace of Human Activity: On Performance, Society, and History as Interminate Teleological Events*. Plymouth: Lexington Books.

Schatzki, T. R. (2011). Theories of Practice. In D. Southerton (Ed.), *Encyclopedia of Consumer Culture* (Vol. III, pp. 1447–1551). Thousand Oaks, CA: Sage.

Scheuerman, W. (2003). Speed, States, and Social Theory: A Response to Hartmut Rosa. *Constellations, 10*(1), 42–48.

Schivelbusch, W. (1986). *The Railway Journey: The Industrialization of Time and Space in the Nineteenth Century*. Leamington Spa: Berg.

Schor, J. (1992). *The Overworked American: The Unexpected Decline of Leisure*. Basic Books.

Schor, J. (1998). Work, Free Time and Consumption. Time, Labour and Consumption: Guest Editor's Introduction. *Time & Society, 7*(1), 119–127.

Schor, J. (2004). *Born To Buy: The Commercialized Child and the New Consumer Culture*. New York: Scribner.

Schor, J. (2010). *Plenitude: The New Economics of True Wealth*. New York: Penguin.

Schor, J. (2016). Debating the Sharing Economy. *Journal of Self-Governance and Management Economics, 4*(3), 7–22.

Schulte, B. (2015). *Overwhelmed: How to Work, Love and Play When No One Has the Time*. London: Bloomsbury.

Scott, J., & Clery, E. (2013). Gender roles: An Incomplete Revolution? In A. Park, C. E. Bryson, J. Curtice, & M. Phillips (Eds.), *British Social Attitudes: The 30th Report*. London: NatCen Social Research.

Schwartz-Cowan, R. (1983). *More Work for Mother: The Ironies of Household Technology from the Open Hearth to the Microwave*. London: Basic Books.

Shaw, J. (1998). "Feeling a List Coming on": Gender and the Pace of Life. *Time & Society, 7*(2), 383–396.

Sheridan, D. (2009). The Mass Observation Archive: A History. *Mass Observation Online* [Online], Marlborough, UK: Adam Matthew. November 26, 2019. Retrieved from http://www.massobservation.amdigital.co.uk/Further Resources/Essays/TheMassObservationArchiveAHistory

Shove, E. (2003). *Comfort, Cleanliness and Convenience: The Social Organization of Normality*. Oxford: Berg.

Shove, E. (2009). Everyday Practice and the Production and Consumption of Time. In E. Shove, F. Trentmann, & R. Wilk (Eds.), *Time, Consumption and Everyday Life: Practice, Materiality and Culture* (pp. 17–34). Oxford: Berg.

Shove, E. (2010). Beyond ABC: Climate Change Policy and Theories of Social Change. *Environment and Planning A, 42*, 1273–1285.

Shove, E. (2012). Habits and Their Creatures. In A. Warde & D. Southerton (Eds.), *The Habits of Consumption*. Helsinki: Open Access Book Series of the Helsinki Collegium of Advanced Studies.

Shove, E., Pantzar, M., & Watson, M. (2012). *The Dynamics of Social Practice: Everyday Life and how it Changes*. London: Sage.

Shove, E., & Southerton, D. (2000). Defrosting the Freezer: From Novelty to Convenience. A Story of Normalization. *Journal of Material Culture, 5*(3), 301–319.

Silverstone, R. (1993). Time, Information and Communication Technologies and the Household. *Time & Society, 2*(3), 283–311.

Simmel, G. (1971[1903]). The Metropolis and Mental Life. In D. Levine (ed.), *On Individuality and Social Form.* Chicago, IL: Chicago University Press.

Simmel, G. (1991). Money in Modern Culture. *Theory, Culture and Society, 8,* 17–31.

Simmel, G. (2004). *The Philosophy of Money* (Third Enlarged Edition). London: Routledge.

Skinner, C. (2005). Coordination Points: A Hidden Factor in Reconciling Work and Family Life. *Journal of Social Policy, 34*(1), 99–119.

Slater, D. (1997). *Consumer Culture and Modernity.* Cambridge: Polity.

Sorokin, P. A., & Merton, R. K. (1937). Social Time: A Methodological and Functional Analysis. *American Journal of Sociology, 42,* 615–629.

Southerton, D. (2001). Consuming Kitchens: Taste, Context and Identity Formation. *Journal of Consumer Culture, 1*(2), 179–204.

Southerton, D. (2003). 'Squeezing Time': Allocating Practices, Co-ordinating Networks and Scheduling Society. *Time & Society, 12*(1), 5–25.

Southerton, D. (2006). Analysing the Temporal Organisation of Daily Life: Social Constraints, Practices and Their Allocation. *Sociology, 40*(3), 435–454.

Southerton, D. (2007). Time Pressure, Technology and Gender: The Conditioning of Temporal Experiences in the UK. In J. Scott & J. Nolan (Eds.), *Equal Opportunities International, Special Edition on Technology and Gender Inequalities, 26*(2), 113–128.

Southerton, D. (2009). Re-ordering Temporal Rhythms: Comparing Daily Lives of 1937 with Those of 2000 in the UK. In E. Shove, F. Trentmann, & R. Wilk (Eds.), *Time, Consumption and Everyday Life: Practice, Materiality and Culture* (pp. 49–63). Oxford: Berg.

Southerton, D. (2011). Introduction. In D. Southerton (Ed.), *Encyclopedia of Consumer Culture* (pp. xxiix–xxxiv). Thousand Oaks, CA: Sage.

Southerton, D. (2013). Temporal Rhythms, Habits and Routines: From Consumer Behaviour to the Temporal Ordering of Practices. *Time and Society, 22*(3), 335–355.

Southerton, D. (2019). Consumer Culture and Personal Life. In V. May & P. Nordqvist (Eds.), *Sociology of Personal Life.* Palgrave Macmillan.

Southerton, D., Diaz Mendez, C., & Warde, A. (2012a). Behavioural Change and the Temporal Ordering of Eating Practices: A UK–Spain Comparison. *International Journal of Sociology of Agriculture and Food, 19*(1), 19–36.

Southerton, D., & Evans, D. M. (2017). Consumption Policies with Different Theoretical Frameworks. In *Routledge Handbook on Consumption* (pp. 213–214). Routledge.

Southerton, D., & Tomlinson, M. (2005). "Pressed for Time"—the Differential Impacts of a "Time Squeeze". *Sociological Review, 53*(2), 215–239.

Southerton, D., Warde, A., & Hand, M. (2004). The Limited Autonomy of the Consumer: Implications for Sustainable Consumption. In D. Southerton, H. Chappells, & B. Van Vliet (Eds.), *Sustainable Consumption: The Implications of Changing Infrastructures of Provision* (pp. 32–48). London: Edward Elgar.

Southerton, D., Warde, A., Olsen, W., & Cheng, S. (2012b). Practices and Trajectories: A Comparative Analysis of Reading in France, Norway, Netherlands, UK and USA. *Journal of Consumer Culture, 12*(3), 237–262.

Spurling, N. (2015). Differential Experiences of Time in Academic Work: How Qualities of Time are Made in Practice. *Time and Society, 24*, 367–389.

Spurling, N., McMeekin, A., Shove, E., Southerton, D., & Welch, D. (2013). *Interventions in Practice: Re-framing Policy Approaches to Consumer Behaviour.* Sustainable Practices Research Group Report, Sept.

Sullivan, O. (1996). The Enjoyment of Activities; Do Couples Affect Each Others' Well-being? *Social Indicators Research, 38*(1), 81–102.

Sullivan, O. (1997). Time Waits for No (wo)men: An Investigation of the Gendered Experience of Domestic Time. *Sociology, 31*(2), 221–240.

Sullivan, O., & Gershuny, J. (2018). Speed-Up Society? Evidence from the UK 2000 and 2015 Time Use Diary Surveys. *Sociology, 52*, 20–38.

Tabboni, S. (2001). The Idea of Social Time in Norbert Elias. *Time & Society, 10*(1), 5–27.

Taylor, F. W. (1911). *The Principles of Scientific Management.* New York: Harper & Brothers. [C2]

Thøgersen, J., & Berit Møller, B. (2008). Breaking Car Use Habits: The Effectiveness of a Free One-Month Travelcard. *Transportation, 35*(3), 329–345.

Thompson, C. (1996). Caring Consumers: Gendered Consumption Meanings and the Juggling Lifestyle. *Journal of Consumer Research, 22*, 388–407.

Thompson, E. P. (1967). Time, Work-Discipline and Industrial Capitalism: Past and Present, 38: 56–97; repr. in Flinn, m. & Smout, T. (eds.) (1974) *Essays in Social History,* Oxford: Clarendon Press.

Thrift, N. (1994). Inhuman Geographies: Landscapes of Speed, Light and Power. In P. Cloke, M. Doel, D. Matless, M. Phillips, & N. Thrift (Eds.), *Writing the Rural: Five Cultural Geographies* (pp. 191–248). London: Paul Chapman.

Thrift, N., & May, T. (2001). *Timespace: Geographies of Temporality*. London: Routledge.

Trentmann, F. (Ed.). (2012). *The Oxford Handbook of the History of Consumption*. London: Oxford University Press.

Urry, J. (2000). *Sociology Beyond Societies*. London: Routledge.

Urry, J. (2009). Speeding Up and Slowing Down. In H. Rosa & W. Scheuerman (Eds.), *High Speed Society. Social Acceleration, Power and Modernity* (pp. 179–198). University Park: Pennsylvania State University Press.

van Spaargaren, G., Koppen, C., Janssen, A. M., Hendriksen, A., & Kolfschoten, C. J. (2013). Consumer Responses to the Carbon Labelling of Food. *Sociol Ruralis, 53*, 432–453.

van Tienoven, T. P. (2019). A Multitude of Natural, Social and Individual Time. *Time & Society, 28*(3), 971–994.

van Tienoven, T. P., Glorieux, I., & Minnen, J. (2017). Exploring the Stable Practices of Everyday Life: A Multi-day Time-diary Approach. *The Sociological Review, 65*(4), 745–762.

van Tienoven, T. P., Glorieuz, I., Minnen, J., Daniels, S., & Weenas, D. (2013). If Only the French Republicans Had Known This: The Week as a Social Fact. *Societies, 3*, 399–413.

Veblen, T. (1935[1899]). *The Theory of the Leisure Class*. New York: American Library.

Virilio, P. (2001). Speed-Space: Interview with Chris Dercon. In J. Armitage (Ed.), *Virilio Live: Selected Interviews*. London: Sage.

Wajcman, J. (2015). *Pressed for Time: The Acceleration of Life in Digital Capitalism*. Chicago: Chicago University Press.

Wajcman, J., Bittman, M., & Brown, J. (2008). Families without Borders: Mobile Phones, Connectedness and Work-Home Divisions. *Sociology, 42*, 635–652.

Wajcman, J., & Rose, E. (2011). Constant Connectivity: Rethinking Interruptions at Work. *Organization Studies, 32*(7), 941–962.

Walker, G. (2014). The Dynamics of Energy Demand: Change, Rhythm and Synchronicity. *Energy Research and Social Science, 1*, 49–55.

Warde, A. (1994). Consumption, Identity-formation and Uncertainty. *Sociology, 28*(4). https://doi.org/10.1177/0038038594028004005.

Warde, A. (2005). Consumption and Theories of Practice. *Journal of Consumer Culture*, 5(2), 131–154.

Warde, A. (2013). What Sort of a Practice is Eating. In E. Shove & N. Spurling (Eds.), *Sustainable Practices: Social Theory and Climate Change* (pp. 17–30). London: Routledge.

Warde, A. (2014). After Taste: Culture, Consumption and Theories of Practice. *Journal of Consumer Culture*, 14(3), 279–303.

Warde, A. (2016). *The Practice of Eating*. Cambridge: Polity.

Warde, A. (2017). *Consumption: A Sociological Analysis*. London: Palgrave Macmillan.

Warde, A., Cheng, S.-L., Olsen, W., & Southerton, D. (2007). Changes in the Practice of Eating: A Comparative Analysis of time-use. *Acta Sociologica*, 50(4), 365–387.

Warde, A., Welch, D., & Paddock, J. (2017). Studying Consumption Through the Lens of Practice: Routledge Handbook on Consumption. In M. Keller, B. Halkier, T. A Wilska, & M. Truninger (eds.), *Handbook on Consumption* [1.3]. London: Routledge.

Warde, A., & Yates, L. (2017). Understanding Eating Events: Snacks and Meal Patterns in Great Britain. *Food, Culture, and Society, 20*(1), 15–36.

Warren, T. (2003). Class- and Gender-based Working Time? Time Poverty and the Division of Domestic Labour. *Sociology, 37*(4), 733–752.

Watson, S. (2014). Mundane Objects in the City: Laundry Practices And The Making and Remaking of Public/Private Sociality and Space in London and New York. *Urban Studies, 52*(5), 876–890.

Weber, M. (1989 [1905]). *The Protestant Ethic and the Spirit of Capitalism*. London: Unwin Hymen. C2

Welch, D., & Southerton, D. (2019). After Paris: Transitions for Sustainable Consumption. *Sustainability: Science, Practice and Policy, 15*(1), 31–44.

Welch, D., & Warde, A. (2015). Theories of Practice and Sustainable Consumption. In L. Reisch & J. Thøgersen (Eds.), *Handbook of Research on Sustainable Consumption* (pp. 84–100). Cheltenham UK: Edward Elgar Publishing Ltd.

Wernick, A. (1991). *Promotional Culture: Advertising, Ideology and Symbolic Expression*. London: Sage.

Whitford, J. (2002). Pragmatism and the Untenable Dualism of Means and Ends: Why Rational Choice Theory Does not Deserve paradigmatic Privilege. *Theory & Society, 31*, 325–363.

Yates, L. (2018). Sharing, Households and Sustainable Consumption. *Journal of Consumer Culture, 18*(3), 433–452.

Yates, L., & Evans, D. M. (2016). Dirtying Linen: Understanding Household Laundry Habits. *Environmental Policy and Governance, 26*(2), 101–115.

Young, M. (1988). *The Metronomic Society: Natural Rhythms and Human Timetables*. London: Thames and Hudson.

Young, M., & Schuller, T. (Eds.). (1988). *The Rhythms of Society*. London: Routledge.

Young, M., & Willmott, P. (1973). *The Symmetrical Family: Study of Work and Leisure in the London Region*. London: RKP.

Zerubavel, E. (1979). *Patterns of Time in Hospital Life: A Sociological Perspective*. Chicago, IL: University of Chicago Press.

Zerubavel, E. (1981). *Hidden Rhythms: Schedules and Calendars in Social Life*. Chicago: Chicago University Press.

Zerubavel, E. (1982). The Standardization of Time: A Sociohistorical Perspective. *American Journal of Sociology, 88*, 1–23.

Zerubavel, E. (1985). *The Seven Day Circle: The History and Meaning of the Week*. New York: Free Press.

Zimmermann, J.-P., Evans, M., Griggs, J., King, N., Harding, L., Roberts, P., & Evans, C. (2012). *Household Electricity Survey: A Study of Domestic Electrical Product Usage*. Intertek Report R66141. Retrieved from https://assets.publishing.service.gov.uk/government/uploads/system/uploads/attachment_data/file/208097/10043_R66141Household ElectricitySurveyFinalReportissue4.pdf.

Index

objective, 15, 38, 39, 43, 44, 62,
90, 96, 101, 154, 161
pre-industrial, 26, 30
timescapes, 13
wealth, 106
zero-sum, 62, 72, 90, 188,
190, 191
See also Time squeeze, pressure
Time diaries, 4, 9, 15, 17, 18,
48–50, 56, 59, 62, 63, 71, 88,
96, 110, 111, 119, 125–136,
138, 143, 144, 147, 148, 150,
158, 159, 161, 163, 165, 178,
182, 183, 185, 187
multinational time use survey
(MTUS), 48
Time discipline, 25–40, 95,
103, 105
Time in practices, 157
Time policies
extending, 21, 78, 179, 189, 191
market-based, 61, 189, 191
substitution, 188
See also Work-life balance
Time-oriented action, 26–30
Time-space compression, 16, 70, 72,
76, 77, 84
Time squeeze
pressure, 5, 16, 17, 60, 69,
96–98, 103, 105, 106, 109,
114, 121, 125, 148, 170, 182,
183, 187, 197
scarcity, 5, 181
Timetables, 13, 30, 60
Timing
collectively timed events, 20, 21,
134, 139, 147, 179, 194,
196, 197

institutionalized events, 12, 18,
112–114, 118, 121, 131, 132,
138–141, 143, 147, 150, 151,
153, 184, 186

U
Urry, John, 76, 181

V
van Tienoven, Theun Pieter, 8,
151–153, 165
Veblen, Thorstein, 32
Video-gaming, 77
Virilio, Paul, 71, 78

W
Wajcman, Judy, 17, 71, 75, 84,
85, 89, 90
Walker, Gordon, 152
Warde, Alan, 9, 34, 35, 138, 155,
156, 178, 179, 195, 197
Weber, Max, 27
Welch, Daniel, 194, 195, 197
Work
flexibility, 19, 50–52, 54, 62, 114,
125, 144
paid, 4, 15, 16, 19, 30, 32,
35–37, 43–49, 53, 54, 56,
59–63, 88, 96, 107–109, 120,
121, 129–131, 141, 143, 158,
182, 183
unpaid, 15, 16, 19, 35, 43–49,
54, 55, 62, 63, 88, 96, 107,
108, 129, 143, 182, 183
work reduction, 47